John Hearsey trained as an architect but was forced to give up his career through illness. Instead he turned to writing books on architectural and historical subjects. His publications include: *Bridge, Church and Palace in Old London* and *London and the Great Fire.*

MARIE ANTOINETTE

John E. N. Hearsey

CARDINAL

CARDINAL edition published in 1974
by Sphere Books Ltd
30–32 Grays Inn Road, London WC1X 8JL

First published in Great Britain
by Constable & Co Ltd 1972

This book is set in Intertype Lectura

Printed in Great Britain by Cox & Wyman Ltd,
London, Reading and Fakenham

ISBN 0 351 16662 9

CONTENTS

LIST OF ILLUSTRATIONS

Colour

Black and White

ACKNOWLEDGMENTS

Photographs and illustrations were supplied by, or are reproduced by kind permission of the following: Biblioteca Estense, Modena, Italy, Plates IX, X, XI; Bibliothèque Nationale, Plates XIII, 7, 22, 27, 28, 37, 39, 44, 51, 52, 59, 60, 71, 72; Bulloz, Plates IV, V, XIII, XIV, XV, 18, 24, 25, 35, 39, 40, 43, 47, 56, 61, 62, 63, 64, 65, 67, 69, 71; Giraudon, Plates 17, 19, 26, 34, 72; Kunsthistorisches Museum, Vienna, Plates II, 1, 4, 5, 6, 9; Musée Carnavalet, Plates XIV, XV, 40, 45, 46, 61, 63, 64; Musée Condé, Chantilly, Plate 19; Musée de Versailles, Plates I, IV, V, VI, VII, VIII, XII, XVI, 8, 10, 11, 12, 13, 14, 15, 16, 29, 31, 32, 33, 36, 55; Musée Jacquemart–André, Paris, Plate 24; Museé de Troyes, Plate 69; Osterreichische Nationalbibliothek, Plates 2, 3, 20, 38; Private Collection, Plates 35, 42; Réalité, Plates 49, 50, 51, 52, 54, 56, 62, 67, 68, 70; Réunion des Musées Nationaux, Plates I, VI, VII, VIII, XII, XVI, 8, 10, 11, 12, 13, 14, 15, 16, 29, 30, 31, 32, 33, 36, 55; Rothschild Collection, Louvre, Plate 65; Schöenbrunn Palace, Plate III; Troll-Wachtmarster Collection, Plate 25; Victoria and Albert Museum, Plate 23; Roger-Viollet, Plates 7, 8, 21, 22, 27, 28, 41, 48, 53, 57, 58, 59, 60, 66.

Preface

What is the place of Marie Antoinette in history? It is not a question that can have a cut-and-dried answer. She was neither the Martyred Queen of her more fervent biographers, nor the wanton who was the sole cause of her country's ruin, as believed by her detractors.

Only in the last three years of her life—she was thirty-eight at the time of her death—did Marie Antoinette really become an individual, thinking for herself but not necessarily about herself. In the history of France her role is passive. Unlike the equally unfortunate Mary, Queen of Scots, she was never a ruler in her own right, but the unwise consort of an incompetent sovereign.

Although the daughter of one of the greatest female rulers Europe has seen, Maria Theresa of Austria, and marked out from birth as the bride-to-be of the future King of France, she never received an education to fit her for such a life. Indeed, on her arrival at Versailles at the age of fifteen Marie Antoinette could not even spell one of her baptismal names correctly in the marriage register.

By the 1780s France had finally emerged, in a weakened condition, from the long series of dynastic wars which had convulsed Europe since the days of Marlborough. Across the Atlantic General Wolfe had turned eastern Canada from a French to an English colony, and in India Clive had driven the fleur-de-lys from the southern part of that country. Internally, France was afflicted by maladministration and failing financial resources; and now many of her citizens were returning from America, where they had been helping the Thirteen Colonies in their fight for independence from Britain, bringing with them new notions about political and social liberty. In an atmosphere of disillusion, coloured with regrets for past glories such as the days of "Le Roi Soleil", when the French monarchy under Louis XIV appeared as the most splendid and powerful in Europe, such ideas soon took root. In the hands of capable ministers an absolute monarchy was tolerable, but now where were such ministers? They did not seem to exist; and for sovereigns the French had a King who thought of little but hunting and a Queen who thought of nothing but pleasure.

Since it is easier to hate a person rather than an abstract institution, the hatred of a whole nation began to fix itself on Marie Antoinette. With no one to restrain her the Queen had moved from merely personal indiscretions and extravagances to interfering in the nomination of ministers for the benefit of her rapacious friends, to squandering millions of francs on her little palace—the Petit Trianon—and intriguing in international politics on behalf of her Austrian relations. Consequently, in an atmosphere charged with rumour and scandal, everyone was prepared to believe the worst of the Queen, even that she really was involved in that amazing confidence trick known as the Affair of the Diamond Necklace.

What was Marie Antoinette actually like as a woman? She was completely of her time, and that time was the Rococo: exquisite, artificial and quite out of touch with reality. As such this Queen of France could only have existed in the second half of the eighteenth century. Had she been brought up in the time of Elizabeth I or of Catherine de Medici she would have been set to work at Latin and Greek and instructed in the ways of kings and queens instead of being allowed to run wild in her mother's palace in Vienna. When she came to France it was under the impression that her first duty was to become a beautiful figurehead, and in that at least she succeeded, sweeping through the galleries at Versailles in exquisite gowns, or leading the applause at the Opera. Living in the enclosed world of Versailles and surrounded by an almost unbreakable circle of self-seeking friends, who not only agreed with everything she said but pandered to her every wish, Marie Antoinette was completely out of touch with reality.

Between the ages of fifteen, when she came to France, and thirty, when she was shaken out of her dream-world by the Affair of the Diamond Necklace, her mind can hardly have developed: fifteen wasted years. But one characteristic was acknowledged by all but her most rabid enemies, and that was her charm. Unfortunately it cannot be said to come across very strongly in the state portraits of

Vigée-Lebrun. When she walked or curtsied it was with a swaying, even a caressing movement, and she could invest the most ordinary remark with a charm which the recipient would never forget. Had it not been for the tragedy and drama of the last years, Marie Antoinette would have remained a minor historical figure, like that other Maria Theresa who was the wife of Louis XIV, or Marie Leszczynska, the neglected spouse of Louis XV. If one of history's greatest upheavals had not occurred when it did Marie Antoinette might be remembered today only for her charming name and for her embellishments of the Petit Trianon. Instead she was to become the living symbol of all that a populace felt was wrong with its country.

The evidence of those last years refutes any argument that Marie Antoinette was simply a feather-brained woman. The tragedy was that she had occupied her mind so long with trivia; for when she did make real use of it one realises that she was indeed a daughter of Maria Theresa: dealing with revolutionary ministers, carrying on a clandestine correspondence with Austria, and educating her two children, all at the same time.

Stupidity can only deaden suffering, never ennoble it, and Marie Antoinette found a nobility of stature in her dreadful cell in the Conciergerie, in the Court-room, and on that last ride to the scaffold which is still undimmed even after the infinite sufferings caused to so many by two world wars and their aftermath. If the fate of Marie Antoinette moves one, as surely it cannot fail to do, it is not as the consort of the King of France and Navarre—a Habsburg married to a Bourbon—but simply as a wife and a mother. Hers was the courage of one woman standing against a whole nation, and her real tragedy lay in the fact that not only was she unable to change with the times, but she was even unaware that they were changing—until it was far too late.

I should like to express my thanks to the staff of the Hove Public Library, especially to J. Dove, Esq., Librarian and Curator, and Miss L. Green, Reference Room, for assistance in obtaining books, both from their own and other libraries. Also, I should like to thank the Library of the Institut Français du Royaume-Uni, London. Lastly, my thanks to all those who have helped bring the book itself into being.

JOHN E. N. HEARSEY

CHAPTER ONE

The Arrival

With good reason the French called November 2nd, 1755, *Le Jour des Morts*—The Day of the Dead. Between thirty and forty thousand inhabitants of Lisbon were killed in a violent earthquake, felt as far away as Scotland, and as if that were not enough, the half-destroyed city was then ravaged by fire. It was therefore excusable if another event which took place that same day passed almost unnoticed by the rest of Europe. The Empress Maria Theresa of Austria had given birth to her tenth surviving child. It was a girl, and like all the other Imperial daughters she would have a Christian name beginning with Marie. Marie Amélie, Marie Anne, Marie Caroline, Marie Christine, Marie Elizabeth, and now Marie Antoinette—Marie Antonia in its original German form.

Almost from the moment of her birth Marie Antoinette was destined to marry into the French Royal House. After the death of the Emperor Francis in 1765, Austria grew increasingly apprehensive of the strength of the Prussians, of the other Protestant German states, and of England across the North Sea. If she could have a country as large as France for an ally, it would go far towards redressing the balance of power in Europe. So, in 1766 Maria Theresa made an outright proposal to Louis XV of France that Marie Antoinette should marry Louis-Auguste, his eldest grandson and future King of France, and on May 24th that year the Ambssador informed the Empress that she could regard the matter as settled. The matter may have been, but it pleased the diplomatist in Louis XV not to appear over-keen, and the months turned into years without anything definite being signed.

Maria Theresa was becoming ever more desirous to settle the alliance with France against Frederick the Great of Prussia, to whom she referred as "Monster", but she never seriously considered Marie

Antoinette being educated in a way befitting a future Queen of France.

The Archduchess Maria Antonia of Lorraine's life in the Schoenbrunn Palace or the Hofburg in Vienna must have been an unending Christmas holiday. Her governesses were, at best, indulgent, and at worst, slightly dishonest . . . like Madame de Brandeiss, who wrote out schoolroom exercises in pencil which were then inked over by her young charge.

Marie Antoinette was taught Italian by Metastasio, a poet and author of innumerable libretti, and her musical instruction was entrusted to Gluck, the composer of *Orfeo*. In time, she became a moderately accomplished harpsichord player and singer, and had a real, though not very profound, love of music. As a child she played duets with Mozart, a year younger than herself, and spent many happy hours in children's games with the infant prodigy. On one occasion the Archduchess and the violinist's son were overheard playing at marriage.

"I shall be your husband, shan't I?" inquired the future composer of *Le Nozze di Figaro*.

"Oh, yes, no one but you!" Marie Antoinette assured him.

Happy though her early childhood must have been it was the worst possible grounding for her future life. "What I want, I have," could have been her motto, for nothing was denied her. If it is true that a person's character is moulded irrevocably in the first few years, then Marie Antoinette could no more help developing into the woman she became than the strict upbringing of Queen Victoria could avoid creating the personality the world knew so well.

As a child the Archduchess was comparatively tall for her age, but not conventionally pretty, as she had a very prominent forehead and the full Habsburg lower lip. Already that lower lip was inclined to pout, foreshadowing the temperament that was to develop in later years. Her eyes were blue, "but not insipid," her complexion beautifully clear and her hair light brown, almost blonde. Charm was her greatest attraction, and nearly all her life it could turn away wrath, however justified.

Maria Theresa had to wait until 1769 to receive the longed-for letter from Louis XV, in which he formally asked for Marie Antoinette's hand in marriage to his grandson, the Dauphin. Easter,

1770, was suggested for the ceremony, which was in a year's time. Maria Theresa then really became aware for the first time of the gaps in her daughter's education, and not much investigation was needed to discover that she could hardly read or write in either French or German, that her grammar was bad and her spelling worse. Something had to be done quickly.

Noverre, famous for his ballets, was engaged to teach dancing, which remained one of her greatest accomplishments. Two actors from a French company in Vienna were employed to give lessons in elocution, but this piece of news was reported back to Versailles, where the idea of the future Queen of France being tutored by actors was not well received, and on the recommendation of the Bishop of Orléans the Abbé Vermond was sent to take over her education. The Abbé Vermond was a sensible individual who could be relied upon to be firm and yet kind. In fact he and the Comte de Mercy-Argenteau, who, in spite of his French sounding name, was the Austrian Ambassador in France, became two of the most sincere but least appreciated well-wishers that Marie Antoinette was destined to have.

At the age of thirteen the Archduchess was like an unbroken filly, and now the Abbé was holding out a bridle. Her reactions were predictable, but he managed to make some headway: "She is more intelligent than most people think. Unfortunately, until she was twelve she was not taught to concentrate in any way whatsoever, and since she is rather lazy and very frivolous, she is difficult to teach. In the first six weeks I managed to instil the outlines of literature, and found that she could grasp my meaning very well when I gave her clear explanations. Then she usually showed a good judgement, but I could not induce her to make an effort to understand a subject of her own accord, though I was convinced that it was well within her power to do so. In the end I came to realise she would only learn so long as she was amused by it."

Now the marriage plans were becoming bogged down over the question of etiquette. From now on etiquette would become the bane of Marie Antoinette's life: she who had always done exactly as she pleased, when she pleased. For example, there was the vital matter of whose name should come first on the marriage contract: Louis XV or Maria Theresa and Joseph II? How much would the dowry be worth? Who would accompany Marie Antoinette on her journey from

Vienna? Who would meet her at the frontier? These and many other questions had to be settled to the social and political satisfaction of both the Austrians and the French, and the messengers who galloped between Vienna and Versailles were so numerous that they themselves almost constituted a procession.

The one person who seemed least interested in all this was the fifteen-year-old Dauphin, whom Mercy, the Austrian Ambassador, dismissed in one cutting sentence: "Nature seems to have denied everything to Monsieur le Dauphin."

Certainly Louis-Auguste was well known for his love of manual labour, which included mixing plaster and working as a locksmith, but Maria Theresa was somewhat surprised when Louis XV sent a portrait of his grandson guiding a plough. Not satisfied, she requested something more conventional, and in return received two portraits. After studying them she said aphoristically to her daughter: "Domestic happiness consists of mutual trust and kindness. Passionate love soon disappears." Looking at the portraits of the Dauphin Louis, she may well have asked if it would ever be kindled.

Time was getting short, and there was so much advice still ungiven. So, two months before the date fixed for Marie Antoinette's departure her mother ordered the girl's bed to be moved into her own room, so that no opportunity might be lost to lecture the child-bride on her future role as Queen. Not all the advice given by the Empress of a huge and ramshackle empire was on the subject of statecraft, for she was aware of at least two of her daughter's shortcomings.

"Don't show curiosity; this is something about which you give me great anxiety. Don't be ashamed to ask advice from everyone and don't do anything of your own accord."

Maria Theresa even drew up a list of rules for regulating her daughter's future life, and when Marie Antoinette was actually en route for France the Empress sent a letter after her: "Let me recommend you, beloved daughter, to re-read it on the 21st of every month (the date of her departure from Vienna). Abide by this wish of mine, this urgent request. The one thing I am afraid of is that you may grow careless or lazy. Never forget your mother, who though far away in Germany will continue to watch over you till her dying day."

Now that Marie Antoinette was actually leaving, Maria Theresa's letters show that in her heart-of-hearts she knew who was responsible for the girl's immaturity. For the next ten years she did watch over her daughter, and as time passed and the reports filtered back to Vienna of Marie Antoinette's conduct at the French Court, so grew her anxiety about the ultimate outcome.

Two magnificent coaches were ordered from Francien in Paris by Louis XV which were to bring the Archduchess from Vienna. The first was upholstered in crimson velvet, embroidered with the four seasons, and the second in blue velvet with the four elements painted on the doors, while bouquets of flowers decorated the roofs. At Versailles itself builders and decorators were working against time to finish a new opera house, while in Vienna construction work was proceeding at the French Embassy where annexes were being erected for an expected one thousand five hundred guests during the festivities surrounding the marriage by proxy which would precede Marie Antoinette's departure for France.

Now the Duc de Durfort, the resident French Ambassador, was appointed Ambassador Extraordinary, and as such made a lavish progress through Vienna in a procession which included the two royal travelling coaches just arrived from Paris and no less than forty-eight six-in-hands together with one hundred and seventeen servants and bodyguards and lackeys. The whole spectacle cost 350,000 ducats, half of which came from Durfort's own pocket, and the following day he sold off the horses to help recover some of the expenses.

The Ambassador Extraordinary was publicly received by Maria Theresa and Joseph II, her eldest son and co-ruler. The Duc de Durfort presented Marie Antoinette with a miniature of the Dauphin, which she pinned to her corsage. Then she was required to forswear her Austrian rights, and received the congratulations of both the Court and the University upon her forthcoming marriage. This in turn was followed by a military review, a gala performance at the theatre, a reception and a ball for three thousand guests in the Belvedere, while the French Ambassador gave a supper for one thousand five hundred at the Liechtenstein Palace, especially borrowed for the occasion. Then, on April 19th, Marie Antoinette was married by proxy to the Dauphin in the Church of the Augustines, where she had been christened less than fifteen years before. Beside her stood her own brother, Ferdinand, himself only sixteen, deputising for Louis far away at Versailles.

Forty-eight hours later it was the 21st of April, the day of departure.

"I am bathed in tears," wrote Maria Theresa after it was all over, and went to church to pray that God would avert the disaster, which, even at that date, she felt must be the inevitable outcome of this political marriage of convenience.

The cavalcade taking one young girl half across Europe consisted of fifty-seven carriages with three hundred and forty horses, which had to be changed as often as five times a day. Ahead of the procession, roads had been resurfaced or even remade, and along the route the people lined the way to cheer and wish God-speed to the youngest of Maria Theresa's daughters setting out for a new and glorious life. All the way it was decorations, flowers, loyal greetings and goodwill. The first night was spent at the vast abbey of Melk, overlooking the Danube, where she was met by her brother, Joseph II, who had gone on ahead. The cavalcade wound through Lambach, Altheim, Alt-Oethingen, Nymphenburg, Augsburg, Günsburg, Riedlingen, Stockach, Donau-Eschingen and Friburg, the young bride's last night on German soil being spent in the Abbey of Schütten.

At the Abbey she was met by another French Ambassador Extraordinary, the Comte de Noailles, who was very much of the *ancien régime* in its least likable aspects. De Noailles was both arrogant about his birth and ostentatious, and when he asked the financially embarrassed French Treasury for a generous sum to finance his present mission, and was offered decorations instead, he replied that he had enough of them already.

Even now all the points of etiquette had not been ironed out, and neither Count Stahremberg, who accompanied Marie Antoinette, nor the Comte de Noailles could agree whose name should come first on the deed of remise relating to the handing over of the bride to the French. Finally a solution was reached by which the document to be seen in France should have Louis XV's name first, while that destined for Austria would have at the top the names of Maria Theresa and Joseph II.

To avoid the risk of either nation feeling slighted if the handing over ceremony took place on the other's territory, a neat solution was found which had been used once before in the past. The actual ceremony was carried out on a small sandy island in the Rhine between Kehl and Strasbourg, where a wooden pavilion had been erected which consisted of a large hall with four ante-chambers, two on either side. Marie Antoinette would enter on one side as an Austrian Archduchess and leave on the other as a French Dauphine.

Leading citizens in Strasbourg lent their furniture, the University made itself responsible for the dais, while tapestries were borrowed from the Archbishop's Palace to hide the bare boards of the walls. For days before the ceremony was due to take place many people bribed their way in to see the pavilion for themselves. Among them was Goethe, who went with a party of fellow students from Strasbourg University. In front of one of the tapestries he stopped short: it depicted the marriage of Jason and Medea. The man who one day would write *Faust* could not keep quiet: "What, is it possible to be so thoughtless as to exhibit before a young queen's gaze this example of the most horrible wedding that perhaps ever took place? Are there none among the French architects, decorators and upholsterers who understand that pictures mean something, that pictures work on the senses and feelings and that they can make impressions and arouse ominous presentiments? It seems to me as though a hideous spectre had been sent to greet this lady at the frontier; this lady who is, we are told, beautiful and full of the joy of life!"

According to legend Marie Antoinette is supposed to have stripped naked in one of the antechambers, putting aside absolutely everything of Austrian origin, and then dressed again in clothes of French manufacture. Apparently the story is an invention of Madame Campan, who became a member of the Dauphine's household, and who wrote her memoirs. Unfortunately they are marred by a number of apocryphal stories more remarkable for their sugar-content than anything else. Moreover, she was not even present at the handing-over ceremony at Kehl.

The truth was that Marie Antoinette put on a fresh ceremonial dress brought from Vienna, while three of her accompanying women also changed their undoubtedly dusty dresses in the adjoining room. Certainly she kept her jewellery, including the watch which was one of the last remaining possessions left her in prison. Hung on a nail by her bed it marked off the hours during the first four days in the Conciergerie in the heart of revolutionary Paris, until it too was confiscated.

In the wooden pavilion a table had been placed in the centre of the main hall, symbolizing the frontier between the two nations, and Count Stahremberg now led her towards it. On the far side stood the Comte de Noailles flanked by two commissioners, while somewhere behind them the son of de Noailles was watching the proceedings through the keyhole of the door from the French side of the pavilion. The Ambassador Extraordinary made a speech full of predictable platitudes, the Austrian Ladies-in-Waiting kissed Marie Antoinette's hand for the last time, and withdrew. Then, through the opposite door Madame de Noailles entered together with two Gentlemen in Waiting. When the door on the German side had closed behind the ladies-in-waiting, Marie Antoinette advanced round the end of the table to meet Madame de Noailles, to whom she was introduced by her husband.

For Marie Antoinette the strain was too much, and in tears she threw herself into the Frenchwoman's arms. After a moment she pulled herself together, and the introductions continued. The prospect was not very attractive for a young girl. Most of the members of her new household were elderly and far from cheerful, having served with Maria Leszczynska, Louis XV's neglected and now dead queen.

But already Strasbourg was waiting. Salvos were fired and the cathedral bells rang out as Marie Antoinette reached the first houses, where a triumphal arch had been set up. There Monsieur d'Autigny, the principal magistrate, started to read a speech of welcome in German.

"Do not speak German, gentlemen," said Marie Antoinette, "from today I only understand French."

Children dressed as shepherds and shepherdesses offered bouquets, girls threw flowers in her path, and small boys were dressed as Swiss Guards. When Marie Antoinette reached the Archbishop's Palace, where she was to stay, she asked that the guard should be mounted by these juvenile Switzers, and her new countrymen were only too happy to grant the request. Then followed the presentations, headed by that of the elderly Cardinal Rohan, and after dinner the Dauphine watched a Feast of Bacchus staged in her honour. No sooner was that over than she was taken to the theatre to see two short plays, then back to the Palace to view the illuminated city, where even the great spire of the cathedral had been hung with lanterns. Hardly was supper over than she crossed the river Ill on a bridge of barges into the park to witness a fireworks display, and although by then it was past midnight her first day in France was not yet over. Off she went to a ball, and only after she had watched several dances was she allowed to return to the Palace and find refuge in sleep. France had opened her arms to this girl from Vienna, and the welcome was completely sincere.

CHAPTER TWO

Wedding at Versailles

While Marie Antoinette slept, Strasbourg danced through the night. The new day began for the Dauphine with yet another public appearance, to hear Mass in the cathedral. A tiny figure at the foot of that vast façade of Gothic tracery and sculpture, she was met by the old Cardinal Rohan's nephew, Louis Prince de Rohan. Although himself a priest, and waiting to step into his uncle's shoes at Strasbourg, this almost too good-looking young man had most decidedly not turned his back on all that was worldly. If one word could sum him up it would be "exquisite". Typical of his age, he was no ornament to his Church, and as the future would show his name would be coupled with Marie Antoinette's in a way which was disastrous for both of them.

Now, with clouds of verbal incense, he welcomed her to France.

"You will be for us the living image of the beloved Empress whom Europe has so long admired and whom posterity will continue to venerate. The spirit of Maria Theresa is about to unite with the spirit of the Bourbons." Then he theatrically blessed the girl, and the Mass began.

The future Baronne d'Oberkirche was among those who saw Marie Antoinette on her arrival in Strasbourg, and twelve years later, on seeing her again at Versailles, she recorded her impression of that earlier meeting.

"At that time Madame la Dauphine was tall and well made, although a trifle too slight. She has changed very little since: it is always the same face—elongated and regular, an aquiline nose, pointed at the tip, very high forehead, eyes blue and vivacious. Her very small mouth was already disdainful in expression. She had the Austrian underlip more pronounced than any member of her illustrious House. Nothing can describe the brilliance of her complexion, the roses and lilies being deftly mingled. Her hair of an ash blonde had only a touch of powder. The poise of her head, her majestic figure, the elegance and grace of her whole person were as they are today."

From Strasbourg the procession of carriages set off on the last part of the journey, through Nancy, Châlons-sur-Marne and Rheims, towards Compiègne. There Marie Antoinette was to meet her husband, her grandfather by marriage and most of her new relations. As a meeting place the Forest of Compiègne has become something of a crossroads in French history. On May 14th, 1770, Marie Antoinette was welcomed by the House of Bourbon. Thirty-six years later it was the scene of another first encounter: between Napoleon and Marie Louise, also from Austria. On November 11th, 1918, the Armistice ending the First World War was signed in a railway carriage in the Forest, and it was in that same carriage that Adolf Hitler insisted on signing terms after the fall of France in 1940.

The evening was beautiful as Louis XV waited, together with the Court, for the arrival of the procession of carriages coming from the direction of Soissons. Drummers, trumpeters and buglers signalled Marie Antoinette's approach, and as the fanfares sounded through the Forest Louis XV, who, in spite of a life dedicated to the pursuit of love, was still good-looking at sixty, got out of his carriage. Already Marie Antoinette had descended from hers, run up to him and was making a profound curtsy. Louis XV raised her, kissed her in a far from perfunctory manner on both cheeks, and gave her a thoroughly appraising look. Then the Dauphine turned to his grandson and the man who was also already her husband, and kissed him too. The Dauphin Louis hardly reacted.

Although only fifteen years and nine months old, Louis was already five feet ten inches tall, heavily built, and clumsy. Undeniably slow-witted, he appeared quite stupid due to the fact that he was distressingly short-sighted, and could not even recognise his friends at three paces. Apart from manual labour, such as making locks, the only thing for which he showed any real enthusiasm was hunting, a passion he retained right up to the day the women of Paris marched on Versailles in October, 1789. This then was the man who would one day rule France with Marie Antoinette as his Queen.

Waiting to be introduced were Mesdames, the three unmarried daughters of Louis XV. In a setting such as Versailles, where cynicism, self-seeking and immorality were more common than their opposing virtues, they were something of a curiosity. Adelaide was the eldest: her beauty had long since vanished, and she had turned into a thoroughly unpleasant old maid, undeniably unconventional. Louis XV affectionately called her "Rag", or "Dishcloth". She played the French horn and the Jews' harp, and also occupied her time making napkin rings. When she gave orders, she practically shouted. Next came Victoire: plump, homely and stupid. The third was Sophie: interestingly ugly, given to walking quickly and looking at people sideways, "like hares do". These were Marie Antoinette's new aunts, and soon they were to try to turn her into a puppet to be manipulated in their absurd intrigues and spiteful quarrels at Versailles. Until the marriage Adelaide had ranked as "first lady", but now she had been dethroned by this Austrian girl, and as might be expected, she was not amused.

The other most important member of the royal family to meet Marie Antoinette that day was the Duc d'Orléans, a grandson of the Regent who ruled during the minority of Louis XV. Then there was the Duc de Penthiève, descended from an illegitimate son of Louis XIV, who was accompanied by his recently widowed daughter-in-law, the Princesse de Lamballe. She was destined to become one of the closest and least self-seeking of Marie Antoinette's friends. Also waiting under the trees were the Dauphin Louis' cousins, the Duc de Bourbon and the Duc de Chartres. The latter was the son of the Duc d'Orléans, and years later, when he had succeeded to that title, he sided with the revolutionaries and actually voted for the death of Louis XVI, only to suffer the same fate soon after.

There was another unofficial member of the household whom Marie Antoinette had not yet encountered: Madame du Barry, the last of Louis XV's mistresses. The trouble was that Jeanne Bécu was the illegitimate daughter of a seamstress, and had actually earned her living by prostitution. Now she was the most influential woman at Versailles, where everyone knew that whoever had her ear, also had the ear of the King. After the death of Madame de Pompadour a faction had deliberately set out to provide the King with a mistress of their own selection, through whom they could rule. Their choice fell on Jeanne Bécu who was still beautiful, though undeniably not over-intelligent. She had, however, a quality hardly known at Versailles—that of kindness. Indeed the old cliché about a prostitute with a heart of gold could have applied to her. A marriage was arranged to give her a title and so the entrée to society, and no sooner could she call herself the Comtesse du Barry than her nominal husband was financially rewarded and told to make himself scarce.

At sixty Louis XV had reached the age and physical condition when he was only sexually attracted by the very young or the very mature, and it was into the latter category that the Comtesse du Barry fitted. The plan worked beautifully: she appealed to Louis XV, and to the scandalised amazement of Mesdames and most of the Court she became his mistress. Before long she and Marie Antoinette would become engaged in a war of attrition that was both funny and contemptible, but at the moment neither had set eyes on the other.

Now Marie Antoinette was seated in the carriage with Louis XV, the Dauphin Louis and Madame de Noailles, and it was the King, not his grandson, who was showing all the interest in her. Afterwards the Dauphin wrote in his diary: "Interview with Madame la Dauphine."

From Compiègne the procession went almost to Paris, to St Denis, where Louis XV's fourth daughter had entered a Carmelite nunnery. Her decision to take the veil had been sudden, at least as far as the rest of her family were concerned. One morning Louis XV told Adelaide that during the night her sister had left them, and she inquired, "With whom?" Now Soeur Thérèse-Augustine was being introduced to Marie Antoinette at the Convent. Then on to the Château de la Muette, the last stopping place before Versailles. More introductions: to the Comte de Provence and the Comte d'Artois, the younger brothers of Louis the Dauphin. One who was not actually introduced, but was very much present among the "ladies of quality" was Madame du Barry, dripping with diamonds.

If the story is not true about what passed at dinner that evening, it is entertaining. Apparently Louis XV asked Marie Antoinette what she thought of the woman—Madame du Barry—who was smiling at her from the other end of the table. "Charming," said Marie Antoinette, and turned to ask Madame de Noallies what was her position at Court.

"Her office?" queried Madame de Noailles. "To amuse the King!"

"In that case," exclaimed Marie Antoinette, "I proclaim myself her rival!"

There only remained two more ladies to meet the Dauphine for her introduction to Louis XV's circle to be complete. They were Mesdames Clothilde and Élizabeth, sisters to the Dauphin, Louis. When the revolution came Madame Élizabeth, a calm and devout woman, shared the royal family's misfortunes: escape, imprisonment and, eventually, execution.

But now Marie Antoinette had reached Versailles and the Palace with its quarter of a mile-long main façade, a monument to the basic lack of self-confidence of Louis XIV, the Sun King. Her marriage in the classical Chapel followed almost immediately, on May 16th. So crowded was the place with those whose birth gave them the right to be present that many of the elaborate dresses with their large paniered skirts worn by the women were crushed and ruined. At one o'clock the ceremony began with the King's entry, heralded by fifes and drums. Then the Grand Master of the Ceremonies preceded the young couple who walked hand in hand. Marie Antoinette was wearing a magnificent dress in gold, silver and rose, while Louis was clad in a suit of white and gold cloth.

The Archbishop of Rheims conducted the marriage service, which was followed by a Nuptial Mass. Then the parish priest brought the register, and when it came to the Dauphine's turn the nervous girl mis-spelt "Marie Antoinette Josepha Jeanne," and then blotted the page.

Once back in the privacy of her own apartments Marie Antoinette received the oath of fidelity from her household, among whom were fourteen waiting-women, five maîtres d'hôtel, six equerries, nineteen valets de chambre, five ushers of the bedchamber, two ushers of the antechamber, two ushers of the Cabinet, two preachers, four almoners, five chaplains, two doctors, two apothecaries, four surgeons, a clock-maker, a tapestry-maker, eighteen lackeys, a stable equerry, a fencing-master, two muleteers, a wig-maker and a Turkish bath attendant. Most can have had little to do, except wait about, scheme and quarrel. But these were not all; there were no less than one hundred-and-sixty-eight servants to prepare her food, and that of her household.

The same evening six thousand privileged guests were allowed to file through the Hall of Mirrors, and watch the King, Louis and Marie Antoinette seated at a table covered with a green cloth, playing a most boring card game then fashionable at Court. The Park outside had been thrown open to the public, and soon those in the Hall of Mirrors were joined by soaking-wet gate-crashers sheltering from the down-pour which had just ruined the fireworks display.

The wedding day ended with a banquet in the newly completed and very beautiful opera house, where the stage had been extended over the auditorium by means of a false floor, on which the table had been set. Now that Turkey was no longer the terror of Christian Europe she had become fashionable, and Turkish music was played by the French and Swiss Guards dressed à la Turque.

Twenty-two sat down to dinner, and another six thousand spectators considered themselves privileged to watch the scene. Marie Antoinette touched hardly anything, but the Dauphin steadily ate his way through every dish that was set before him. Said Louis XV, who knew all about such matters. "Don't overload your stomach to-night."

The Dauphine stopped eating and asked, "Why not? I always sleep better after a good supper."

Louis XV gave Marie Antoinette a pitying glance.

Eventually the day came to an end with the ceremonial putting to bed of the young couple. The Archbishop of Rheims was there to bless the bed and sprinkle it with holy water. The King handed the Dauphin his nightshirt, the Duchesse de Chartres helped Marie Antoinette into her nightdress, and the young couple, still hardly more than children, got into bed behind the curtains. Then these were drawn back so that they could acknowledge the bows and salutations of the departing courtiers.

The following days the Dauphin wrote one word in his diary: *Rien*—Nothing. It transpired that he was incapable of consummating the marriage.

CHAPTER THREE

Splendours and Miseries

All through the remainder of May the wedding festivities went on—receptions and presentations for the privileged and, in the Park, firework displays and dancing for the general public. The culmination was to be a grand firework display in Paris itself on the evening of May 30th, and what was more Marie Antoinette could herself be present—unofficially.

In the second half of the eighteenth century Paris had hardly begun the sprawl beyond its medieval walls, and the Place Louis Quinze, later the Place de la Concorde, was almost on the western edge of the city. Not far from it were the ramparts, and there a fair was to be held as part of the celebrations. The fountains ran with wine, and it was reckoned that something like three hundred thousand people crowded into the Place Louis Quinze to watch the fireworks. By the time Marie Antoinette's carriage had reached Cours la Reine (opposite Les Invalides) the display was almost over, and the spectators were already surging towards the fair. This was nearly a century before Baron Haussmann gave Paris a new appearance with the wide avenues familiar today—the streets were much narrower then.

A fireman's cart was overturned, people stumbled against it, the crowd behind pushed those in front, and in a matter of moments the streets north and west of the square were a mass of writhing humanity. Marie Antoinette's coach was stopped and, when told what had happened, she returned to Versailles in tears. After the disaster one hundred and thirty-two identified bodies were buried in the Cemetery of the Madeleine. Marie Antoinette's first sight of Paris had been an occasion for tragedy in the Place, and so would her last, twenty-three years later. Not only that, but she, too, would be buried in the same cemetery. Both she and the Dauphin, who had not accompanied her, were shaken by the disaster and sent money to help the most needy.

Marie Antoinette became enmeshed in the routine at Versailles. Her mercurial temperament would not be moulded to fit the strait-jacket of Court etiquette which, since the days of Louis XIV, had hardened into a series of empty and useless formulae—worrying, for example, about how far down the chest the hat should be held when addressing a royal bastard. To expect this high-spirited and completely undisciplined young girl to conform was like trying to make a butterfly flutter in a straight line.

In a letter to her mother, Marie Antoinette gives a very full account of how she was expected to spend her day:

"I tell you that I get up at ten, or at nine, or at half past nine, and having dressed I say my morning prayers; then I breakfast and go from there to my aunts, where I usually find the King. This lasts till half past ten; then at eleven I go to have my hair done. At twelve they have the levée and everyone can come in, all who are not common people. I put on my rouge and wash my hands before everybody, after which the men go out and the ladies remain, and I dress myself before them. At twelve there is Mass; if the King is at Versailles I go with him and my husband and my aunts to Mass: if he is not there, I go alone with Monsieur le Dauphin, but always at the same hour. After Mass, we dine together before everyone, but that is finished at half past one, as we both eat very fast. From there I go to the Dauphin, and if he has business I return *chez moi*; I read, I write, or work, for I am making a waistcoat for the King which hardly progresses at all, but which I hope by the grace of God may be finished in some years' time. At three I go again to my aunts, where the King comes at that hour; at four o'clock the Abbé comes to me, and at five o'clock every day the harpsichord or the singing master till six. At half past six I nearly always go to my aunts, when I do not go out; it should be understood that my husband almost always goes with me to my aunts. At seven they play till nine, but when it is fine I go out and there is no play *chez moi*, but *chez* my aunts. At nine we have supper; when the King is away, my aunts come to supper with us, but when he is here, we wait for the King, who usually comes at a quarter to eleven. While I wait, I place myself on a large sofa and sleep till the King's arrival, but when he is not here we go to bed at eleven. I beg you, my very dear mother, to pardon me if my letter is too long, but it is my one pleasure to converse with you. I again beg your pardon if my letter is dirty, but I had to write it at my dressing-table two days running, having no other times to myself; and if I do not reply very correctly, please believe me it is owing to care in burning your letters."

A description of Marie Antoinette at this time tallies with that given by the Baronne d'Oberkirche who saw her at Strasbourg.

"Her figure was small but perfectly proportioned. Her arms were well-formed and of a dazzling whiteness; her hands elongated, with tapering fingers and pink transparent nails; her foot charming. When she had grown and filled out, her foot remained equally charming, but her figure altered and became slightly too full."

The person whose duty it was to try to make Marie Antoinette conform was Madame de Noailles, attached to the Dauphine's household as a Lady of Honour. Hers was a thankless task, and before long Marie Antoinette had nicknamed her "Madame Etiquette". Madame de Noailles was a most upright woman and extremely devout, though in later years this degenerated into religious mania. She was also prim and snobbish, even by the standards of the *ancien régime*. Count Mercy, the Austrian Ambassador, left a candid picture of her:

"In spite of her defects it is perfectly certain that Comtesse de Noailles is the member of the Court who has least drawbacks in her special place, but she has so little character or cleverness that it is impossible to make her see reason as regards the best means of discharging her duties."

From now on everything Marie Antoinette did was reported back to Vienna by the Austrian Ambassador. Had she known who it was who was relaying information to her mother the Dauphine would probably have liked the middle-aged bachelor from the Low Countries a lot less. As it was, thanks to him she was continually bombarded at long range with very necessary advice, which she seldom took.

"I can continue to report much that is good and little to the contrary about the Dauphine's behaviour," he wrote to the Empress. "The worst thing she does is listen to the advice given by Mesdames. She is careless of her appearance, and bored by ceremonial, which she avoids whenever she can."

Even the fact that Marie Antoinette had stopped wearing a whalebone corset which was intended to cover a defect—one shoulder-blade protruded more than the other—was relayed, and resulted in a maternal admonition.

While Madame de Noailles said, "Don't do this, and don't do that," and nearly drove the girl insane trying to make her conform to the rule of etiquette, Maria Theresa weighed in with some very blunt speaking:

"They say that you do not bother to speak to and notice the important personages; at table and at play you only talk to your young ladies, whispering and laughing with them." Maria Theresa was justified: Marie Antoinette had started making fun of nearly everyone in sight, and apparently she knew how to put into her remarks just enough wit to give them a cutting edge. She was an Austrian, and possessed that Viennese characteristic in which the borderline between wit and malice was indistinguishable. Certainly French wit could be extremely bitchy, but witty malice from one so young was not appreciated in the hide-bound, self-important atmosphere of Versailles.

Maria Theresa wrote to warn her daughter that if it was true she was making fun of everybody and laughing in their faces, it would end with her amusing about five or six of her young friends, but losing the goodwill of everyone else.

The Dauphine wanted to ride, to be free, and to do as she liked. But horses were out of the question: she might ride a donkey, providing it was completely docile. The Dauphine accepted the compromise, and orders were given to find "very gentle and tranquil" donkeys, and on such an animal Marie Antoinette rode out into the adjoining forests, accompanied by her young ladies in waiting on equally spiritless mounts.

Vienna heard, and disapproved. Maria Theresa would never have allowed such an outing, not even on a donkey, and in her considered opinion Louis XV was spoiling the girl.

Another attempt to escape from the all-enveloping life at Court was the Dauphine's idea of following her husband and his young friends in a coach whenever they went hunting. However, a very effective damper descended on the Dauphine and her friends when Mesdames invited themselves along too. Even so, that did not stop

Marie Antoinette from stocking the carriage with cold food which she distributed to the members of the hunting party when they stopped for a breather in some forest clearing.

Maria Theresa was perfectly right in all that she wrote to Marie Antoinette; but it would have been more to the point if she had shown more interest in her daughter's upbringing when she was still under her care in Vienna, instead of waiting until it was too late, and then indulging in a correspondence which lasted until her death in 1780. In the Hofburg she had never bothered what books Marie Antoinette read; indeed, she never seems to have inquired whether she could even read. But now she was telling her firmly that it was her duty to fill her head with good reading, blaming her for having neglected the matter in the past. In Maria Theresa's opinion the donkeys were to blame. Time had been wasted on them which should have been devoted to reading, and she should make an effort to catch up during the winter, "since you know only a little about music, drawing, dancing or painting or other accomplishments."

Soon the young girl must have come to dread her mother's letters, like cold blasts of reality from Central Europe blowing through the hothouse atmosphere of Versailles. Her natural inclinations were to play with her two brothers-in-law, the Comte de Provence, aged fourteen, and the Comte d'Artois, who was a year younger. Dressing up was already a favourite amusement, a withdrawal into a make-believe world which was to become more and more pronounced as the years passed.

Although Marie Antoinette ranked as the First Lady in France, that position was occupied, albeit unofficially, by Madame du Barry. It was not long after the Dauphine's arrival that Mesdames took her aside and in tones of spinsterish indignation and self-righteousness made it quite clear who, and what, was the du Barry. There may or may not have been a bad fairy at Marie Antoinette's christening, but there were certainly three of them at her wedding: Mesdames Adelaide, Sophie and Victoire. Making mischief was their delight, and now they had drawn the Dauphine into their web. The results were to have international consequences that not even they could have foreseen.

Marie Antoinette informed her mother that it was pitiful to see the King's infatuation for the du Barry, who in her opinion was the most stupid and impertinent creature imaginable. But although she assured Maria Theresa she would do nothing either for or against the woman, it was not long before she was an active partisan in the camp of Mesdames.

Unlike Louis XV's other mistresses Madame du Barry was indiscreet, and perhaps a little brazen. An English visitor recorded a dinner party:

"Next to him (the King) sat Madame du Barry, speaking familiarly and taking pieces off his plate to show her consequence, affecting great affability and talking and smiling all round the table."

Mesdames did their work well, and Marie Antoinette, still not sixteen, took a malicious delight in snubbing the du Barry on every possible occasion, public or private, formal or informal. So much so that in the end Madame du Barry complained in tears to Louis XV. From then on the incident snowballed. Louis XV's attitude to the Dauphine changed, and Mercy had to intervene. He was granted an interview with the King in Madame du Barry's private apartments. There, after she had left them, Louis XV humiliated himself to the extent of asking Mercy to put in a word with Marie Antoinette, and persuaded her to treat everyone as they had a right to expect.

"All she (Madame du Barry) wishes is that Madame la Dauphine should speak to her just once."

Mercy went to the girl and pointed out that her behaviour was actually jeopardizing the alliance between France and Austria, as Louis XV was becoming spiteful. Maria Theresa entered the lists:

"You make me laugh by imagining that I or my Minister would ever advise you to do anything against honour or even against the simplest propriety."

The Austrian Chancellor Kaunitz wrote to Mercy telling him that in his opinion it was offensive to the King and his circle if anyone went out of their way to avoid being civil to the King's friends, and that anyone must be regarded as a member of that circle who had the King's confidence: "No one is entitled to question whether he is right or wrong."

The courtiers were even taking bets, as to whether the two women would ever speak to one another.

With a bad grace Marie Antoinette agreed to make the first move. The remark, whatever it was, could only come from her as by etiquette a person of inferior rank, even a Countess, could not be the first person to address the Dauphine. It was arranged that Marie Antoinette should speak to Madame du Barry that Sunday evening, July 10th, 1771. But she talked about it to Mesdames, and when the moment came for the young girl to address Madame du Barry, the mischief-making Adelaide cut in saying:

"It's time to go! Come along, we will go and wait for the King with my sister Victoire!" and Marie Antoinette was whisked out of the room. Louis XV was furious. His mistress had been publicly humiliated yet again, and the Dauphine continued to be insolent to her.

Politics of a rather shameful nature hung in the balance. Austria needed France as an ally since Prussia and Russia were planning to partition Poland, and Maria Theresa wished to be in a strong enough position to demand a share of that unfortunate country.

Maria Theresa took a personal hand in the childish feud between Marie Antoinette and Madame du Barry, and asked what all the fuss was about, simply over saying "good day" to someone or making a trivial remark about a dress or some such thing. The trouble was, the Empress went on, her daughter was too much under the influence of Mesdames; as far as she was concerned Madame du Barry was simply a lady of the Court who had the right of entry to the King's chosen circle, and as his first subject Marie Antoinette owed it to him to be obedient and submissive.

The Dauphine wrote back defending her conduct:

"If you saw all that goes on here as I do you would realize that this woman and her clique will not be content with a word, and the whole thing will start up again."

Even Marie Antoinette could not hold out forever and on New Year's Day, 1772, at least some of the courtiers lost their bets. According to custom the ladies of the Court were offering their greetings. The Duchesse d'Aiguillon presented Madame du Barry to the Dauphine. Marie Antoinette spoke at her rather than to her, "There are a lot of people here at Versailles today."

She had kept her side of the bargain. Louis XV was delighted, and Austria had his moral support in the dismemberment of Poland. But the Dauphine had had the last word. She never again addressed a single remark to the du Barry, but this was something that neither the King nor his mistress could yet realise. Now Madame du Barry thought she would consolidate her position, but all she in fact did was to overplay her hand. First she wrote a number of letters to Marie Antoinette, assuring her of her eternal devotion, and received no reply. Then she thought of Böhmer, the Court Jeweller. He had made a pair of monstrously expensive earrings which Madame du Barry knew Marie Antoinette had admired. Through a go-between the du Barry offered to persuade Louis XV to buy them for her. The girl did not even bother to give an answer.

There was something very wrong with the Dauphine's private life, and after she had been at Versailles a few months most of those in the Palace knew what it was. Her over-excited state and unending pursuit of amusement, alternating with periods of gloom, had a very real reason. For want of a minor operation the Dauphin Louis was incapable of consummating the marriage, and for seven years Marie Antoinette was continually having her emotions stirred without ever a hope of true satisfaction. Only in 1777 did Louis finally and in fear and trembling agree to have the operation, and then afterwards complacently declared that he wished he had had it sooner.

From the start of the marriage the Dauphin was extremely sensitive about his failure as a bridegroom; the crowning humiliation having come with a lecture and exhortation by those three archetypal old maids, his aunts. The result was that he became almost aggressively he-mannish in his sports and recreations. Whatever it was he did, it had to require strength rather than skill or intelligence—plastering, working at his forge, making locks and, above all, the hunt. It was as though he was sublimating all his humiliation and sense of inferiority in hunting. From early morning until late in the evening he was in the saddle. Then, lost to the world, he snored through the night, and was up early the next morning to resume the round. Both her confessor, the Abbé Vermond, and Monsieur de Mercy were moved by Marie Antoinette's situation, and "un chien Mops"—a pug dog—was sent from Vienna. Vermond wrote:

"The Dauphine amuses herself with her little dog. Monsieur de Stahremberg thought it might be useful, which it is, as the distraction of a moment, but this is succeeded by deep thought. My heart is wrung by all this."

Quite suddenly, in the summer of 1771, something in Marie Antoinette snapped. Just once too often Louis came into her apartments dirty and dishevelled from hunting. She lashed him with her tongue. Mercy recorded what happened when the Dauphin turned and fled for his own rooms, followed by his wife who catalogued "somewhat strongly, his way of life. This language so upset Monsieur le Dauphin that he began to weep." Then Marie Antoinette started to cry as well. At least some sort of emotional contact had been established between the couple, and afterwards the Dauphin showed a little more consideration.

It was at about this time that the girl started to amuse herself with amateur theatricals. She and her brothers-in-law, Provence and Artois, and their equally young wives, Marie-Josèphe of Savoy and Marie-Thérèse of Savoy, had a little folding theatre in the Dauphine's apartments which could be hidden away in a cupboard in a matter of moments if a spoilsport like Madame de Noailles was heard approaching. Only the Dauphin was there to watch them, but here at least he and Marie Antoinette had an interest in common. She was even beginning to like the boy.

Apart from the one abortive sortie into Paris on the night of the disaster in the Place Louis Quinze, Marie Antoinette had never set foot in the captial, although it was only twelve miles from Versailles. Now, on June 8th, 1773, she and the Dauphin would see and be seen by the Parisians. Mesdames were as much to blame as anyone for the delay. They knew that the Dauphine's acclamation in Paris would set the seal on her acceptance as the First Lady of France, and that idea was resented by Adelaide in particular. Delays were engineered, and excuses made for not going, but eventually the day came when the young couple made a happy entry in procession into the capital. After a service in Notre Dame they were received by the Abbot of St Geneviève outside his church, and also by the heads of the University. Then they went on to the Tuileries Palace. Today the plan of the Louvre is rather like that of a pair of open tongs. The Tuileries Palace, built on the site of a tile factory, was at the west end, but in the eighteenth century there was no long northern arm to the Louvre, that had still to be built, and what is now the Place du Carrousel was then filled with houses. The Palace overlooked the Tuileries Gardens, and until its destruction in 1871 following the Franco-Prussian War and its aftermath, it was the Paris residence of the French monarchy.

"We made our entry into Paris," wrote the Dauphine. "We were well received with all imaginable honour. Although that was very pleasant, what really touched me was the affection and enthusiasm of the poor people, who were delighted by the sight of us, although they are weighed down by taxation. While driving to the Tuileries the crowd was so large that we were brought to standstill for three-quarters of an hour without being able to go on or go back. Dearest Mother, I cannot begin to describe the affection and delight they showed towards us, and before we at last drove away, we kissed our hands to them, which pleased them very much. How lucky we are to be in the position where we can have such widespread popularity at so small cost. Though the cost is small, such love is extremely worth having. That fact was impressed upon me, and I shall never forget it."

Marie Antoinette had conquered Paris as she had conquered Strasbourg three years earlier. When she stepped out on to the balcony of the Tuileries overlooking the gardens and the Place Louis Quinze in the distance, she was visibly shaken.

"My God," she exclaimed, "how many there are of them!"

"Madame," replied the Maréchal de Brissac, "I hope that His Highness the Dauphin will not misunderstand me, but in front of you are two hundred thousand people who have all fallen in love with you."

In 1773 that was the truth. Twenty years later there would be an equally huge crowd filling what by then was called the Place de la Révolution, but their mood was very different.

CHAPTER FOUR

An End and a Beginning

All Paris had fallen in love with Marie Antoinette, and she returned the compliment by falling in love with her capital by adoption. The city was the absolute antithesis of Versailles in its strait-jacket of musty etiquette. Here there was no one to raise their eyebrows if she did not conform, or involve her in their petty intrigues, or, worse still, plague her with lessons. Two or three nights a week, she and a few close friends drove to Paris; to the theatre, to parties and to the Masked Balls held at the Opera. There she could live in her make-believe world, believing that because she was wearing a mask, no one would recognise her. Even if the Opera Balls were not the quickest way to lose a reputation, they certainly never improved one, and were a recognised meeting place for prostitutes. While all this was going on, the Dauphin Louis was sleeping like a log at Versailles, worn out by a hard day's hunting.

The Balls held during the Carnival season were Marie Antoinette's particular delight, and during those of 1774 she first became acquainted with Count Axel Fersen, the son of a Swedish Field Marshal. He was gallant, she was charming, and they thoroughly enjoyed each other's company. Had she been free to marry whom she chose, and had she not been handicapped by her Imperial birth, they might have made a devoted couple. Count Fersen was good-looking and with a strong enough character to have made Marie Antoinette realize she had met her match. For that, she would probably have loved him all the more. As it was, they flirted mildly and went their very different ways. Before her life was over, though, she would be addressing him in her private correspondence as "the most loved and loving of friends". But that was still fifteen years away in the future.

Now that Marie Antoinette had found an escape from the domineering Mesdames and the old-hen fussings of Madame de Noailles, she began to develop as an individual, to acquire poise and dignity. Mercy was delighted with the impression she was making: "One could fill volumes with the many remarks which were made, the comments on the appearance, charm and gracious, kindly air of the Archduchess." Maria Theresa however preferred to reserve her judgement.

The first time that Marie Antoinette made her mark, and scored a personal victory, was in the operatic war then being waged in Paris. Music had been brought into politics by the factions which surrounded Madame du Barry and Marie Antoinette respectively. When Madame du Barry professed to admire the Neapolitan composer, Niccolo Piccinni, her followers promptly extolled him as their idol. In retaliation, Marie Antoinette's circle chose the German, Christoph Gluck, as their musical champion. When he came to Paris in 1772, he was assured of a royal welcome in every sense of the word, for Marie Antoinette was genuinely glad to see the man who had tried to teach her music during her childhood in Vienna.

Gluck had come for the first Paris performance of his opera, *Iphigénie*, and it took all Marie Antoinette's charm to smooth the singers' outraged feelings and the indignation of the orchestra at being shouted and stormed at by this bluff German who knew what he wanted and meant to get it.

In the hope of starting a fierce musical quarrel Madame du Barry's followers espoused Piccinni from Italy, but the personal warfare between this man and Gluck was merely a figment of the imagination of the journalists of the more fashionable periodicals. The two musicians liked each other, refusing to be provoked. Eventually, after Gluck's return to Vienna, Piccinni became Marie Antoinette's singing master, a post he held until the Revolution.

When the leading tenor in *Iphigénie* fell ill just before the premiere, Gluck refused to let an understudy take his place—the performance must wait, or he would go back to Vienna then and there. The Court was scandalised because the Dauphin and Marie Antoinette were coming, together with their entire circle of Gluck supporters. The Dauphine intervened—the composer had his way and the opera was performed by the original cast.

One can imagine what the fashionable and superficial audience really thought of *Iphigénie* which, in its day, was considered revolutionary for breaking away from the outworn conventions, but they smiled bravely and whenever Marie Antoinette applauded they rapturously followed suit. Perhaps the triumph that night belonged more to the Dauphine than to Gluck, but he was "made" as far as Paris was concerned, and German music became the fashion.

Mozart, known to Marie Antoinette as a child, visited Paris a few years later. If only she had shown the slightest interest, she could have turned his visit into the financial success he so badly needed. She did not, and he left almost empty-handed, saddened by the death of his mother. He bequeathed the ungrateful city his handsome but superficial 31st Symphony together with one of his most charming minor masterpieces the *Flute and Harp Concerto*, written for the Comte (later Duc) de Guines. Later de Guines was to prove one of the most worthless of Marie Antoinette's friends.

It was one thing to indulge in musical intrigues, but politics were another matter, and it was Maria Theresa's fervent hope that Marie Antoinette would not interfere in what she could not understand.

"I say outright that I do not want my daughter to have a marked influence in affairs. I know only too well from personal experience what a weight it is to rule a huge kingdom. What is more I know my daughter's frivolousness and her aversion from concentrating—and she does not know a thing! All that makes me thoroughly afraid if she should try to govern a kingdom as ramshackle as France at the moment." This letter to Mercy betrays her considered opinion of the Dauphin as the future ruler of France.

In April, 1774, the old roué Louis XV felt unwell, and took to his bed, in the Grand Trianon in the Park at Versailles. His doctors consulted together, and he was brought back to the main palace. Etiquette insisted that should he wish to die he must do so in the state bed, and nowhere else. Fourteen different medical men were unable to diagnose the trouble, until a servant happened to hold up a light in the darkened room, and those nearby noticed the King's face was covered with angry red spots. Louis XV had smallpox, probably caught from a milkmaid.

He took thirteen days to die, slowly and horribly. Those in line of succession, including of course the Dauphin and Dauphine, were not allowed near the King, but Mesdames were permitted to go to him. They showed courage, and despite the infection and the nauseating smell stayed with their father almost until the end. For the first time in nearly forty years Louis XV asked to confess his multitude of sins. But his confessor would not grant absolution: the confession of sins must be made in public. The following morning the Host was brought from the chapel in a procession which included the Archbishop of Paris, the Dauphin and Marie Antoinette, the Counts of Provence and Artois and their wives. The young princes and princesses of the blood stopped and knelt in the doorway, while the Archbishop and supporting clergy went into the sick chamber to the King, whose face was quite black by now. In a voice that was inaudible to the onlookers Louis XV made his lengthy confession, and received Holy Communion. Then the Archbishop came out; "Gentlemen, the King instructs me to tell you that he asks God's pardon for his offences and for the scandalous example he has set his people."

Those near Louis XV heard him mutter, "I wish I had been strong enough to say that myself."

Everyone knew the end was inevitable. Already Madame du Barry had been sent away to the Château de Rueil, and the fickle courtiers were ready for a change of allegiance.

A candle was kept burning at a window in Louis XV's room to signify that he still lived. Then, just after three in the afternoon of May 10th, it was snuffed out. The traditional cry went up: "The King is dead! Long live the King!" Then there was a noise like thunder echoing through the tense and silent Palace—the sound of the courtiers running to the Dauphin's apartments. There they acclaimed their new sovereign, King Louis XVI and Queen Marie Antoinette.

Unfortunately it is only in the lavender-scented memoirs of Madame Campan that the young couple are supposed to have fallen on their knees, embraced each other in tears and exclaimed, "Oh God, protect us, we are too young to reign." A pity, but for one thing it would have been completely at variance with Marie Antoinette's character.

The funeral was hasty. The late King's body was taken at top speed to St Denis, the burial place of the French monarchs, in the middle of the night. Perhaps only Madame du Barry was truly sorry: certainly not France as a whole. The long reign which had begun with admiration for the splendour of the monarchy, ended in contempt and near-bankruptcy mingled with bitterness due to the crushing taxation which fell heaviest on those least able to bear it—the poor people. To the peasant at his plough and the common men Versailles was little more than a gilded sink of iniquity, a luxury which France could not afford. Now that Louis XV, once called the "Well Beloved", was dead, there was hope once again. France had a young King and Queen—it would be a young people's world, with progressive ideas and, at long last, some likelihood of reforms.

Marie Antoinette certainly regarded it as a young people's world, though not in the way her more sanguine subjects might have hoped.

"When one has passed thirty," declared the new Queen, "I do not know how one dares show oneself at Court."

Among the first to go was the tiresome Madame Etiquette. Very firmly Madame de Noailles was told that her services would no longer be required, and her family were among the first to change their opinion of Marie Antoinette. In later years Madame de Noailles became a noted eccentric and entered into heavenly correspondence with the Virgin Mary. To humour her, her confessor would reply in letters purporting to have come from the Virgin Mary herself. Madame de Noailles spent most of her time inquiring about points of etiquette, as might be expected, and on one occasion the confessor made a slip-up which she noticed. This she explained to her own satisfaction at least by saying that while Joseph was descended from the royal house of David. Mary was only a bourgeoise, and so need not be expected to know the niceties of such procedures. Silly old woman she may have been, but like nearly all the others of the *ancien régime*, she knew how to die when the time came. A priest left a moving account of how he risked his own life to stand in the crowd and give absolution to Madame de Noailles and her daughter as they passed in a tumbril on their way to the guillotine.

From Vienna Maria Theresa, who day by day became more Cassandra-like in her unheeded warnings of disaster, wrote to Mercy to say that she was very upset to hear of the death of Louis XV, and even more worried about her daughter's future, "which cannot fail to be either wholly magnificent or extremely unfortunate". Yet again she commented on her daughter's light-headedness and inability to concentrate, and doubted if it was a defect she could ever overcome.

Nor did Maria Theresa spare Marie Antoinette herself. In the midst of all the excitement the young girl must have fallen silent as yet another of her mother's letters was handed to her. Maria Theresa could not find it in her heart to compliment the girl on her new-found dignity, which had a high price, and warned that this price would go on rising if she did not continue to lead a quiet and reasonable life, such as she had done under the guidance of Louis XV. This had endeared her to the ordinary people. Also, the Empress insisted, she must not be the cause of heavy expenditure, and should try to make herself useful to her husband if he should ask her opinion on any serious matters. At the same time Maria Theresa wrote to Mercy, "I fear that her good days are passed."

News of Marie Antoinette's activities were faithfully reported back to Vienna, only to evoke further rumblings and parental advice. She need not expect her good luck to last for ever, warned Maria Theresa, and if she were plunged into misfortune it would be her own fault, "because you lead such a superficial life, and never try to concentrate on anything. What books do you read? Yet you put your finger into every pie, interfere with state business, even with the selection of ministers. You will recognize the truth some day, but then it will be too late. I hope I shall not live to see misfortune overtake you, and I pray God to cut short my days before this happens.'

The old Empress's prayer was granted. She died in 1780, thirteen years before the final catastrophe overtook her daughter.

Why should Marie Antoinette worry? Her mother was far away in Vienna, and letters were only letters after all. Besides, Louis was going to be crowned at Rheims, and so there were the Coronation preparations to be made.

Somehow it is difficult to visualise Louis XVI's coronation on June 11th 1775, in that most perfect of medieval cathedrals which symbolised a more idealistic if not necessarily a better age.

The ceremony was extremely long, lasting for about five hours, and, if Louis at the age of twenty-one found it exhausting, it must have been nearly insupportable for the seventy-eight-year-old Archbishop of Rheims, weighed down by his magnificent vestments.

After the actual coronation Louis was enthroned before his people, and although in the coronation church of France, the congregation showed no inhibitions and clapped and cheered, and Marie Antoinette wept with emotion. The Golden Age had begun, she was sure of that.

CHAPTER FIVE

Payment Deferred

In much the same way that a queen ant is surrounded by a swarm of ants, so Queen Marie Antoinette was now surrounded by countless servants. At Versailles her household had swollen to no less than five hundred persons. Five hundred individuals who perforce could have had little to do, except quarrel over their rights and jealously claim their salaries.

Within the walls of the Palace, life was dominated by etiquette to a degree that is almost unbelievable today. If her first Lady of Honour or her First Waiting Woman was absent Marie Antoinette had to go thirsty, because while they had the right to hand her a glass of water, none of the other members of her household had sufficient status to do so. Getting dressed in the morning was in itself a major operation requiring considerable deployment of forces. Madame Campan, who held the post of Reader to Her Majesty, left an account of Court procedure when the Queen was at Versailles, or for that matter at any of the other royal châteaux in the Paris region such as Fontainebleau, Rambouillet or Compiègne.

The ritual was presided over by the Lady of Honour and the Mistress of the Robes, who both took part "as if they were acting together", and assisted by the First Waiting Woman together with two Waiting Women. Among themselves there were distinctions about who performed what duties. It fell to the Mistress of the Robes to hand the Queen her petticoat and dress, while it was the Lady of Honour who had the right to pour out the water for washing the hands and also to offer the chemise. If a Princess of the royal family happened to be present, then a different procedure had to be observed. The Princess took over the duties of the Lady of Honour, "though each of these ladies observed these customs more carefully, as they were privileges."

Beautiful clothes had always had a special fascination for Marie Antoinette, and now it was as though the millennium had come. Her dresses were numbered in hundreds: satin, silk, brocade, gold thread, silver thread, material sewn with pearls or precious stones. All were the masterpieces of Mademoiselle Bertin and her team of seamstresses. At least in one respect did Marie Antoinette break through the etiquette. No one except the oldest of the nobility were supposed to be received in the Queen's private apartments but Mademoiselle Bertin, a woman of the people and dictator of fashion in Paris, achieved the seemingly impossible, by crossing that threshold.

At this time if Marie Antoinette considered she had any duty at all, it was as the leader of fashion. Extravagance followed on extravagance, and before long the inevitable letter came from Vienna. While Maria Theresa considered one should follow fashion up to a point, extremes should be avoided. If a queen was attractive and charming, she had no need of such follies, and indeed simplicity enhanced her daughters high position. Since it was she who set the tone, Maria Theresa reflected, everyone else would follow wherever she led.

If Marie Antoinette's dresses were extravagant, her hairstyles were fantastic. In this she was aided and abetted by a sublime idiot, Monsieur Léonard, the most fashionable hairdresser in Paris. Every morning he drove out to Versailles in a coach drawn by six horses to dress the hair of the Queen of France and Navarre. By one of those odd twists of fate which recur throughout Marie Antoinette's life, it was thanks to Léonard's losing his nerve and dismissing troops sent to escort the royal family that Louis and his Queen failed to escape over the frontier into the Austrian Netherlands in 1791.

However, that lay in the future and in the 1770s Monsieur Léonard's genius was at full stretch inventing one towering folly after another to adorn the heads of the Queen and her circle. The hair was combed upwards to a height of about eighteen inches above the forehead, and, with the addition of plumes, most of his creations attained an overall height of at least three feet. In the Opera House at Versailles the flat-topped doorways to the boxes had to be turned into semi-circular arches to allow the followers of fashion to enter without almost having to go on their knees.

Before plumes became the rage the hair was topped with a remarkable collection of childish objects. One day it would be a garden, another a country scene, complete with windmill, or tiny figures hunting. Some were frivolous to the point of being dangerous; ladies even wore revolutionary bonnets on top of the hair, after there had been bread riots in Paris. At the suggestion of the ineffable Léonard, Marie Antoinette would be willing to put on the revolutionary bonnet, but when the charade was over and she had to face the mob in the Tuileries Palace she staunchly refused to wear that emblem of the French Revolution, the Phrygian Cap of Liberty, though her husband would not prove so strong-minded.

Böhmer and Bassenge, two Germans, were the Court Jewellers, and like Mademoiselle Bertin and Monsieur Léonard, they were frequent and welcome visitors at Versailles. What Marie Antoinette wanted, she had, whether rings, bracelets, brooches, earrings or necklaces. It was a case of buy now, pay later. Every action has its equal and opposite reaction, in this case it was one of Maria Theresa's most outspoken letters:

"A queen only succeeds in cheapening herself by this outlandish behaviour and she makes herself even more cheap by unwise spending, especially in hard times. I know only too well how extravagant you are, and I shall not remain silent because I love you too much to indulge in idle flattery. If you are not careful, you will lose, through these follies, the good will that you had at the beginning. Everybody knows that the king is thrifty, so you will receive all the blame. I hope I do not live long enough to see the disaster which will probably result."

There was one item that even Marie Antoinette dare not purchase, or ask her husband to acquire. Böhmer and Bassenge had made a diamond necklace that for sheer cost must still be without rival. This necklace consisted of six hundred and forty-seven perfect stones weighing two thousand eight hundred carats, and may have been worth something in the region of one and a quarter million pounds at today's values. The jewellers had fashioned it on the off-chance that Louis XV would buy it for Madame du Barry, but he died before he could give it to her, and the two men were left with the priceless necklace on their hands. Marie Antoinette was interested, but refused to consider its purchase, though it was not to be the last she or France were to hear of the famous diamond necklace.

Little time was to elapse after the death of Louis XV before Marie

Antoinette started to make herself felt in politics, if only in the furthering of personal feuds. The Duc d'Aiguillon and his wife had supported Madame du Barry at Court, and that in itself was sufficient reason to ensure the Queen's enmity. For a start she engineered the dismissal from the Cabinet of Monsieur de Maurepas, the Duc's uncle.

Surrounding the Queen was an almost unbreakable circle of friends, few of whom possessed any redeeming qualities, and who did not hesitate to use that friendship to further their own ambitions. The men were led by the King's youngest brother, the Comte d'Artois; but his brother Provence stood aloof. All his life Provence remained a thoroughly devious character, and even at this juncture he may have felt that if he played his hand carefully the throne might one day be his, and, in fact, he did become Louis XVIII, after Napoleon's exile to Elba. So, reluctant to have his name associated with the Queen's circle, which was already unpopular, he sided with the younger branch of the royal family, headed by the Duc d'Orléans and the Duc de Chartres, which was centred at the Palais Royal in Paris. In later years the Palais Royal became a hotbed of intrigue and mischief-making against Louis XVI and Marie Antoinette.

Not all the Queen's friends were of her own age. The Swiss Baron de Besenval was over fifty, but he had a gift for talking amusing nonsense, and in a group where the unforgivable crime would have been to talk seriously, his place was assured. Another witty time-killer was the Duc de Lazun, whose somewhat familiar attitude was enough to start tongues wagging. For Count Esterhazy, Marie Antoinette not only arranged payment of his debts, but also obtained for him the command of a regiment. Perhaps the most dubious character was Montfalcon, who called himself Count d'Adhémar, and was something of a philanderer, though it was as a singer who could accompany himself on the harp that the circle opened to receive him.

Another was the Comte de Guines for whom Mozart wrote his *Flute and Harp Concerto*. Although he was French Ambassador in England most of the Comte's time was spent at Versailles. He was not above using diplomatic privilege as cover for smuggling activities, and when caught out, blamed his secretary. The matter came to trial, at which he declared that the Duc d'Aiguillon, one of Madame du

Barry's friends, was trying to ruin his reputation. Marie Antoinette jumped to the defence of de Guines, and through the intervention of the King he was acquitted. The quarrel intensified and Marie Antoinette found herself involved in something more than trying to help one of her friends. To the outsider it looked as though she too was engaged in trying to destroy d'Aiguillon, and there was much gossip when he rode past her carriage at a military parade and she showed her displeasure by pulling down the blind. Later he went into self-imposed exile in southwest France. It was not the end of the smuggling affair; through the Queen's machinations Turgot, the Controller General of Finances, was dismissed for having ordered the recall of de Guines. That same day de Guines was raised to the rank of Duke. Turgot was something of a rough diamond and unpopular with the nobility, but had he been allowed to continue in office he might have been able to save France from bankruptcy on the eve of the Revolution.

If the men in Marie Antoinette's circle were for the most part worthless, and, with the exception of the Prince de Ligne, exercised a detrimental influence over her, that of Madame de Polignac and her family was catastrophic. In the Queen's case the unending round of pleasure and the search for novelty were linked with the fact that for the first seven years her marriage remained unconsummated. Highly strung, affectionate and wanting to love and be loved, she found her only outlet in mild flirtations with men, or a series of adolescent friendships with women. They may have been quite innocuous, but in the malicious atmosphere of Versailles it was not long before the gossips began to whisper about their exact nature: sotto voce speculations made the scandal twice as entertaining, and it travelled twice as fast.

Marie Antoinette had known the Princesse de Lamballe since the days when she had been among the party which welcomed her at Compiègne on her arrival from Austria. Slowly their liking for each other grew into a lasting friendship, though certainly it had its ups and downs. Unlike Madame de Polignac, her friendship was disinterested, and not a means for personal enrichment or for the advancement of relatives. Completely loyal, Madame de Lamballe returned from the safety of England to revolutionary France, only to suffer the most appalling death during the September Massacres in 1792.

Although Jules de Polignac was the favourite's husband, the Comte de Vaudreuil was quite openly her lover, and between them they were to rule the Queen during the long sultry years as the storm-clouds gathered heralding the Revolution. Portraits of Madame de Polignac show a face of little-girl innocence quite at variance with the character as shown by her actions. When she first met Marie Antoinette the latter asked her why she so seldom appeared at Court, and Madame de Polignac replied that it was because she was not sufficiently well-off to come more often. Then she said that before they became too close friends perhaps she ought to leave the Court, as she could not afford the privilege of being the Queen's friend. Marie Antoinette would not hear of this, and before long Madame de Polignac had arrived on the scene in no uncertain manner. She became the Queen's First Lady-in-Waiting, and Marie Antoinette began squandering money on her family to a stupefying extent. First, debts which amounted to four hundred thousand livres, were paid; her daughter received a dowry worth eight hundred thousand livres, her father a pension, and Madame's nominal husband was made a Duke and given the position of Postmaster General. Small wonder that the courtiers gossiped and looked on knowingly, or that pamphlets which may or may not have been libellous started to circulate.

Marie Antoinette sighed, and wrote to her mother: "There have very generally been two tastes attributed to me, that for women and that for lovers."

It hardly seems a likely remark to have made to Maria Theresa, who was the self-appointed guardian of morals in Austria, had there been any truth in all these insinuations.

Mercy was really worried and wrote: "It is unexampled that in so short a while the royal favour should have brought such overwhelming advantages to a family as to the de Polignacs."

Versailles thrived on scandal, intrigue and cliques, and there was even a Lamballe faction and a de Polignac faction. The former centred on the Duc de Chartres and the Palais Royal, while the de Polignac family gravitated towards the Princesse de Guénémée, governess to the King's young sister, Madame Élizabeth. Enough spite was generated between these two factions to have powered a turbine, and before long the more powerful de Polignacs were interfering with the nomination of ministers and even Army appointments. The whole scene was summed up by the Duc de Lévis:

"She (the Queen) thought it absurd to suppose that the loyalty of the common people could depend upon the number of hours which the royal family spent in a circle of bored and boring courtiers. Except for a few favourites, chosen for some whim or because of successful intriguing, everyone was excluded from the royal presence. Rank, service, reputation, birth, were no longer warrants for admission into the intimacies of the reigning family. Versailles, a scene of such magnificence in the days of Louis XIV, when all Europe was eager to go there for lessons in good taste and good manners, now became nothing more than a minor provincial town, which one visited unwillingly and which one left as quickly as possible."

Vermond, the confessor to Marie Antoinette who had known her since she was thirteen years old, tried to make her see reason. She was not careful enough about the reputations and morals of her friends. All kinds of misbehaviour, immorality and bad reputation seemed to be passports for admission to the Queen's society. Maria Theresa added her voice, saying that she could no longer remain silent, and that she spoke for her daughter's good: "Do not let your frivolousness lose the goodwill you started out with, for the King is known to be very easy-going, and you will get all the blame."

But why should Marie Antoinette be expected to listen to these tedious old people? She had coined the phrase "strait-laced", and anyone over forty was dismissed as a "centenarian". When speaking to Mercy of one of her mother's admonitions she exclaimed: "What does she want of me? I am terrified of being bored."

Little by little the old society was withdrawing from Versailles: middle-aged Dukes and Duchesses, Counts and Countesses became exasperated with driving out to the Château only to find that at the last minute Marie Antoinette had decided not to attend a presentation or reception and had gone off for the day into the vast park with some of her amusing friends.

First it was Yolande de Polignac and her voracious relations who set Paris talking, then it was the young Comte d'Artois and the craze which he introduced into France from England. Until he took it up horseracing was unknown to the French, but on a course on the edge of the Bois de Boulogne, racing soon became the latest thing for all the young bloods. Marie Antoinette was invited to attend, and on numerous occasions the Parisians were treated to the undignified spectacle of the Queen of France and her young friends behaving like over-excited adolescents as their horses won or lost.

As usual Maria Theresa had something to say on the subject. She would not have minded so much if her daughter indulged in her pleasures in the King's company; what upset her was that almost without exception she was on her own, or rather accompanied by "all that is youngest and worse in Paris", and among a group in which she was usually the eldest. The newspapers, Maria Theresa went on, which used to be full of stories about Marie Antoinette's "kindness and generosity of heart, have suddenly changed their tone. In them I read of nothing but accounts of horseracing, gambling, the turning of night into day so that I can no longer bear to look at them."

The Austrian Empress had every right to be worried about gambling. Although Louis XVI had made gaming illegal in France, it was carried on openly at Versailles, and every night thousands of pounds changed hands. If the King was reported to be on his way the cards vanished from sight, and when he appeared it was to gaze short-sightedly at his wife and her friends having a quiet evening talking together. Of course he knew gambling went on, but not the scale or size of the stakes involved. In order to improve the standard of play professional card-players from Paris were allowed into Versailles, and it was open knowledge that cheating went on at the Queen's table.

After a minor scandal had been caused by gambling past midnight into All Saints Day, November 31st, 1776, all that Louis said was, "Really! You are all a worthless lot!" Not long after he paid his wife's debts, which amounted to nearly half a million livres, a sum which surprised even her.

It was obvious that Louis XVI had no control over his wife, her friends or her recreations, and as usual the only real adverse comment came from Maria Theresa: "I know only too well what the outcome will be: you will lose prestige with the public, and especially abroad."

Not only was there gambling to keep Maria Theresa awake at night. The number of pamphlets in circulation was increasing. Every day they rolled off clandestine presses, criticising Marie Antoinette, her extravagances and her friends. Some inevitably found their way back to Vienna, and the Empress' anger grew. But at Versailles the Queen was hurt, puzzled, but unmoved. Perhaps her remark to Mercy: "I am terrified of being bored," is the clue to her behaviour in the years 1770–7. More than anything she desired a normal married life with children of her own on whom she could lavish affection, and the pursuit of pleasure may have been nothing more than an unsuccessful attempt to escape from the empty reality of her life. When the Duchesse de Chartres gave birth to a child which was stillborn, Marie Antoinette wrote to her mother, "However upsetting, I only wish the same thing could happen to me." A cry from the heart, if ever there was one.

CHAPTER SIX

The Little Kingdom

Once Louis XIV had been glad to slip away to the Grand Trianon from the overpowering splendours of the main Palace at Versailles, which he himself had created, and in the last years of his great-grandson's reign Louis XV had been equally glad to seek out the nearby Petit Trianon, where he and Madame du Barry could be alone together. Built by the architect Gabriel at the suggestion of Madame de Pompadour, the Petit Trianon was intimate, and furnished in perfect taste. But Madame de Pompadour did not live to see it completed, and it was the du Barry who sat alone with the King in the dining-room, undisturbed by the presence of servants, while the fully-laden table rose through an opening in the floor from the kitchens below.

Soon after the death of Louis XV his grandson gave it – a charming and unexpected gesture—to Marie Antoinette. Now, at the Petit Trianon, the young girl of twenty really was the queen of a tiny make-believe kingdom, set in the bigger but equally unreal world of Versailles. She called it her "Little Vienna", a name that was to be thrown in her teeth when the day of reckoning came concerning the money she had lavished on it and the entertainments held there.

At the Petit Trianon the Queen's servants had their own livery, scarlet and silver, and rules were posted up in the grounds. "The Queen forbids that her garden be deemed a public place, allows entrance only by the gate and under the escort of a Swiss Guard; she forbids persons attached to the service of Trianon to bring their families or friends into the grounds on the days when she dines there alone or with the royal family; even in her absence such persons must be accompanied."

Under Salic Law in France the King was the supreme authority, and eyebrows were raised when such rules bore the subscription, "By order of the Queen." She was Queen of the Trianon and here all were her subjects; even Louis XVI only came by invitation, stayed an hour or two and then returned to the Palace, leaving his wife and her friends to amuse themselves until they too returned late in the evening. On one occasion when he looked like outstaying his welcome, someone put the clock on an hour, and off Louis went at ten o'clock, thinking it was his bedtime, which was not until eleven.

Marie Antoinette dreamed of pursuing a life of pastoral innocence where everything was beautiful and simple and nothing as ugly as reality was allowed to intrude. At the Petit Trianon a miniature village, the Hameau, was constructed beside a lake. It included a farmhouse with a thatched roof (which contained a billiard room), cowsheds, dovecots and barns—all were newly built and then aged artificially with cracks and signs of weathering painted on the walls.

In a setting of exquisite unreality, Marie Antoinette and her friends must have been like Meissen or Nymphenburg groups of figures come to life, as, dressed as shepherdesses, they collected eggs, made butter and milked the immaculate cows into urns of Sèvres porcelain. The flight from reality had hardly reached its zenith, however, before the first rumblings could be heard from the outside world.

"In the first instance, the public heard with pleasure that the King had given the Trianon to the Queen. It now begins to be uneasy and alarmed at Her Majesty's expenses there. By her orders the gardens have been demolished for the creation of an English garden that will cost at least one hundred and fifty thousand livres. The Queen has had a theatre made at Trianon; as yet she has given only one performance there, followed by a supper. This fête was most costly, and there is fear that it may be repeated, as well as the dinners that follow the hunting and coursing parties at La Muette."

The entertainments were undeniably costly, above all the fête given on September 3rd, 1777, to celebrate the completion in the grounds of the Temple of Love—a charming rotunda with Corinthian columns. A fair, complete with booths and a market place was set up, including a sweet shop, a bakery, and what could be described as a delicatessen. In a tavern the drinks were poured by ladies of the Court, while the Queen dispensed lemonade. All her life Marie Antoinette was extremely abstemious, drinking only a little wine, and that diluted. Then there were the sideshows and an open air theatre, and dancing to the band of the French Guards in Chinese costume. It must have been an enchanting evening, but the bill which went to the almost bankrupt Treasury was for no less than four hundred thousand livres.

Although the Petit Trianon served as an extremely expensive diversion for Marie Antoinette, it was becoming increasingly obvious to Mercy that in itself it was not sufficient. Day by day the Queen's emotional frustration was becoming more and more acute. Both the Duc de Lazun and Count Fersen had left the Court at Versailles rather than risk being the cause of Marie Antoinette losing her reputation. Fersen was already on very friendly terms, and at least on her side it would only have taken a spark to set that friendship afire; so, not wishing to cause unhappiness or disgrace, he departed overseas to join Lafayette who was helping the thirteen states fight George III in the American War of Independence.

So worried was Mercy that he wrote to Joseph II in Vienna, begging him to come to Versailles. There he must have a straight talk not only with his sister about her irresponsible behaviour, but also to Louis about the operation he had been avoiding for seven years. Joseph II, irked by having to live in the shadow of his redoubtable mother, was something of a showman, and particularly enjoyed playing the part of a most democratic Emperor. He travelled to France under the assumed name of Comte de Falkenstein, taking cheap lodgings in Paris and mixing with the ordinary people. Just how calculated was the act can be gathered from a letter to his brother Leopold in which he remarked that he—Leopold—was the more worthy of the two. Joseph admitted he was a charlatan, but added that in France one had to be, and that his simple way of life was no more than a pose. He was deliberately overplaying his part, but he knew it, and had already found that it had aroused an interest and enthusiasm that was most embarrassing.

Joseph II's unbiased opinion of his brother-in-law is informative, and confirms the world's opinion, then and now. Louis was weak, but not a fool. He had some ideas of his own and quite good judgement, but was apathetic both mentally and physically. His conversation was quite intelligent, but he was devoid of culture or curiosity.

Brother and sister were delighted to see one another, though Marie Antoinette must have been justifiably apprehensive, knowing that Joseph II had not come all the way from Vienna simply to bring greetings from their mother. The couple met and talked by the hour in the grounds of the Petit Trianon.

Joseph considered his sister an amiable and refined woman, though not yet completely adult, and not given to thinking carefully. She was basically well-behaved and virtuous, with a sharp wit and at times surprisingly perceptive. "Her initial reaction is always sensible, and if only she would abide by it and give more thought to the matter in hand, instead of listening to all who offer advice on all sides, she would be really perfect."

In addition to lecturing Marie Antoinette on her frivolity and the doubtful friends with whom she surrounded herself, Joseph II also lectured the King about his failure as a husband. There at least he was successful, and Louis plucked up courage to have the operation. Quite apart from the constitutional question—no heir to the throne—he was the butt of every tavern wit in France, and was spared neither in songs nor in pamphlets.

Joseph II said goodbye to Marie Antoinette on May 30th, 1777, before setting out on the long road back to Vienna.

"The Queen, who had made too great an effort to put a brave face on the parting, gave way to a rather violent fit of the vapours that same evening. She wished for solitude, and spent the day at the Petit Trianon, followed by the Princesse de Lamballe, the Comtesse Jules de Polignac, and only one lady-in-waiting."

Seven years before Maria Theresa had given her daughter a list of rules which she hoped would guide her life in France. Now, Joseph II had done much the same thing on his own behalf. Marie Antoinette had been left with a thirty page homily, in which he did not spare her feelings, particularly with regard to her behaviour towards her husband—Did she respond to the affection he showed? asked Joseph. Was she not vague and indifferent when he caressed or spoke to her? When she was bored, did she not show it? Did she go out of her way to make herself indispensable? Did she do anything to show that she loved him more than anyone, and that his success was all important to her?

All her young life Marie Antoinette was offered advice: now it was coming in torrents from her brother— "Did you ever give a thought to the results of gambling, and the undesirable people who are always to be found on such occasions, and of the overall atmosphere of such a place? Think of the upsets you have had at the Opera Balls, and of the misadventures you yourself have told me about. Do you really think that no one recognises you? Believe me, everyone knows who you are, and in fact the place has very bad reputation. In that case, why do you go? Why do you rub shoulders with a crowd of loose-livers, fast women and strangers, listening to improper remarks, and possibly making them yourself? The King is left alone all night at Versailles, while you lower yourself by mixing with the scum of Paris!"

Perhaps the future would be different, though, and all that had gone before might seem a folly excusable under the particular circumstances. At any rate, on August 30th, 1777 Marie Antoinette wrote to her mother:

"I have attained the happiness which is of the utmost importance to my whole life. More than a week ago my marriage was thoroughly consummated." Nearly a year later, at the beginning of August, Marie Antoinette came to Louis and in a mock-aggrieved voice said:

"I have come, Sire, to complain of one of your subjects who has been so audacious as to kick me in the belly."

CHAPTER SEVEN

'The Trianon Set'

In the months before the birth of the royal couple's first child Marie Antoinette found herself drawn into the world of international politics. Up to now her political activities had been confined either to her own intrigues or those of her place-seeking friends, and that within the realm of France. But now she was expected to act in the interests of her relations in Austria. Maximilian Joseph, Elector of Bavaria, had just died, and Joseph II saw the occasion as an excellent opportunity to add that state to the Austrian Empire. The support of France was vital to discourage Prussia from coming to the aid of Bavaria. But France, who had been openly aiding the rebels in the American colonies, was on the brink of war with England. When Marie Antoinette, acting on promptings from Vienna, approached Louis, he told her that the French ambassadors had already been told to inform the courts to which they were accredited that the partition of Bavaria would only take place against his wishes.

Maria Theresa did not press her daughter to act. Years of political experience had taught her that in such a situation Marie Antoinette must tread very carefully, or the French ministers might publicly discredit her and so make further intrigue on her part impossible. Mercy urged the Queen to use her influence, but without success. Maria Theresa wrote impatiently to her Ambassador:

"She is so occupied with her pleasures that she is almost incapable of thinking clearly on major matters. We will have to be content with what can be obtained by remonstrating with her.'

The fact that Marie Antoinette was expecting her first child had increased her prestige in France, and now Mercy tried to turn this to political advantage. The upshot was that the Queen had interviews with Maurepas and Vergennes, and while France did not agree to the swallowing of Bavaria, she would still be prepared to fight alongside the Empire against the Prussians if they attacked Austrian soldiers stationed in the Low Countries.

Having drawn her daughter into politics, Maria Theresa then had second thoughts about the wisdom of her action, and wrote to Mercy:

"I only hope she is not too impetuous, with the only result that she makes a nuisance of herself to the King, is mistrusted by the Ministers and odious to the nation."

The beginning of the year 1778 saw Marie Antoinette launched into the sphere of international politics, the disastrous consequences of which were to ensue, and in December she became a mother, eight years after her marriage to Louis. The start of her labour pains was announced by the ringing of bells, and the sound brought not only the courtiers running to her door, but what seemed like half the peerage of France. As the day of her confinement drew near the peers started to converge on Versailles, for by a barbarous custom they had the right to be present in the room when their queen gave birth. More than fifty of them had crowded into Marie Antoinette's room, the most important seated in armchairs round the bed, waiting and watching, while others at the back even stood on the furniture for a better view.

The Queen's labour went on right through the night, and it was not until half past eleven the following morning that she finally gave birth to a daughter. After her prolonged ordeal Marie Antoinette was far from well. "Air and warm water," ordered the *accoucheur*. "She must be bled in the foot." In the eighteenth century bleeding the patient was the doctor's answer to nearly every ill then known. This was done, and the Queen started to improve. Louis himself forced open one of the large windows, which had been sealed for the winter with gummed paper, and the gaping crowd was driven from the room. At last Louis had become a proud father, and his wife was safe.

All France celebrated: bells were rung, guns fired in salute and bonfires lit. That same afternoon the infant was baptised, Marie Thérèse Charlotte, usually referred to as Madame Royale.

Some seven weeks later, February 8th, 1779, Marie Antoinette went to Notre Dame to be Churched. Just before her arrival one hundred good-looking couples had been married in the cathedral in a mass wedding. Each of the brides received a dowry from the Queen herself. Although Paris was supposed to be celebrating a happy occasion, the truth did not escape Marie Antoinette. With anger she realised that the inhabitants were not finding it difficult to restrain their enthusiasm. Too much gossip had already circulated about what was supposed to go on at the Petit Trianon and about her meddling in politics.

If nothing could ever make the royal union into a love-match, at least the Queen was now genuinely fond of her husband. The birth of Madame Royale had consolidated the marriage as nothing else could have done. In the child they at least had something in common, and Marie Antoinette had the right to feel she was at last fulfilling her role as a mother and as the provider of heirs to the French crown. Even so, the pattern of her life had become too firmly set for any radical changes in her basic character.

All too soon the general public had something to talk about. When Marie Antoinette planned to visit the Shrove Tuesday Masked Ball at the Opera that year, she decided she really would go in disguise. As soon as she reached Paris she changed into an old and anonymous-looking carriage, which promptly broke down, leaving its occupants standing and laughing in the street. While waiting for it to be mended the royal party invaded the nearest house, which belonged to a merchant. The carriage could not be repaired on the spot, so eventually Marie Antoinette reached the Opera House in a hired cab, an unheard-of occurrence. All was harmless enough in itself, but by now the people were willing to think the worst of their Queen, and the story circulated that she had gone to the merchant's house to meet a lover.

Two years earlier Marie Antoinette had laid herself open to talk by her indiscreet mingling with the townspeople of Versailles in the grounds of the Palace. On warm evenings it was the custom to hold serenade concerts on the terrace, to which the public were admitted. On one occasion Marie Antoinette, dressed in simple clothes, sat on a bench and talked to a clerk from one of the Ministries. By the time the story had gone the rounds nothing had been left to the imagination. In a pamphlet she was accused of leaving her husband alone in bed to abandon herself "to bacchantes or satyrs and to become one with them through their brutal pleasures."

If the Queen did not deserve all that was said about her walks on the terrace, she did lay herself open to adverse comment when she had measles. Up to that date, the spring of 1770, she had never slept at the Petit Trianon, but had always returned to the Palace however late the hour. Now convalescing after measles made an excellent excuse to break the custom.

"Today I am going to establish myself at Trianon," she wrote to her mother, "and stay there for a change of air till the end of my three weeks, when I can go to the King again. I prevented him from shutting himself up with me; he has never had measles, and it would be most vexatious if he caught the illness, especially at this moment when there is so much business."

Turning the Petit Trianon into a sanatorium was in itself an excellent idea, but in addition to a few ladies of her household she also took the four brightest male members of her circle—the Duc de Coigny, the Duc de Guines, Count Esterhazy (whom Maria Theresa described as a "puppy"), and Baron Besenval. There they made it their duty to entertain the Queen from seven in the morning till eleven at night. At the Palace the four were asked with smiling malice by the rest of the Court which four ladies would be chosen to nurse the King in similar circumstances. Another who found his way across the Park to the Petit Trianon at this time was "the King's younger brother, Artois, flippant as he always is, adding to the unseemliness of the gatherings."

In spite of what the pamphleteers thought, the Queen's pleasures were not brutal, except for their effect on the Treasury. In 1780 the little theatre in the grounds of the Petit Trianon came into its own. In addition to occasional plays and operas given by professional groups it was the scene of amateur theatricals to the exclusion of nearly everything else. Mercy reported back to Vienna:

"For the past month (September) all the Queen's occupations and all her amusements have been concentrated on one unique object: the two little pieces to be given on the stage of the Trianon. The time needed to memorise the parts, and that needed for the numerous rehearsals, added to the other accessory details, have more than sufficed to fill her days. A kind of amusement restricted to so small a number of persons becomes a marked sign of favour for those who are included, and quite equally a cause for jealousy and protest among the many who are left out. All protests have no effect, and it has been a great cause of mortification, giving rise to talk which has spread from Versailles to Paris itself."

The cast at this theatre included Marie Antoinette herself; Madame Élizabeth; Madame de Polignac, her daughter, her sister-in-law, and Vaudreuil her lover; Artois; Adhémar, and Esterhazy. Neither Louis nor Provence took part, preferring to remain on the far side of the footlights.

The Queen made an attempt to forestall the inevitable letter from Vienna by dragging in her husband:

"The King seems very happy here; he sups here every day and comes to see me in the mornings, just as he does in my apartment at Versailles. I choose this time for my stay here because it is the month in which the King hunts almost every day and has less need of me."

Nothing could break the circle which surrounded Marie Antionette, but Mercy took it on himself to try to give a timely warning:

"I made her see how cleverly her set sought to profit by any opportunities of mingling very serious and important things with things of pure amusement. Everyone who approaches the sovereigns has always some design made up of ambition, intrigue, or other personal ends. A great Court must be accessible to a great number of people; otherwise hatreds and jealousies turn every head and give rise to complaints, bitterness and a sort of alienation. These observations did not seem to annoy the Queen; she told me that when the time comes to go to Marly there will be no question of theatricals, that she only thought of them as a very passing recreation, and that throughout next winter she intends to give herself up to Court life at Versailles." In addition to her undeniable charm, Marie Antoinette had the less attractive characteristic of easing herself out of a tiresome situation simply by saying whatever it was her hearer wanted. Soon after Maria Theresa wrote to her daughter about her obligations:

"I am very glad to hear you intend to resume your receptions at Versailles. Believe me, I know the boredom and the vanity, but if you do not give them, the troubles that will follow will be far worse than the petty inconveniences of receptions, especially as you have such a hot-tempered country to deal with."

That was to be Maria Theresa's last letter to Marie Antoinette. In November, 1780, she became ill with a lung infection, and on the 29th of that month she died in the arms of her eldest son, Joseph II. Tiresome and forever scolding she may have been in her dealings with her wayward daughter, but when she died the young Queen had lost the only person who could really take her to task with even a slight hope of being heeded. In more ways than one November 29th was a sad day for the youngest of the Empress' children.

The following summer Joseph II returned to Versailles, as Maria Theresa had wished him to do, for another heart-to-heart talk with his sister. This time Marie Antoinette was less inclined to listen to his lectures. She gave a fête in his honour at the Petit Trianon, and the second of Gluck's two operas on the Iphigenia legend was performed in the theatre. At least as far as her appearance was concerned the Queen was determined that Joseph II should have nothing to complain about: "When their majesties went together from Versailles to Trianon, they rode in a berlin-coupé drawn by four horses without pages, guards, or suite. The Queen was dressed in a muslin coat with a blue sash, and her hair tied with a simple ribbon, no rouge and no diamonds."

After a stay of only a week Joseph II left, and his sister buried her face in her hat to hide her tears.

Now it was Madame de Polignac who was expecting a baby, and after the arrival on May 14th, 1780, Marie Antoinette caused a thorough upheaval by going to La Muette so she could be near her friend at Passy, where she was recovering from her confinement. The wits of the day excelled themselves in their speculations as to who was the other parent of Madame's baby. Then next year it was the Queen who was the expectant mother, and on October 22nd, 1781, Louis became a father for the second time. His diary was more like a case-book. He noted that his wife's pains increased at half past twelve in the afternoon, and that at exactly a quarter past one by his watch she was safely delivered of a boy. At least on this occasion the room was not crowded to suffocation with sightseers determined to miss nothing. Only Provence, Artois, Mesdames, Madame de Polignac and four or five Ladies in Waiting were present, and they took turns to wait in an adjoining room.

1 Francis I and Maria Theresa with eleven of their sixteen children, in the Hofburg palace.

2 (*Above*) The Belvedere in Vienna, the great Baroque palace built by Prince Eugène of Savoy in the seventeenth century.
3 (*Below*) The City of Vienna, from an eighteenth-century engraving. In the centre stands the Hofburg palace with the cathedral of St Stephen behind.

4 (*Above*) Emperor Joseph II with his brother, the Archduke Leopold, painted by Batoni in 1769. Joseph became Emperor and co-regent with his mother after Francis I's death in 1765.
5 (*Above right*) Marie Antoinette at the spinet. As a child, she was taught music by Gluck.
6 (*Right*) Marie Antoinette in riding clothes; portrait by Krantzinger.

7 (*Above*) Engraving of the Dauphin – the future Louis XVI – guiding a plough. Louis XV sent Maria Theresa a similar portrait, much to her surprise.
8 (*Below*) Louis XV presenting to his grandson, the Dauphin, a portrait of Marie Antoinette; painting by Gauthier D'Agoty.

9 The feast held in Vienna on 2 April 1766 to celebrate the marriage of Marie Antoinette with the Dauphin Louis. Marie Antoinette is shown at the head of the table with her brother, the Emperor Joseph II. Painting by Auerbach.

Louis XVI with his brothers and one of his sisters. 10 (*Above left*) Louis XVI; portrait by Van Loo. 11 (*Above right*) The Comte de Provence, who was to reign as Louis XVIII of France from 1814 to 1824; portrait by Van Loo. 12 (*Below left*) The Comte d'Artois, who became Charles X of France in 1824; portrait by Van Loo. 13 (*Below right*) Madame Clothilde, Louis' elder sister; portrait by Drouais.

The unmarried daughters of Louis xv.
14 (*Above*) Madame Sophie, noted as walking quickly and looking sideways 'as hares do'; portrait by Drouais. 15 (*Above right*) Madame Victoire; portrait by Drouais. 16 (*Right*) Madame Adelaide, nicknamed 'Rag' or 'Dishcloth' by her father; portrait by Labille-Guiard.

17 (*Above left*) Madame du Barry, the last of Louis XV's mistresses. Her feud with Marie Antoinette enlivened the Court at Versailles during the last days of Louis XV's reign; portrait by Drouais.
18 (*Above right*) The Princess de Lamballe, who became one of Marie Antoinette's closest friends; portrait by Duplessis.
19 (*Below*) Louis Philippe, Duc d'Orléans, with his son the Duc de Chartres, cousins to Louis XVI. Orléans, known as Philippe Egalité, voted for his cousin's death, but was himself guillotined in 1793. Chartres became Louis Philippe, last king of France. This painting by Carle Verner shows them meeting in the hunt, in 1788.

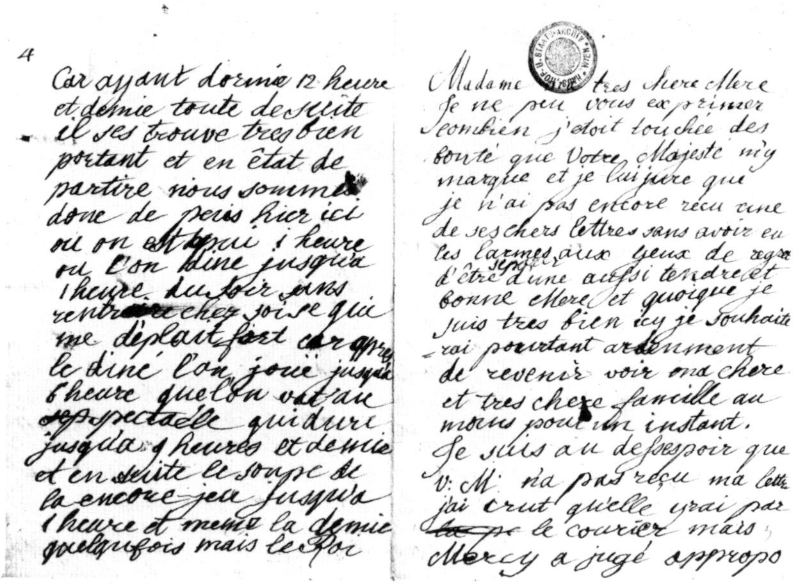

4

Car ayant dormie 12 heure
et demie toute de suite
il ses trouve tres bien
portant et en état de
partire nous sommes
donc de peris hier ici
ou on est venu i heure
ou l'on dine jusqua
1heure du soir sans
rentrer chez soi se qui
me déplait fort car apres
le diné l'on joue jusqua
6heure quelon vat au
spectacle qui dure
jusqua 9 heures et demie
et en suite le soupe de
la encore jeu jusqua
1heure et meme la demie
quelquefois mais le Roi

Madame tres chere Mere
Je ne peu vous exprimer
combien j'etoit touchée des
bonté que Votre Majesté m'y
marque et je lui jure que
je n'ai pas encore reçu une
de ses chers lettres sans avoir eu
les larmes aux yeux de regr
d'être separer d'une aussi tendre et
bonne Mere et quoique je
suis tres bien icy je souhaite
rai pourtant ardemment
de revenir voir ma chere
et tres chere famille au
moins pour un instant.
Je suis au desespoir que
V: M: n'a pas reçu ma lettre
j'ai crut quelle yrai par
le courier mais
Mercy a jugé appropo

20 (*Above*) Marie Antoinette's first letter to her mother, after her marriage.
21 (*Below*) As Dauphine, Marie Antoinette was highly popular and conquered Paris. This painting by Gauthier D'Agoty shows Louis and Marie Antoinette bestowing charity.

22 (*Above*) On Marie Antoinette's wedding day, nuptial mass was celebrated in the chapel at Versailles. In the evening she played cards with the King and the Dauphin in front of six thousand guests in the Hall of Mirrors.
23 (*Below*) To conclude the festivities, a huge banquet was held in the newly completed opera-house of the palace.

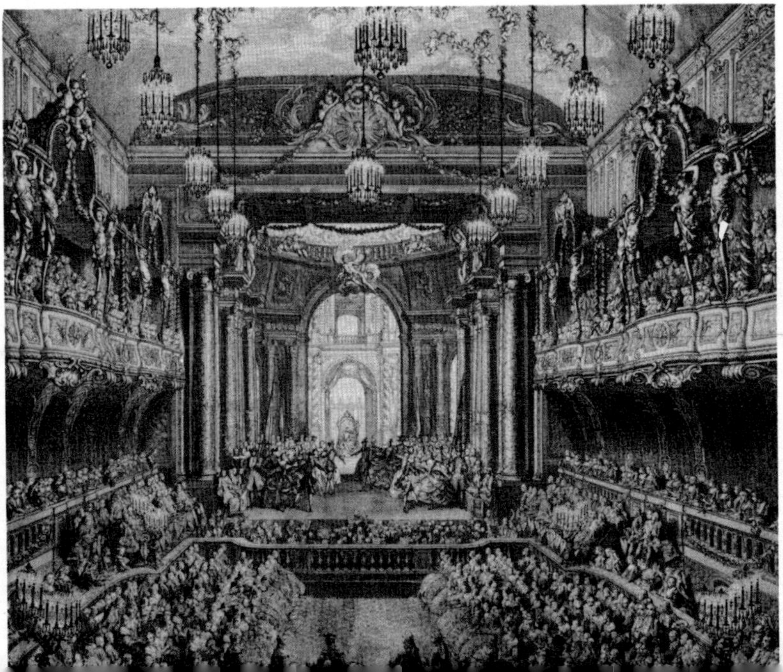

24 (*Above left*) The Comte de Vaudreuil, Madame de Polignac's lover, a member of the close-knit circle which surrounded the Queen at Court. Portrait by Madame Vigée Lebrun.
25 (*Above right*) Count Axel Fersen, 'the most loved and loving of friends'. Portrait by Pasch.
26 (*Below*) Madame de Polignac, whose influence over Marie Antoinette was to prove catastrophic. Madame Vigée Lebrun has portrayed her in this portrait wearing the simple pastoral clothes which became so popular with the Queen and her circle.

In 1774, Louis XVI gave to his Queen the Petit Trianon at Versailles. Marie Antoinette called it her 'Little Vienna' and spent much of her time there with her closest friends. 27 (*Above*) The Petit Trianon viewed from the English Garden; from a late eighteenth-century engraving. 28 (*Below*) An evening party at the Temple of Love; from a late eighteenth-century engraving.

29 (*Above*) The construction of the baths of Apollo at Versailles in 1777; painting by Robért.
30 (*Below*) The world of pastoral innocence, so desired by the Queen and her friends, was reflected in the art of the period, as exemplified by this painting by Pater.

31 (*Left*) Marie Antoinette's jewel cabinet at Versailles.
32 (*Below*) The park at Versailles illuminated for evening festivities; painting by Moreau le jeune.
33 (*Right*) In 1778, Marie Antoinette gave birth to her first child, Marie Therèse Charlotte, Madame Royale. This event is portrayed in stone by Pajou.
34 (*Far right*) In 1782, Marie Antoinette gave birth to her second son, Louis Charles, who eventually became Louis XVII. This engraving shows the masked ball given by the City of Paris to celebrate the birth.
35 (*Below right*) Portrait of Madame Royale by Kucharski.
36 (*Below, far right*) Miniature of the Dauphin Louis Charles.

37 (*Left*) A scene from Beaumarchais' devastating social comedy, *Le Mariage de Figaro*. The play was banned in Paris by Louis XVI, but Marie Antoinette wore away his resistance and it was first performed publicly on 27 April 1784.

38 (*Below*) Gluck, who had been Marie Antoinette's music teacher in Vienna, went to Paris in 1772, to supervise the first performance there of his opera *Iphigénie*. Nine years later, when Joseph II visited Versailles to see his sister, the opera was performed in the theatre of the Petit Trianon. In this painting, Gluck is shown presenting *Iphigénie* to the Queen.

According to a Swede (not Axel de Fersen), who wrote to King Gustav III, the Queen's rooms were filled with people who were both laughing and crying at the same time. Strangers embraced, and even those who had little regard for Marie Antoinette were swept away on a wave of enthusiasm. Madame de Guénémée, the royal governess, was wheeled to her own rooms, beaming with joy and holding the infant in her arms.

At first no one had told Marie Antoinette the sex of the child, and she feared it was another daughter. Then Louis said "Monsieur le Dauphin begs leave to enter."

"They brought her the child and those who witnessed the scene say they have never seen anything so touching."

The mother did not nurse the baby herself, that duty falling to the appropriately named Madame Poitrine: "She is a simple peasant, the wife of a gardener at Sceaux; she has the manners of a grenadier and swears with the greatest of ease, and is neither surprised nor disturbed by anything."

From now on, when Marie Antoinette took herself off to the Petit Trianon, she was accompanied by the two-year-old Madame Royale and the little Dauphin. This son had the title of Duc de Normandie, but he was a sickly child, and died in 1789; it was his younger brother who became the uncrowned Louis XVII after the execution of his father, and who disappeared so mysteriously in the Temple Prison.

The year following the Duc de Normandie's birth saw the Petit Trianon welcoming illustrious foreign visitors. About one hundred years before—in the time of Louis XIV—Peter the Great had stayed at the Grand Trianon, and now it was the son of Catherine the Great who visited Versailles. The Grand Duke Paul, later Tzar Paul I, and his wife travelled incognito under the name of the Comte et Comtesse du Nord, and Marie Antoinette casually referred to them as "the Norths". But evidently she got on well enough with them, and received a number of confidences from the Grand Duke about Court life at St. Petersburg, which he detested, and also about his mother's nymphomania.

A few months after Paul had departed for his homeland the

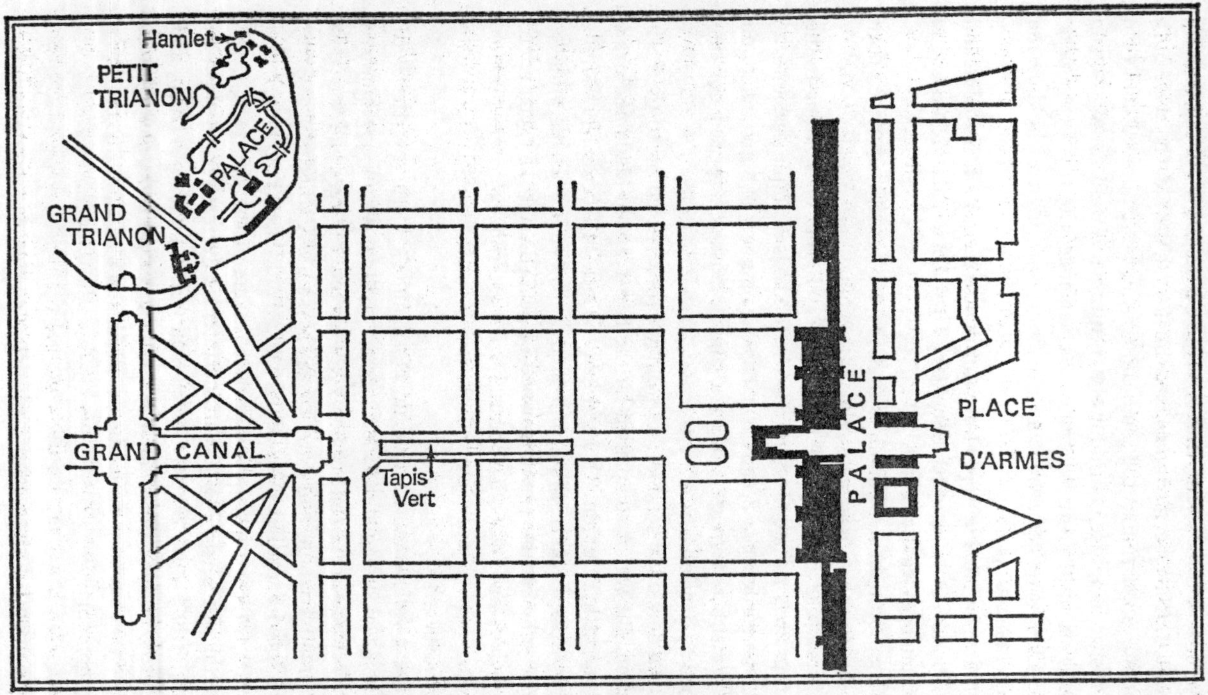

A sketch map of the Palace and Park of Versailles shows the relation between the isolated Trianon palaces and the main palace

Queen's household received a violent shake-up when Monsieur de Guénémée suddenly went bankrupt for an astronomical sum. His wife was governess to the royal children (Joseph II described her salon as a gambling hell), and she felt it her duty to resign. Marie Antoinette wanted to retain her, but Louis was relentless, and she had to go. Who would fill the post?

By December, 1782, Madame de Polignac had succeeded in exasperating her friend with her rapacious demands, and relations became somewhat strained. Obviously, Madame de Polignac or one of her family asked Baron de Besenval to put in a good word on her behalf. "Baron Besenval succeeded in persuading her that any other choice would make people think that she had not enough power to give this important post to her whom everyone regarded as her special friend." Of course, Madame de Polignac received the office of governess to the royal children.

Whatever Marie Antoinette did, it was bound by now to be wrong. For years she had been criticised for her elaborate dresses, but now the *gaulle*, a simple white muslin dress, was in fashion. Madame Vigée-Lebrun exhibited a painting of the Queen in the Salon of 1783, in which she was wearing a *gaulle* and a simple but becoming hat. At once Marie Antoinette was accused of dressing like a chambermaid, and of trying to ruin the silk-weavers of Lyons at the expense of the Flemish muslin makers. Angrily, the sitter had the portrait withdrawn. It was only a small episode, but it epitomised the dislike building up against the Queen.

First Marie Antoinette had antagonised the powerful de Noailles family by her brusque dismissal of "Madame Etiquette", then there was Madame du Barry—exiled from any of the royal palaces—while Mesdames took themselves off to Bellevue. In fact, practically anyone who did not belong to the "Trianon Set" thought they had a grudge, real or imaginary, against the Queen.

The aunts may have been spiteful, but the Duc de Chartres was dangerous. Recently he had inherited his father's title of Orléans, and he was of the stuff that Pretenders are made. What was more he had a particular reason for hating Marie Antoinette: a well-timed reference by her to his inglorious part in a naval engagement against the English ruined his chances of becoming Lord High Admiral of France. Although he was the King's cousin, it was at his residence in Paris, the Palais Royal, that the thinkers with revolutionary tendencies first gathered, to discuss how to cure the ills plaguing their country. Of Louis' brothers, Provence kept his own counsel, while young Artois was still little more than a silly young coxcomb, though he too was destined to wear the crown of France as Charles X.

If Marie Antoinette ever gave thought to her unpopularity, it was soon banished. Count Fersen was back from his adventures in America. In 1779 the warmth of affection between them had not gone unnoticed by the Swedish Ambassador. He informed his King that the favour in which the Queen held him had given offence to several people, and that he himself could not help believing there were grounds for suspicion. "During the last few days (before Fersen left for America) the Queen could not take her eyes off him, and as she looked they were full of tears."

A scheme had come to nothing by which Fersen might have married the formidable daughter of Monsieur Necker, the Swiss financier. Instead Mademoiselle Necker became Madame de Staël, and perhaps the only woman before whom Napoleon quailed. In a letter to his sister Fersen made an illuminating statement:

"I am unable to belong to the one I want to, the one who really loves me, so I wish to belong to no one." At least back again at Versailles he was near that someone.

CHAPTER EIGHT

Love into Hate

As the years passed, so the flood of pamphlets increased, mostly directed at the Queen. Nor were they all the work of discontented royalists or republican sympathisers. By the mid-1780's some of the bitterest enemies Marie Antoinette had made were among her husband's own relations. The birth of the first Dauphin was a particular blow to the Comte de Provence, since it seemed likely to end forever his chances of coming to the throne. In a letter of remarkable candour written to Gustav III of Sweden, he said,

"It has not been easy for me to master the inner man, who still rises in revolt from time to time, even if I cannot entirely subdue him."

Pamphlets appeared in the Palace itself, for the most part brought from Paris by disloyal and sniggering courtiers. One jingle ran that if Louis wanted to see a cuckold, a whore and a bastard, he had only to look at his mirror, his wife and his son. Marie Antoinette even found scandal-sheets folded up and slipped into her table-napkin at meal times, while others were cached among the papers on the King's writing-desk. The wit was verbal as well as printed; jokes circulated about Madame de Lamballe and the Duchesse de Polignac, while others of a contradictory nature made the Queen appear as a second Messalina. A number of these stories reached Marie Antoinette's ears:

"We are suffering from an epidemic of satirical verses, directed against the notables of the Court, both men and women, and French wit has not refrained from aiming its shafts even against the King. Nor indeed have I been spared."

Never in all history can more mud have been thrown, scandals circulated, or libels printed than at this time, and nearly all directed at Marie Antoinette. The worst offenders were the courtiers and hangers-on who owed their very existence to the system they were now helping to eat away with their corrosive malice. The monarchy, like Louis XV in his last days, was starting to decompose alive, and the smell nauseated not only the extremists in France, but also the moderates who, in spite of everything, still wished to cling to the old forms and ideas.

Yet in all this there was one name which was never mentioned and never coupled with that of the Queen—Count Fersen. Usually Marie Antoinette was arrogantly indifferent to public opinion, but where Fersen was concerned she was—for her—astonishingly discreet.

Fersen wished to stay in France, at Versailles if possible, and the obvious thing was for him to obtain a commission in a foreign regiment connected with the French Army. This was in days when commissions were bought and sold like used cars, and for one hundred thousand livres Axel de Fersen could have command of the Royal Swedish Regiment. Senator Fersen, Axel's father, could not help financially, and the Count raised a loan. That same day the debt was discharged by Louis himself.

Fersen may have been Marie Antoinette's lover, but it was not a wholly idealistic relationship. When he went off to Italy he soon acquired a mistress, first in Florence, and then another in Naples. He returned to Versailles in the summer of 1784, at the same time as Gustav III, the Swedish king who wished to model his court on the elegance and splendour of Versailles.

"We are in a whirl of feasts, pleasures and entertainments of every kind," wrote Axel de Fersen somewhat breathlessly. "This giddy life suits Count de Haga (Gustav III) very well. It does not suit me nearly so well and I am exhausted. We have already had a grand opera at Versailles and a state ball."

Eight years later it would be at a masked ball in the Opera House in Stockholm that Gustav III was shot by a conspirator, and carried, in a leather armchair, back to his Palace to die.

For Marie Antoinette history was to repeat itself: in 1784–5, when she was again pregnant, she meddled once more in international affairs at the behest of her Austrian relatives. Just as Peter the Great had wanted a "window on the west" in the shape of St. Petersburg, which could be reached by shipping from the Baltic, so Joseph II wanted an outlet to the North Sea for his Austrian Empire. To be exact, he wanted control of the mouth of the River Scheldt. Marie Antoinette was brought into the scheme, and she sounded out the Minister Vergennes. His answer almost amounted to a snub; France would not countenance such aggression. Then Joseph II sent a brigantine up the Scheldt. The Dutch fired on it, and eighty thousand Austrian soldiers prepared to march. The Dutch asked for French aid, and the situation started to deteriorate. Marie Antoinette interfered, as a result of pressure from Mercy, the Austrian Ambassador; and Louis wrote to Joseph II offering to mediate in the quarrel. That was not what Austria had been hoping for; and in spite of Marie Antoinette, their schemes did not come to fruition. Instead, Louis stated that France would aquiesce to Austria's aggression if Prussia was also agreeable. He, or rather his ministers, knew perfectly well that Frederick would never agree to anything that increased the Empire's size or strength. Again Marie Antoinette was urged to push Austria's claim, but her attempts were half-hearted, and eventually an incident which threatened to set half Europe ablaze ended with the Dutch apologising for firing on the brigantine, and having to pay an indemnity.

The French ministers must have felt guilty about failing to support the Netherlands, for they paid a portion of the fine imposed by Austria. Years later, when Marie Antoinette had to face the Revolutionary Tribunal, one of the charges was a garbled version of France's share of the indemnity. But by then the story had become so twisted that she was accused of sending millions of pounds worth of French gold out of the country to help Joseph II finance a war against the Turks.

Even if the details were not known to the ordinary citizen everyone was aware that Marie Antoinette had harangued ministers, dictated letters to the King and generally tried to influence the course of events. Consequently, when she went to Paris in May, 1785, after the birth of her second son (the future uncrowned Louis XVII), she was cold-shouldered to an alarming degree. There were only a few people in the streets, and they had come to stare. Back at Versailles Marie Antoinette wept and asked Louis what she had done that they should treat her so.

Until it was too late, something would always happen to sweeten the bitter taste of reality. At Versailles the risk of war was trivial compared to the excitement caused by the first Paris performance of Beaumarchais' acid social comedy, *Le Mariage de Figaro.* The servant who comes off best at the expense of his master was nothing new in Italian opera, but here in a play was a barber-turned-valet outwitting and ridiculing his master, a Count and dedicated amorist. Further edge was given by the play being in modern dress, and the whole plot hinged on the fact that the Count was courting popularity by abolishing *droit de seigneur* on his estate, though at the same time he intended to have his way so far as Suzanne, Figaro's bride, was concerned. Beaumarchais was not only a playwright, but also a notorious pamphleteer who had seen the inside of prisons both in Paris and Vienna. It was he who first spread the news right round France that Louis was incapable of consummating his marriage. Not unnaturally, *Figaro* was banned in Paris and in Vienna as well.

Since no play succeeds like a banned play, *Figaro* became widely read, if not performed, and Beaumarchais gave one reading after another of it in fashionable salons in and around Paris. *Figaro* attacked and debunked everything these people stood for, and yet they adored the piece. It was as though they were appreciatively running their fingers along the blade of the guillotine itself. Not without reason would *Le Mariage de Figaro* be called the prologue to the French Revolution. If the piece could not be publicly performed, then it must be given privately, and this was done in the theatre owned by the Comte de Vaudreuil, Madame de Polignac's lover.

Although it was on Louis' orders that *Figaro* had once been banned, when the audience was actually arriving, it was Marie Antoinette who wore away his resistance. At last, on April 27th, 1784, the play was given in Paris with only minor alterations, and the loudest applause came from those it openly attacked.

If, for once, the Queen was not the leader of fashion, she could at least follow, by staging a Beaumarchais play in her theatre at the Petit Trianon. *Figaro*'s predecessor, *Le Barbier de Séville* (a less provocative piece though), was to be staged with advice from the Comédie Française. Artois would be Figaro and Vaudreuil the Count Almaviva, while Marie Antoinette would take the leading feminine role of Rosine.

The Queen could think of nothing else now, and devoted most of her time to learning her part. On the morning of July 12th, 1785, she was waiting in her private apartments for Madame Campan to come and hear her lines. A few minutes earlier Böhmer, the Court Jeweller, had given her a letter, at the same time handing her some jewellery. Now Marie Antoinette read it, and then gave it to Madame Campan when she entered, saying that as Madame was good at solving the puzzles in the journal *Mercure de France,* perhaps she could solve this one which that fool Böhmer had just handed her.

"Madame," it read, "We have reached the peak of happiness in presuming to assume that we have shown our respect and devotion to Your Majesty's commands by our acceptance of your latest terms, and we find great satisfaction in the thought that the most beautiful jewel in the world is to adorn the greatest and best of Queens."

Marie Antoinette commented that to her the letter was only another proof of Böhmer's madness, and that she had not the slightest idea what he meant by complimenting her on the beauty of her diamonds. She thought the jeweller had created some new piece which he now hoped she would buy.

"Please remember to tell Böhmer,' she said to Madame Campan, "that I no longer like diamonds, and that I shall never buy another stone as long as I live, and that if I have money to spend I prefer to add to my properties at Saint-Cloud. Please, go into all details so as to get this idea out of his head."

Madame Campan asked if she should deliver the message at once, but the Queen said that the next time she saw him would do. A candle was always burning on her writing-desk for melting the wax with which to seal letters, and she made a twist of Böhmer's note and burnt in the flame, saying, "This is hardly worth keeping."

Without realising it, Marie Antoinette had lit the fuse which would explode into the most extraordinary scandal and confidence trick ever perpetrated: the Affair of the Diamond Necklace.

CHAPTER NINE

The Blood of the Valois

Jeanne de Saint-Rémy was born in 1756, the daughter of a down-at-heel aristocrat who had married a servant at the family château of Fontette. Baron de Saint-Rémy could claim descent, albeit illegitimate, from Henri II, the last Valois king of France. His wife reasoned that since Henri II was a cousin of the first Bourbon, that made the Baron a cousin of Louis XVI, though how many times removed was a matter of no account. Therefore, she said, he should go to Paris and obtain a pension from the King, or, better, a place at Court.

The father, mother, elder brother and four-year-old Jeanne set out to walk to Paris, leaving behind them all the debts at Fontette which had been piling up over the years. The whole family did not even rate as shabby-genteel; they were little better than beggars, and Jeanne was taught to repeat: "Take pity on a little child who descends in a direct line from Henri II, one of your country's greatest kings." If a passer-by showed interest, the Baronne unrolled a parchment scroll of her husband's family tree, which also included a sketch of the coat of arms, including three golden *fleur-de-lys* surmounted by a crown. Below was the Valois motto: "From my ancestor, the King, I derive my name, the lilies and my blood." The child repeated the patter whenever she met a likely looking stranger. Some laughed and passed on, while others gave her a few coins.

Then the Baron died, and the Baronne took to the streets, finally abandoning Jeanne, her brother and another infant daughter, to run away with a soldier from Sardinia. The children continued to beg, and one day Jeanne—with her tiny sister clinging to her back—jumped on the foot-board of a magnificent coach on the road to Passy, just outside Paris. She eyed the occupants, a finely clothed nobleman and his wife, and thrust a bunch of wild flowers at the latter, the Marquise de Boulainvilliers. Jeanne said her piece; the

Marquise was amused, then intrigued, and questioned her at length. Finally she asked where the children had a room and gave Jeanne a gold coin. The following day she sent a groom, who led them back to the Château de Boulainvilliers at Passy. The result was that the Marquise took them under her wing. Jeanne and her sister received a convent education, and the brother eventually went into the Navy.

The Marquise believed the story about the family connection with the Valois was genuine, and decided to support the claim for the restoration of estates at Fontette which had been seized by creditors. The Judge at Arms of the French nobility confirmed Jeanne's claim to descent from Henri II, and gave her a certificate to prove it. The two sisters were granted a small pension out of state funds. Then Jeanne's delusions of grandeur began in earnest. Unfortunately for her she had acquired a taste for high living at the Château de Boulainvilliers, but except for the pension she had no money of her own, and so was unable to live in the style to which she intended to become accustomed.

One night in 1779 Jeanne and her younger sister decided that their education had lasted long enough, bundled their possessions together and escaped over the convent wall to Bar-sur-Aube, near Fontette. Word soon went round that the Saint-Rémy heiresses had returned to unravel the legal tangle and reclaim their rights. Bar-sur-Aube opened its doors, and they were included in the town's social round. Above all, Jeanne had great talents as an actress in amateur theatricals, and it was through them that she met Nicholas de la Motte, an Army officer on leave.

Obviously de la Motte did not waste his time, and on his next leave he married Jeanne, within a month of her giving birth to twins, who did not survive. The couple then set up house on the money he raised by selling his carriage and horse, which he had acquired on hire-purchase!

Monsieur de la Motte resigned his commission: later Jeanne described the regiment he was in as: "So provincial. That regiment made us both a laughing stock." By now she was quite obsessed by her ancestry, and was forever telling people:

"I can never forget that my forefathers occupied the highest positions at the Court of their King, some of them ruling as governors over the French nation. Why, to them it must have seemed only a brief hour since their family had occupied the throne itself. This is the royal blood that flows in my veins!"

When the couple heard that the Marquise de Boulainvilliers was visiting the Prince de Rohan, they set off for his palace at Saverne. There the Marquise introduced her foster-daughter to the Prince. Already, the first strands of the web which would finally entangle him were being spun.

Soon after the Marquise died of smallpox, and Jeanne and her husband were thrown back on their own initiative. By then they were signing themselves the Comte et Comtesse de la Motte, or when they wanted extended credit, de la Motte-Valois. Now they had become three, for Rétaux de Villette, a friend from de la Motte's "provincial" regiment, had joined them.

Jeanne decided it was time to further her acquaintance with Louis de Rohan. Since the day he had welcomed Marie Antoinette at Strasbourg, he had served as French Ambassador in Vienna, to the scandal of Maria Theresa and the delight of the more flighty Viennese social world. Hunting and womanising came before his diplomatic and ecclesiastical duties, and it was not long before the Empress requested his recall. Now, when Jeanne de la Motte crossed his path for the second time, he was Bishop of Strasbourg, and a cardinal.

Good-looking, greying at the temples, and in his forties, Cardinal Rohan dressed with the care of an extremely fashionable (and wealthy) woman. Incredibly conceited, his family ranking next in the social hierarchy to the Princes of the Blood, he might have stepped straight out of Mozart's *Cosi Fan Tutte*.

Jeanne's request for an interview was granted, he read her petition, and promised to help. Then, acting in his official capacity of Grand Almoner of France, he gave her a purse with a few gold coins, saying that he expected her to give him her full confidence. The restitution of her properties should be easy with her Valois name and her infinite charms. At that Jeanne started, and Rohan broke off in mid-sentence.

Later she received a second invitation to visit his Paris mansion. She went, extravagantly dressed. The Cardinal received her in his private study, which was more like a courtesan's boudoir. Seating himself beside her on a sofa he asked for details about herself, some of which were willingly given. Rohan was distressed to find that Monsieur de la Motte neglected his wife, so young and so charming. "A woman indeed fashioned expressly by nature for the conquest of men's hearts," was what he said as he clasped her hands in a state of glassy-eyed lust. Through his cousin, de Soubise, he said he would arrange a commission for de la Motte, away from Paris.

This second meeting was more advantageous to Jeanne than the Cardinal: when he obtained a commission for de la Motte in the Comte d'Artois' Bodyguard, he meant only the husband to go to Versailles. Jeanne had other ideas. She too would go and live near the Court "to attract the attention of the Queen".

At Versailles Jeanne rented rooms for herself in the town, and made Rétaux de Villette her personal secretary. Had de la Motte objected to this arrangement, it would merely have been a case of the pot calling the kettle black. Then Jeanne set about bombarding Court officials with her petitions for the restoration of the Fontette estates. They fell on deaf ears, so she tried the direct approach and joined the crowds of well-dressed people who were allowed to throng the public rooms in the Palace. To attract attention she staged a faint in Madame Êlizabeth's antechamber, and let it be known that she was a destitute noblewoman, overcome by starvation. Always sympathetic, Madame Êlizabeth gave her two hundred francs.

When the Court moved to Fontainebleau, the de la Mottes followed. While her husband made a sizeable income from gambling at cards with the other officers, Jeanne was little better than a prostitute, receiving one courtier after another in her room. She was no nearer breaking through the de Polignac circle which surrounded the Queen.

Baffled, the de la Mottes returned to Paris, where they rented a house and lived far beyond their practically non-existent means. The staff included a valet, three ladies' maids, a blackamoor page boy and a messenger. Jeanne really was at her wits' end, and she searched for a good tale to satisfy all her creditors. Then she had the idea of telling everybody that she and the Queen had become friends. Marie Antoinette's circle being what it was, the story was quite feasible, and Jeanne took every opportunity of telling her acquaintances about the Queen and herself: the Queen had been so moved to hear of the misfortunes of a Valois; the Queen had received her in secret; the family properties would shortly be restored. She even went around showing letters apparently written by Marie Antoinette, which contained affectionate sentiments and began: "To my cousin, the Comtesse de Valois". They were in fact forged by Villette.

At Versailles Jeanne tried the fainting trick again. This time she staged a scene under the windows of the Queen's apartments, and afterwards she claimed that she had had convulsions and a miscarriage. The Queen was not even in her rooms at the time, but the audacious Jeanne said that Marie Antoinette saw it happen and was so upset that when Louis came in he asked what was the matter, and Marie Antoinette was supposed to have replied: "She is a Valois, the wife of Count de la Motte. They are a young couple and I pity them with all my heart."

All this was related to Cardinal Rohan. Jeanne and the Cardinal were two excessively ambitious people who were prepared to use each other as stepping stones to forward their own plans. Jeanne wanted to use de Rohan as a way of reaching the Queen, and de Rohan—believing her stories about her friendship with his sovereign—saw her as a means to win back the royal favour he had dismally lost some years before.

His stay in Vienna had coincided with the time when Austria hoped for a share of Poland, when that country was about to be partitioned by Prussia and Russia. De Rohan was unwise enough to write a letter to Madame du Barry telling her all about it, saying that Maria Theresa had a handkerchief in one hand for the tears she was shedding for Poland's fate and in the other a sword with which to cut off a portion of that country. Madame du Barry read out the letter at a dinner party, where it was thoroughly enjoyed. The story went the rounds, and eventually reached Marie Antoinette's ears. Her pride was touched; someone had dared to make fun of her mother, a Habsburg. As far as de Rohan was concerned, after his return to France, he did not exist. At the baptism of the Dauphin the Queen stood on one side of the font, de Rohan on the other, without a glimmer of recognition on her part.

De Rohan was exceedingly ambitious, his overwhelming desire being to follow in the steps of Cardinal Richelieu and Cardinal Mazarin, and direct the very destinies of France. Now, perhaps the charming Comtesse de la Motte could speak on his behalf. He flattered

Jeanne, and then admitted the truth, that he was persona non grata at Court: "Do you realize Countess, that my fate as well as yours rests entirely in your hands?"

Jeanne thought he must be joking, but he assured her he was not: "For you, your moment, your chance has come. Such a moment never recurs. I have established as a certainty the fact that the Queen has a liking for you."

"A liking for me!" interrupted Jeanne. "You must mean that Her Majesty has taken pity on me—that her tender heart has been stirred by my misfortunes."

De Rohan pressed his case, that she could help both of them at the same time.

"Put all your faith then in the Queen, and remember that my fate, along with yours, rests in your hands."

When Jeanne had been in the care of the Marquise de Boulainvilliers she had for a while been apprenticed to a fashionable Paris dressmaker. Quickly she turned this to her advantage at the expense of Madame de Polignac, who, she declared, was the stumbling-block.

'I remember the Polignacs when they were impoverished non-entities; when my employer sent me to try to collect her bills, Madame de Polignac could only pay in promises. Why, before she came into favour with the Queen, Madame de Polignac could not obtain credit from a single merchant in Paris, and had not a decent dress to her name." With appealing innocence Jeanne then asked: "Does the Duchess fear my revealing to the Queen what I know of her past? Does she fear the advantage of my name and rank over hers?"

De Rohan assured her she must not be too easily discouraged, and begged her to speak to the Queen directly about him. Jeanne now risked having her bluff called, so there was nothing for it, she must faint again. This time she chose the Hall of Mirrors just as Marie Antoinette was going through on her way to Mass. She never even noticed the dark-haired woman with a good figure lying prostrate on the floor.

However, back with the Cardinal, Jeanne made out she had spoken most favourably about him to the Queen.

"I spoke of your good works in your diocese, of your grateful parishioners daily singing your praises and blessing you for your benefactions."

According to Jeanne, Marie Antoinette replied: "I am grateful, of course, to hear such a glowing report of Cardinal Rohan, although I must admit it takes me completely by surprise. I never dreamed Monseigneur capable of such nobility of action. He does not generally enjoy so good a reputation as you give him. Other versions have led me to think of him in quite another light."

De Rohan must have winced at these observations, but Jeanne had not yet finished: "I dared to add that the upset of your disgrace had affected your health, but said that your greatest distress was caused by the fact that you were not allowed to put your case in person to a sovereign worshipped by all France."

According to Jeanne the Queen then asked how de Rohan hoped to clear himself of his shameful conduct, and she had requested that he should be allowed to state his case.

"My entreaties were successful. I am authorised to ask you for your self-justification, which is to be written in your own hand and to be delivered to the Queen by me."

De Rohan wrote the letter, which Jeanne promised to deliver the next time she saw the Queen at Versailles or the Petit Trianon. Incidentally, all the dialogue in this greatest of eighteenth century comedies was written either by Jeanne in her memoirs or by the accused and the witnesses in their statements before the trial in 1786.

A few days later Jeanne handed him a letter on gilt-edged paper with the *fleur-de-lys* in one corner.

"I have read your letter, and I am glad that I need no longer consider you guilty. I cannot yet grant you an audience, but as soon as circumstances allow, I shall inform you. In the meanwhile, remember, be discreet."

After that several more letters were apparently exchanged between Marie Antoinette and the ambition-blinded Cardinal, each one from the Queen a little warmer than its predecessor.

Then Jeanne started turning the whole confidence trick to her financial advantage. First came a letter telling the Cardinal that she wished to make a charitable donation in secret to a proud but indigent family. As she happened to be short of funds, she commissioned him, as the Grand Almoner of France, to lend her the sum of sixty thousand francs, and send them to her by Madame de la Motte.

With calculated foresight de Rohan asked for a loan from Cerf-Beer, a Jewish financier, telling him that he would gain the Queen's favour, and also her protection for him and his race. Cerf-Beer agreed, and Rohan passed on the money to Jeanne.

The lengths to which she carried her deceptions can still amaze. To add colour to her stories Jeanne told de Rohan that she frequently went to the Petit Trianon. In point of fact she had scratched an acquaintance with the concierge, and so could describe features accurately. Often she would tell the Cardinal in advance of her supposed comings and goings, and on one occasion when she knew he would be watching outside the gate, she asked Villette to accompany her out of sight. After Villette disappeared, de Rohan hurried up to ask excitedly who he was. "Desclaux, the Queen's confidential messenger at the Petit Trianon," she lied without hestiation.

What had gone before was nothing to what was to come. Jeanne had stood in the Hall of Mirrors in the crowd watching the Queen pass by on her way to Mass on many occasions, and she noticed that Marie Antoinette had a curious mannerism. Every time she passed the open doorway in to the Oeil-de-Boeuf apartments she turned her head and glanced in, probably without even being aware what she was doing. The gesture was not unlike a nod.

"I have just left Her Majesty," Jeanne told de Rohan, "and she asks me to give you this message: station yourself tomorrow, as if by accident, in the Oeil-de-Boeuf at the time when she passes down the Hall of Mirrors to High Mass. If you are there, she will nod to you as she passes, a signal of her approval of your present conduct."

Of course de Rohan did as he was told: the Queen glanced through the open doors, and he felt sure she had given him the promised nod. He was in ecstasy; now it was only a matter of time before he was fully restored to royal favour. Along came another note, on paper with the *fleur-de-lys* in one corner, requesting a further loan, once more of sixty thousand francs. Like the first it was met by Cerf-Beer, but now de Rohan gave orders that if necessary his own private funds could be drawn on to meet the Queen's wishes.

The weeks slipped by, but still the Queen did not make any public statement about the Cardinal, who thought he would soon receive a high ministerial post. Something had to be done to stop him getting restive, and only a meeting with the Queen herself would do that. As in the last act of *Le Mariage de Figaro*, the meeting would be a comedy of mistaken identity in a garden in the dark.

Jeanne informed de Rohan that although Marie Antoinette was unable to give him an audience, she would meet him in private. They would rendezvous in the Palace park late one night, when she would tell him all the things she hesitated to put in writing on the subject of his imminent return to public life. The meeting was to be in the Grove of Venus near the Trianon on a moonless night in July, 1784. Since it was well known that the Queen liked walking in the park on warm nights, the scheme did not sound too far-fetched.

Who was to impersonate the Queen? Monsieur de la Motte soon found the answer in the form of a twenty-three-year-old prostitute called Mademoiselle d'Oliva, whom he had picked up in the gardens of the Palais Royal. This girl bore a remarkable resemblance to Marie Antoinette, but was extremely slow on the uptake. Monsieur de la Motte took her back to his wife, who played the *grande dame*: "You may trust me, my dear, I am a very highly placed person attached to the court at Versailles." Jeanne flashed a letter forged by Villette before Mademoiselle d'Oliva, who was completely mystified. Jeanne went on: "I am the Queen's confidante. She and I are just like that." Jeanne entwined her fingers, and went on to explain that the Queen had a job for someone who resembled her closely. It was something to do with play-acting, and the bait was one thousand five hundred francs, and more from the Queen if the girl acquitted herself well.

The next night Mademoiselle d'Oliva was driven to Versailles, and taken to the de la Mottes' apartments. The tricksters disappeared, and returned saying that the Queen was amused to see what would happen. Then they dressed up the girl to resemble Marie Antoinette in a simple *gaulle* dress, like the painting by Vigée-Lebrun which caused so much trouble when it was hung in the Paris Salon. Mademoiselle d'Oliva was given a letter in a plain envelope, and told she would have to hand it to a "very great nobleman" who would meet her in the Park. The little prostitute's professional instincts were now aroused.

"This *seigneur*," she asked, "will he expect to embrace me? And if so, am I to allow him? But what, what if he should expect more?"

Jeanne assured her that was highly unlikely. Between eleven and twelve that night she and her husband took Mademoiselle d'Oliva into the grounds of the Trianon. There she was given a rose, and told that all she would have to say was: "You know what this means." She did not, but that was beside the point. Jeanne added that the Queen was watching, "not ten steps away". Then the so-called Countess de la Motte-Valois put on a black domino, and went off to meet de Rohan. She pretended to be slightly disconcerted, saying that she had just heard that Madame (Comtesse de Provence) and the Comtesse d'Artois intended to accompany the Queen on her walk. Therefore the meeting must be brief, but it would at least be long enough for the Queen to assure him that he had her goodwill.

De Rohan hurried off to the Grove of Venus, where Mademoiselle d'Oliva was waiting. She held out the rose, saying, "You know what this means," and forgot to hand over the letter. Jeanne ran up, telling him to leave at once as the royal ladies were coming to accompany the Queen on her walk. Behind the hedges Monsieur de la Motte and Villette provided the sound of approaching footsteps. De Rohan fled, convinced that at last, after years of waiting, he had met his Queen.

Monsieur de la Motte accompanied Mademoiselle d'Oliva back to her hotel room, where they waited for Jeanne to join them. She eventually entered in high spirits, saying that she had just come from the Queen, who had informed her: "I am highly pleased, my dear Countess, with the person you found for me. She played her part marvellously, and you may tell her that her future is assured."

Meanwhile, no doubt, Cardinal Rohan was contemplating the rose the little prostitute had just given him, and the hem of whose dress he had kissed, and thinking himself the luckiest and happiest man alive.

CHAPTER TEN

The Countess de la Motte-Valois

In the year 1784 there was an even more improbable character in Paris than Cardinal Rohan: the so-called "Count" Cagliostro. The Count surrounded his origins in mystery, claiming that he might have been born in Malta, or possibly Trebizond—he was not quite certain which—and that he had been brought up in the holy Moslem city of Medina, and then wandered through Africa and the Middle East. In Egypt he claimed to have been admitted to the mysteries which had been handed down from one generation to the next in the Great Pyramid, while in Africa he said he had visited a city ten times the size of Paris. Perhaps his thick Sicilian accent was the truest guide to his origins.

Whoever he was, he held fashionable Europe spellbound; but his dabbling in the occult, his claims as a seer and his reputation had been enough for the police to run him out of nearly every capital in Europe. Not only did he claim to have witnessed the launching of the Ark on the flood-waters, the Marriage at Cana and the Crucifixion, but he even said he knew the secret of making gold and diamonds.

De Rohan was proud to call him a friend, and wore a ring which contained a stone cut with his crest, which Cagliostro was supposed to have created. What was more natural than that the Cardinal should consult "The Friend of Man" about his future? Recently he had received a letter, apparently from Marie Antoinette, which both puzzled and excited him.

"The time is not yet ripe for your public triumph, but there is a secret transaction of great personal interest to me, which I will entrust only to you. The Countess de la Motte will speak for me and explain what it is all about,"

When asked, Jeanne said that the Queen had entrusted de Rohan with a mission: to purchase a necklace she had set her heart on acquiring. If there was any mystery about the transaction, it was because she did not wish the King to know about it until it was all over.

"Because no one knows that Her Majesty has extended the hand of friendship to you, no one will ever suspect that you are acquiring it for her," explained Jeanne.

Now de Rohan had gone to his friend Cagliostro to ask his advice. The pug-faced "Count" put on a robe covered with signs of the Zodiac, and in a darkened room filled with incense went into a trance which lasted nearly all night.

"Your mission will be successful," he told de Rohan with the aid of his evil genius. "It will bring you the highest honour. You will hasten the dawn of that glorious day which will reveal your rare talents to the world. France, all humanity will benefit by your talents. Get the contract and request Her Majesty to sign it. Purchase the necklace, and so also the undying love of your sovereign. Make it a stepping stone to destiny. Your destiny. Your name shall resound through France and to the farthest corner of the civilised world."

At least the last part of Cagliostro's prophecy was to come true. De Rohan walked straight into Jeanne's trap. On the fringes of Court circles it was known that Marie Antoinette bought jewellery in secret from Böhmer and his partner, Bassenge. Suddenly she found she was in debt to the Court Jewellers to the tune of half a million francs, and was forced to ask Louis to settle the account. All he said was: "I am not surprised at your financial difficulties in view of your passion for diamonds."

After that Marie Antoinette did stop buying so much jewellery, especially diamonds, and this just at a time when Böhmer and Bassenge hoped they might interest her in the necklace they had made some twelve years before, which they thought Louis XV would buy for Madame du Barry. When that came to nothing, they approached Louis XVI at the time of his coronation, at the birth of Madame Royale, and again after the birth of the first Dauphin. He might have considered buying it to please his wife, but Marie Antoinette was the one who said "no". Böhmer even approached Madame Campan's husband to see if she could make the Queen change her mind. Again he had no luck and was forced to take it round the courts of Europe in the hope of finding a purchaser. No one was interested, and finally in desperation he made a scene during an interview with the Queen in her private apartments. In tears and on his knees he told her that if she refused to buy the necklace he would be ruined, bankrupted and dishonoured; he even threatened to go and throw himself in the Seine.

Sharply Marie Antoinette told him to get up, adding that if he did commit suicide she would be sorry, but it would be through no fault of hers.

"Never mention it again. Break up the necklace and try to sell the diamonds separately. Then you will have no reason to drown yourself."

Böhmer could not bring himself to do the sensible thing and break up the piece and sell the stones individually. Instead he sought out Jeanne, who as everyone knew, was such a great friend of the Queen's. He asked her help, adding that she would get a commission.

Böhmer took the necklace to Jeanne's apartments: "After all, a look costs nothing," he told her as he opened the two-foot long jewel case. Jeanne, like everyone else who saw the piece, consisting of six hundred and forty-seven stones, all flawless, was dazzled. Then it was that she must have had the idea of using the Cardinal in a confidence trick to obtain it for herself.

In due course de Rohan received a letter, apparently from Marie Antoinette, commissioning him to purchase the necklace. He went to the jewellers in the Rue Vendôme and explained that he had been instructed to inquire the lowest price they would accept. Böhmer told him that they were so anxious to be rid of it that they would sell for one million six hundred thousand francs, a sum lower than the cost of the stones, the setting and the labour. De Rohan said he would report the conversation, and even considered purchasing the necklace out of his own pocket. Unwisely he told the jewellers: "I do not know whether I shall ever be allowed to tell you who this purchaser is, but I will give you my personal signature as a guarantee on the contract."

Villette forged a letter from Marie Antoinette agreeing with the arrangements he was making, and enclosed her terms: "The first instalment, in the amount of four hundred thousand francs, shall not be payable for six months; successive instalments of similar sums shall be payable every six months thereafter. If these conditions are accepted, the necklace is to be delivered Tuesday, February 1st (1785)."

Böhmer and Bassenage induced de Rohan to admit that he was acting for the Queen, and asked for proof. This Jeanne willingly provided in the shape of a forged document with her signature. Villette signed the contract "Marie Antoinette de France".

On the day of the handing over of the necklace de Rohan wrote to the Court Jewellers informing them that the Queen had instructed him to make the first payment at the end of August, and that the interest on the remainder of the agreed price should be paid at the same time as the instalments, until the whole sum had been paid off. The letter bore his signature.

At dusk on February 1st, 1785, de Rohan took the necklace to Jeanne's apartment in Versailles. A seat was offered him in a room lit only by a single small lamp. After a few minutes there was a knock at the door, and a voice said: "In the name of the Queen." Jeanne went towards the door with the jewel case, and handed it to a man in the Queen's livery. His face was familiar to de Rohan, and afterwards Jeanne explained that he was the Queen's confidential messenger from the Petit Trianon.

"You saw him with me that night," she reminded de Rohan. "That night" was the occasion when Villette had accompanied Jeanne through the Palace gates when they knew the Cardinal was watching from the shadows.

Before long the impatient de Rohan began to wonder why Marie Antoinette was not wearing the new necklace in public. As usual, Jeanne had an excuse ready: "Her Majesty's exquisitely delicate sensibilities make it difficult for her to wear it in public until it is paid for."

Of course, as soon as the Cardinal had left the apartment that evening Jeanne or her husband had broken up the necklace, with the intention of selling the stones separately. Villette had a narrow escape in Paris when trying to dispose of some of them, and the dealer became suspicious. The man called in the police, who questioned Villette closely. Coolly he told them he was acting for the Comtesse de la Motte, and since she was known as a "general dealer", there the inquiry ended, after the police satisfied themselves that there had been no jewel thefts in the recent past.

Caution was advisable though, and Monsieur de la Motte went over to England. In London he disposed of most of the stones in Bond Street, putting the money into letters of credit. Since Jeanne was finding de Rohan's presence in Paris something of an embarrassment, she had a letter forged requesting him to return to his diocese of Strasbourg while she—the Queen—made final preparations for his return to public life. De Rohan believed the letter, and obediently went to his palace at Saverne.

Jeanne left nothing to chance. She prepared her friends for the coming change in her living standard by telling them that her husband had had simply fantastic winnings on the English racecourses. Some sort of an explanation was needed, for the de la Mottes behaved like a couple of *nouveaux-riches*, filled their mansion with furniture and *objets d'art*, and even had a carriage made in England, which was then the latest status symbol. When they went to the country to wipe the eyes of old acquaintances in Bar-sur-Aube, they were covered in jewels. Monsieur de la Motte even sported a large *fleur-de-lys* in diamonds on the lapel of his coat.

Spring turned into summer, and when the day for the payment of the first instalment was near, Jeanne sent de Rohan another forged letter, recalling him to Paris. Back he came, as obedient and trusting as ever. Bluntly she told him that Marie could not raise the four hundred thousand francs, and that it would be an excellent thing for him if he offered to lend her the money. If he could not do it quickly, get a loan from the banker St James, she advised.

De Rohan showed St James the forged contract, promising that if he helped, he would see he got a decoration—perhaps even the Cordon Bleu. Then it struck the hard-headed banker that there was something strange about the whole transaction, and he even succeeded in arousing de Rohan's suspicions. The Cardinal again questioned Jeanne why Marie Antoinette had not yet worn the necklace in public, and was told that the Queen considered the price too high, and that it must either be reduced or revalued, because until then she would not wear it.

De Rohan sent for the two jewellers, then and there making them write a letter thanking the Queen for purchasing their necklace. This time it was not delivered via Jeanne, but by Böhmer himself when taking jewellery to the Palace.

This then was the situation on the morning of July 12th, 1785, when Marie Antoinette read the letter from Böhmer and Bassenge while waiting for Madame Campan to hear her lines for *Le Barbier de Séville*.

After a few days had elapsed, and Böhmer had heard nothing from the Queen, St James sought out the Abbé Vermond, who was still her confessor. The Abbé promised to take up the matter with Marie Antoinette, and when he did so she realised it was a plot to compromise her in some way not yet clear. She, in her turn, asked the advice of the Baron de Breteuil. The Baron hated the Cardinal, and saw the episode as a chance to discredit him for once and all. First he would obtain signed statements from St James and the jewellers, and then if the first instalment was not paid, they would all go to the King. St James willingly gave the Baron a signed statement. also telling him that de Rohan had been consulting Cagliostro. That in itself was enough to make anyone doubt the Cardinal's integrity.

At the end of July de Rohan had an opportunity to compare the Queen's signature with that on the letters apparently passed on by Jeanne. Although he was horrified at the difference he still could not believe the worst. He went to Jeanne and accused her of deceiving him. Theatrically she told him: "You insult me at the very moment when I have succeeded in making the Queen tear away the veil of secrecy which has up to now hidden her feelings towards you. Soon you will have reason to be ashamed of your suspicions." Immediately afterwards she persuaded Villette to forge a letter telling de Rohan that she (the Queen) could raise thirty thousand francs, and she hoped the jewellers would be prepared to wait until the end of the month for the rest. After a frantic day Jeanne raised the thirty thousand francs, which de Rohan handed on to Böhmer and Bassenge. They argued, and several mornings running the Cardinal awoke to find them standing by his bed.

Meanwhile, Jeanne was stripping her house of its contents, and sending them away to Bar-sur-Aube.

Desperate with worry, Böhmer spoke to Madame Campan at

her residence at Crespy, on August 3rd. The jeweller asked how it was that the Queen did not seem to have understood his letter. Madame Campan told him that she too had read it and, like her royal mistress, she could make neither head nor tail of it. As soon as her other guests had departed, the couple went into the garden to talk. As they did so a storm broke, but they were too preoccupied to notice the rain teeming down.

"Her Majesty burnt your letter without even being able to make up her mind what it was all about," explained Madame Campan.

Böhmer was horrified, and insisted that Marie Antoinette owed him money.

"Money, Monsieur Böhmer? We settled the Queen's account with you in a full a long time ago."

Böhmer explained that she owed the jewellers one million six hundred thousand francs for the necklace which had originally been made for Madame du Barry. Then he added that Cardinal Rohan had been entrusted with the transaction. Madame Campan could hardly believe her ears.

"You must be mistaken! The Queen has not addressed a single word to Cardinal Rohan since his return from Vienna ten years ago. No man is in such disfavour at Court."

Böhmer tried to contradict her, but Madame Campan insisted: "I do not know what dreadful plot is afoot, but I do know that you have been robbed."

"In truth, Madame, I am getting frightened myself, for his Eminence assured me that the Queen would wear the necklace at Pentecost, but I have not yet seen it on her. It was after that date that I made up my mind to write the letter to the Queen."

Madame Campan advised Böhmer to go at once to Baron de Breteuil, Minister of the King's Household and Keeper of the Crown Jewels. That same evening Paul Bassenge went to Jeanne. Calmly she told him that the Cardinal was in a terrible situation as the Queen's signature on the contract had turned out to be a forgery. She added that she did not know how the Cardinal would extricate himself from the situation, but if they were wise they would make him stand by the guarantees he had given. A few hours later, in the middle of the night, Jeanne was with the Cardinal, informing him that Marie Antoinette had just told her that she would deny ever having received the necklace, or authorising him to act for her; she would order his arrest, and bring about his downfall. Jeanne even asked for asylum in his house until she could escape from Paris, as the police were already watching her own home.

There she stayed, in the Palais-Cardinal, for twenty-four hours, until she felt the coast was clear. Then she set off for Bar-sur-Aube, following the last wagon-load of her furniture.

Now events were moving fast towards their unprecedented climax. On August 9th, Marie Antoinette was at the Petit Trianon, being rehearsed in her lines by Madame Campan for the production of *Le Barbier de Séville*, due to be performed in the little theatre the following evening. It was the Queen who mentioned Böhmer first.

"Did you know that imbecile came here a week ago asking to speak to me, claiming that he had been sent by you! As I had nothing to say to him I refused. What on earth can he want with me? Do you know?"

Madame Campan told all she knew, but Marie Antoinette found it almost impossible to believe the central figure in the transaction could be de Rohan.

The next day Böhmer was summoned to Versailles. He begged the Queen to admit that she had the necklace and pay the instalment due, otherwise he would go bankrupt and everything would come into the open. Back in Paris Böhmer and Bassenge called on de Rohan, insisting that he must stand by his guarantees. The Cardinal became slightly arrogant, and said he was acting on the Queen's orders. Böhmer explained he had just seen Marie Antoinette, and that she denied all knowledge of the necklace. He then asked de Rohan what he had done with the diamonds.

"The Comtesse de la Motte—I saw the case handed over to the Queen's messenger on February 1st. What is more I have the authorisation to hand which was signed by the Queen."

"In that case," answered Böhmer, "you have been cruelly deceived."

The jewellers reported back to Baron de Breteuil, and wrote out a statement.

Sunday, August 15th, was Assumption Day, as well as the Queen's official birthday. Baron de Breteuil, Monsieur de Miromesnil, Keeper of the Seals, and Count de Vergennes, the Foreign Affairs Minister, were in the King's study together with their two sovereigns. They were discussing the affair. Marie Antoinette asserted her innocence, and demanded public condemnation of de Rohan. Then Louis ordered the Cardinal to be fetched. When he entered, the King handed him the jewellers' statement and also the declaration made by St James, the banker.

De Rohan was asked if he had purchased the necklace. He said yes, on the instructions of the Queen.

"Who instructed you to make the purchase?" asked Louis.

"A lady called the Comtesse de la Motte-Valois. I thought that by undertaking the commission I was paying court to the Queen."

Marie Antoinette interrupted to ask how could he possibly believe she would have chosen him—of all people.

"I now realize that I have been duped. It was my great desire to please Your Majesty that blinded me." He took out the forged letter authorising him to act as intermediary. Louis examined the signature.

"But this is not in the Queen's handwriting, and the signature is not even in the proper form. How is it possible that a prince of the house of Rohan, a Grand Almoner of France could believe that the Queen would sign herself Marie Antoinette de France. Everyone knows that Queens only sign their baptismal name. Not only is it a bad imitation of the Queen's handwriting, but it shows ignorance of protocol."

The Cardinal was too overcome to answer lucidly, and the King told him to go to the Library where he would find pen and ink, and write out his statement. After he had left the room Vergennes and Miromesnil were in favour of hushing up the affair, while the implacable de Breteuil—backed by Marie Antoinette—wanted to make a public example of the man.

Fifteen minutes later de Rohan returned, handed over his statement and was told to leave again. De Breteuil suggested his immediate arrest, and Louis, suddenly angry at the sight of his wife in tears, ordered him to do just that. By then de Rohan, robed for Mass, was walking down the Hall of Mirrors which was filled with people waiting to see the royal family pass by on their way to Chapel.

"Arrest Cardinal Rohan," shouted de Breteuil. Everyone turned to stare, hardly believing their ears. It was true; there in public the great Cardinal Rohan was being arrested by officers of the guard. He turned towards the wall, bent down as though to straighten a buckle, and scribbled a note. As he was taken back to his house in Versailles he passed it to his valet who galloped off to the Palais-Cardinal in Paris. There he helped burn papers in a small portfolio, believed to have been the majority of those supposedly sent by Marie Antoinette.

Not long afterwards de Rohan himself arrived with de Breteuil and Monsieur de Crosne, the Lieutenant General of Police. Everything was sealed, and the Cardinal handed over the forged authority. At 11.30 p.m. the Comte d'Agout arrived with a *lettre de cachet* bearing the King's seal, ordering the Cardinal to be escorted to the Bastille at once; half an hour later Comte de Launay, the Governor, came to collect his prisoner.

In the country, Jeanne heard of the arrest and spent the night burning papers, apparently including de Rohan's love-letters to her. Only an hour later, at 4 a.m., the police arrived to take her back to Paris. They had no warrant for the arrest of Monsieur de la Motte, so while she drove one way, he drove hell-for-leather in the opposite direction, towards the Channel coast and across to the safety of England.

In the small hours of the following morning Jeanne was received at the Bastille by de Launay, in his dressing-gown. At once she was interrogated, and when charged with stealing the diamond necklace she burst out laughing and said it was utterly ridiculous, adding that if she had was it likely she would have gone on living quietly at Bar-sur-Aube? She demanded that de Crosne send someone to search the house there, and then threw all the blame on Cagliostro.

Both Cagliostro and his wife were arrested, and when de Crosne started to question the so-called Count, the latter said magnificently that he could think of no misdeed to account for his arrest, unless it might be in connection with the assassination of Pompey—although in that case he had been acting on the Pharaoh's orders. Poker-faced, de Crosne remarked that he would refrain from going into criminal matters that happened to be the concern of his predecessors in office.

There was one very guilty fish, however, which had slipped through the net. Villette had escaped to Switzerland.

At Versailles there was deep discussion as to how the affair should be handled. Marie Antoinette felt her honour had been touched.

"It seems to be thought that I received a necklace for which I had not paid. I want to find out the truth of the matter in which someone has dared to use my name." The Rohan family wanted the case tried in a regular court of justice, but Marie Antoinette wished it to be referred to the Parliament of Paris for judgement. The Parliament of Paris was not a legislative assembly, as its name might suggest, but more in the nature of a High Court of Justice.

Finally, after much discussion, Marie Antoinette agreed that the choice should be left to de Rohan himself. From the Bastille he wrote to Louis regretting that he could not directly confront Madame de la Motte, leaving the judgement to the King himself (a perfectly legal procedure since the sovereign rated as the supreme judicial authority in France). He ended: "I implore Your Majesty to issue the necessary orders to refer my case to the judgement of the Parliament of Paris, before a joint session of the Grand' Chambre and the Tournelle."

The trial, when it finally got under way, became not so much a case of de Rohan versus the Queen as the Queen versus the people of France—and the Queen was to be the loser.

CHAPTER ELEVEN

Trial

All through the spring of 1786 both the Bastille and the Palais de Justice were busy with comings and goings as statements and depositions were taken both from the accused and from the scores of witnesses. Among the latter were Böhmer and Bassenge, the de la Mottes' entire domestic staff, the banker St James, notaries and tradespeople and even Desclaux, the Queen's confidential messenger at the Petit Trianon. Madame du Barry was called, and her visit to the Palais de Justice was more like a royal occasion than anything else. Gallantly the examining magistrates did not query the seven years she lopped off her age, which she gave as thirty-five. According to her, she had been approached by Jeanne who suggested she should become the ex-favourite's *dame de compagnie*. But after hearing all about the Valois ancestry, the du Barry decided Jeanne was not for her: "I am not of such noble lineage myself as to aspire to a Valois in my retinue." She also informed the magistrates that Jeanne used to sign herself, "de France", saying, "I have been officially recognised by the Crown as a descendant of the royal house of Valois; I always sign myself thus."

Another witness who rather spoilt the "blood of the Valois" image was Jeanne's personal maid, Rosalie. Like the maid in a French farce, Rosalie was pert, wasp-waisted and wore a towering cap. She recounted that although the de la Mottes had silver plates and dishes, on a number of occasions when they were handed round at dinner there was nothing on them. "And I said, let us go to bed early, Madame; sleep takes the edge off hunger."

Among those in the Bastille was Cardinal Rohan, living in great style, and giving champagne suppers for his friends. Then there was Cagliostro and his wife. When the latter arrived and was asked to sign her name, all she could do was to put a cross on the paper. Also there was Nicole d'Oliva, brought back from Brussels and soon to have a baby. Protesting vehemently, Villette was whisked back from Switzerland by the French Resident in Geneva, and on admittance to the Bastille, he was asked his occupation: "Stud bull to Madame de la Motte." For a man so crooked and so cunning, he went to pieces remarkably quickly, asking if Nicole d'Oliva had talked, adding that she was the only one who could involve him in the affair as he knew Jeanne would never talk.

Handwriting experts were called in to examine the forgeries, and they agreed the writing was an attempt to disguise the writer's own hand, but even so it was similar to Villette's. After being assured that forgery did not carry the death penalty, he admitted it was his work: he had copied some writing given him by Jeanne, including the fateful words "Marie Antoinette de France", and "*Approuvé*" in the margin of the contract.

On May 12th, 1786, Jeanne, Villette and Nicole d'Oliva were brought face to face. D'Oliva kept bursting into tears, and finally induced Villette to admit that they had been in the Grove of Venus together. At this Jeanne's outraged innocence was spectacular. She insisted the whole thing was nothing more than a practical joke to pay out de Rohan for an infidelity. She declared that it was obvious to her that if Villette promised to confess he would receive a lighter sentence: "I repeat that I am not guilty, and I therefore calmly await the judgement of the Parliament of Paris without asking any man's favour."

Frequently she interrupted the proceedings by having either fainting fits or convulsions, the latter being noisy and dramatic.

After the hearings had been completed, the examining magistrates sent their report to the Grand' Chambre and the Tournelle of the Parliament of Paris in joint session. The text of this report, along with the records of the proceedings, was then forwarded to the Prosecutor General, de Fleury, so that he could prepare his conclusions and recommendations for the guidance of Parliament.

Briefly, they were that the Cardinal really believed he was buying the necklace for the Queen; that the signature "Marie Antoinette de France" had been forged by Villette; that the necklace had been delivered to Madame de la Motte, and that her husband had sold the stones in London.

The actual basis of the trial was a charge brought by Louis XVI against Cardinal Rohan of *lèse-majesté*. Sixty-two or sixty-four judges took part, but all the princes of the blood and peers of the realm, who had the right to vote, abstained.

Villette appeared first. He admitted writing "Marie Antoinette de France", but on another's instructions. Since Jeanne refused to implicate herself by admitting she knew anything about the letters, that charge could not be proved. At least de Rohan was cleared of the forgery charge.

When Jeanne was called, her attitude veered between brazen and injured innocence. Of course she denied everything, and implied that since the letters from Marie Antoinette to the Cardinal were written in such familiar terms, they must have been lovers. Then it was de Rohan's turn. He entered in purple, the colour of mourning for Cardinals, and behaved with quiet dignity. Candidly he admitted, "I was utterly blinded by my overwhelming desire to regain the Queen's good graces." His defence was reasoned, and when he withdrew the whole High Bench stood to salute him. But comedy was never far away, and when Nicole d'Oliva was called, the Sergeant at Arms returned to say could they wait a few minutes as the prisoner was nursing her son, recently born in the Bastille. Justice in all its majesty thawed and smiled, and word was sent that she need not hurry.

D'Oliva's evidence was for the most part inaudible because of her sobs. "When the pretty creature appeared about to faint, half the members of that austere tribunal were on their feet to rush to her assistance." There was hardly a dry eye in the chamber when she left.

Next came Cagliostro, over-dressed and swaggering. The President asked who he was and where he came from: "I am a noble voyager, Nature's unfortunate child." His defence ended with the ringing phrases: "I do good because that is my mission in life. And yet what harvest have I reaped for the services I have rendered the French nation? Out of the bitterness of my heart I tell you my reward has been slander—and the Bastille."

At 6.00 a.m. on the morning of May 31st, 1786, the Grand' Chambre and the Tournelle of the Parliament of Paris were declared to be in session. Before the day was over all the accused would know their fate, for good or bad. The Prosecutor General opened the proceedings by reading his recommendations to the Court. Then the emphasis of the trial started to shift, and as the day wore on it became obvious from the remarks made by council that it had indeed become a case of de Rohan versus the Queen.

Advocate-General de Séguier, for de Rohan, openly accused the Prosecutor General of showing partiality for the King in the hope of preferment. At this de Fleury, the Prosecutor General, said that for de Séguier to defend the Cardinal was a case of one libertine defending another. De Séguier lashed back, "I do not deny that I occasionally visit public women. I don't even care if people see my carriage waiting before their door. But people will never see me stoop so low as to sell my vote for power and fortune."

The President, d'Aligre, summed up in de Rohan's favour, and at 9.00 p.m., after a session which had lasted eighteen hours, he was acquitted of all charges. A huge crowd had gathered outside the Palais de Justice, and cheers went up, mixed with cries of "Long live the Cardinal! Long live Parliament!" He had become a symbol of opposition to Marie Antoinette and all she stood for. Many believed she had been involved in the affair from the start, and a popular song circulated to the effect that the King and Queen were supposed to have blackened the Cardinal, but he would be whitewashed by the Court.

At Versailles, after the acquittal, Marie Antoinette is reputed to have asked her friends to sympathise with her, since the schemer who wanted to ruin her, or to obtain money by forging her signature, had been completely exonerated by the Parliament of Paris.

What of the others? M. de la Motte was sentenced in his absence to the galleys, Villette was banished, Nicole d'Oliva was reprimanded, Cagliostro left the Court without any new stains on his character; but Jeanne was sentenced to be branded on both shoulders as a thief, and imprisoned for life.

On June 21st, 1786, the sentence was carried out at six in the morning in the courtyard of the Palais de Justice. First she received a token flogging tied to the tail of a cart: "It's the blood of the Valois that you are desecrating. Save me from my executioners! It is the Queen, the Queen should be in my place! My only crime is that of having served her too well!"

Jeanne writhed, scratched, kicked and screamed. Half her clothes were torn off, and it took six men to hold her down to be branded. V for *Voleuse* (thief) was burnt on to one shoulder-blade, but she then twisted round with such force to bite the executioner right through his leather jerkin, drawing blood, that the second branding mark was received just above the left breast.

Half dead, she was taken to the Prison of Salpêtrière. There she remained until June 2nd, 1787, when she and another girl escaped with outside help. Perhaps the truth will never be known today, but the escape may have been engineered as part of a deal between the Duchesse de Polignac and Monsieur de la Motte in London, for the return of a packet of letters in his possession. Jeanne escaped to England via Luxembourg, and once in London she poured out a non-stop flow of vitriolic and pornographic pamphlets, letters and an autobiography, *Vie de Jeanne St-Rémy de Valois*, all directed against the Queen, who had a reputation for lesbianism, and Jeanne did not hesitate to inform her readers that that was how she found royal favour.

During the Revolution (before Louis XVI was formally deposed in August, 1792) someone of whom Jeanne was terrified called at her lodgings near Westminster bridge in June, 1791. She jumped from the third floor window, suffered multiple injuries, died two months later, and was buried in St Mary's Churchyard, Lambeth.

To return to the events immediately following the trial. The day after de Rohan's acquittal Baron de Breteuil went to the Palais Cardinal to ask de Rohan, in the King's name, for his resignation as Grand Almoner of France, and to hand over his Cordon Bleu. The Cardinal was given a *lettre de cachet* from Louis, ordering him to go into exile at his Abbey of Chaise Dieu in the Auvergne, far from the delights and refinements of the capital. Everyone saw the Queen's hand in this spiteful action, and her popularity dwindled to vanishing point.

Later de Rohan was allowed to go to his diocese of Strasbourg, and after the outbreak of the Revolution he crossed the Rhine to estates which he owned on the German side. There he did all he could to help clergy escaping from the Terror, and at the time of his death in 1803 he was a completely reformed character and a genuinely devout churchman.

For Marie Antoinette the Affair of the Diamond Necklace was one of the most crucial events in her life, although she was only indirectly involved. People had criticised her extravagances and frivolity for some ten years now: the lucrative positions occupied by her friends and their relations: the money spent on clothes, on improvements at St. Cloud and at the Petit Trianon with its village and theatre. Now her enemies had a burning-glass through which to focus their dislike, for few were prepared to give Marie Antoinette the benefit of the doubt in anything that was said about her, or with which she was concerned. After her interference on Austria's behalf in the crisis over the Netherlands they had nicknamed her "The Austrian". Now they called her "The Austrian Bitch".

Not long after the trial Marie Antoinette was greeted with hisses when she entered her box at the Comédie Française, and Madame Vigée-Lebrun's latest portrait of her was withdrawn from the Salon lest it provoke demonstrations. Then in the autumn, Monsieur de Crosne of the Paris police wrote a tactfully worded letter suggesting it might be better if she postponed any intended visits to the capital. Genuinely puzzled by it all, she asked, "What harm have I done them?"

The Queen was now thirty-two years old, and at last showing signs of settling down. She had become genuinely fond of her husband and adored her three surviving children; a fourth, Sophie-Béatrix, was born in 1786, but died within a year. But even if she now preferred to spend more time at home, as it were, and less time in the frantic pursuit of amusement, it was too late. The damage had already been done.

Marie Antoinette realised at last that she had gone too far. Mademoiselle Bertin, her dressmaker, was dismissed, and the gambling tables vanished from her rooms. There was one inevitable result; the Queen soon found out who were her friends, and the truth was as ugly as the insincerity had been.

To Mercy the way in which people openly expressed their opinions of Louis not only in their own homes but in the streets as well was almost unbelievable. He informed Joseph II that the wasting of money by the Court was "painted in the darkest colours", while everyone agreed that the Estates General must be summoned, as if there was no government in France. It would be useless, concluded

Mercy, to try arresting the offenders, as there were so many of them, and it would only lead to a revolt.

Madame Campan also realised that the Affair of the Diamond Necklace had marked a turning point in the Queen's life, and that from then on the tide would be running against her.

"The carefree joyous days were gone, never to return. It was farewell to those tranquil and informal holidays at her beloved Trianon; farewell forever to those brilliant fêtes and galas which served as a showcase for all the glittering splendour, the sparkling wit, the exquisite good taste of French Court life. What was more, it was farewell forever to respect and reverence for institutions of monarchy."

Not only was the glory of the monarchy departing, but now the long overdue auditing of the nation's accounts was at hand. Calonne, the Controller General of Finances, disclosed the situation: one thousand two hundred and fifty million livres had been borrowed to prop up the economy. Since everyone knew that Louis was thrifty, all fingers pointed at the Queen. Soon she had a new nickname, "Madame Déficit". Ironically enough, the remark by which the world remembers Marie Antoinette was one she never even uttered. "Let them eat cake," supposed to have been spoken after hearing the peasants were hungry for bread, was current over one hundred years earlier, and attributed to Marie Theresa, the wife of Louis XIV. Now, in the vindictive atmosphere which prevailed, it was again circulating at Marie Antoinette's expense.

Perhaps the "starving peasant" aspect of the French Revolution has been overstressed. Many agricultural workers were in fact better off than their opposite numbers in the towns. It was there that the bread was in shortest supply. When the struggle came it was not simply the workers versus the rest of the nation, but, as much as anything, a conflict engineered by the less well-off white-collar workers. Avidly they read Voltaire, Rousseau and Diderot, and their radical new ideas about liberty and the individual were reinforced by the tales told by those just returning from fighting in the American War of Independence. Did the monarchy justify its existence? Why should privilege be automatic for some and denied to others? Those were only two of the questions being asked, and judging by the details which came to light during the trial of Jeanne de la Motte, the answer must be "no." For many the monarchy had ceased to be a divine institution; they had seen its feet of clay all too clearly.

Before long Calonne was out of office, and his place taken by Loménie de Brienne, Archbishop of Toulouse, at the suggestion of Marie Antoinette. Economies must be made at Court, he decided, and he drastically reduced the size of her household for a start. Baron de Besenval was particularly bitter about this: "It is a terrible thing to live in a country where one cannot be sure of having one day what one had the day before."

Not only were banknotes hardly worth the paper on which they were printed, but the coinage was debased: either inflation or complete bankruptcy faced the country. When Loménie de Brienne laid two edicts before the Parliament of Paris for the imposition of a stamp duty and a land tax, the lawyers refused to accept them, implying that the Estates General should be called. Instead, the edicts were registered at Versailles and the Parliament of Paris exiled to the city of Troyes. With the backing of Marie Antoinette, Louis was trying to assert himself as an absolute monarch. The outcome was disastrous. Demonstrations were held in Paris, and with reluctance Parliament was allowed to return to the capital. Then on November 19th, 1787, Louis issued loans for four hundred and twenty million livres. Although described as loans they were more in the nature of orders, and the Duc d'Orléans declared the registration of the edict to be illegal, openly clashing with his cousin and sovereign.

Calonne had failed, and now so had de Brienne, but there was one man who might be able to save France from total disaster: the Swiss financier, Monsieur Necker. Once before Monsieur Necker had been called in to try and sort out the tangled skein of finance, but he was resented by the other ministers because he was a Calvinist, a foreigner and a commoner. When he finally tendered his resignation to the King it was on a small half-sheet of writing paper. Certainly he had little reason to love the royal family: on one occasion the Comte d'Artois—in his early thirties—called him a "fornicating foreign bastard". So it now fell to Marie Antoinette to receive the ruffled Swiss in her private apartments and use all her charm to persuade him to help her country by adoption. Afterwards, as he returned to Paris amidst cheers of "Long live Necker!", Marie Antoinette remarked prophetically: "I tremble at the thought that Necker's recall has been my doing. It seems to be my fate to bring misfortune, and if he should fail like his predecessors, or damage the King's authority, I shall be hated even more than I am now."

For the first time in her life Marie Antoinette was, without realising it, assuming the role of a daughter of Maria Theresa. Once she could not make up her mind which dress to wear and could not read a book or a letter to the end, but now she was making decisions—admittedly in the Crown's own interest at the expense of the nation as a whole—and trying to assume a role which was hers by birth but not by training.

Mercy quickly realised that her lack of experience was having disastrous results, and in a letter to Joseph II told him that the Queen was quite occupied with trying to arrange internal affairs, economies, reforms and even the debates in the Assembly. Unfortunately all these affairs were dealt with in a haphazard manner, and this resulted in a confusion which made things worse.

Ten years earlier, after his first visit to Versailles, Joseph II wrote to his sister:

"I tremble when I think of your happiness, because things cannot go on like this indefinitely. The revolution will be a cruel one, and possibly caused by you yourself."

At this time Marie Antoinette and Louis had their own private grief. Slowly but inevitably the eight-year-old Dauphin was dying of rickets. Never strong, his health was now declining sharply during the latter part of 1788. His spine was deformed and protruding, and it was painfully obvious even to his mother that he could not have much longer to live.

As in England just before the outbreak of the Civil War, the French were starting to align themselves for the inevitable struggle. On one side were the King and Queen and the peers and ministers still loyal to them, and on the other those who had been antagonised by the Court, headed by the Duc d'Orléans and the liberal thinkers gathered round him at the Palais Royal. And on both sides a new and curious phenomenon appeared, the no longer inarticulate mass of the people.

Daily the demands for the summoning of the Estates General grew louder. Almost unbelievable though it sounds, the French legislative assembly had not been called since 1614, in the days of Louis XIII, Finally Monsieur Necker made Louis realise that they must be summoned, and at the beginning of May, 1789, the nobles, the clergy and the commons—the Three Estates—converged on Versailles. Altogether there were one thousand one hundred and sixty-five of them, and there had been an innovation: the commons would be equal in number to the nobles and the clergy together.

They were to meet in the curiously named *Salle des Menus Plaisirs*, the Hall of Lesser Pleasures, in the centre of the town. First they would have an audience with the King in the Palace. Even now, with the country tottering on the brink of a revolution, etiquette still had to be observed. Strict adherence to protocol even included such distinctions as opening both halves of the great doors of the Royal Chamber for the nobles, half for the clergy—and leaving them shut in the face of the commons, amongst whom was a lawyer named Maximilien Robespierre.

On Monday, May 4th, the Estates General went in procession, together with the royal family, to a service in the church of St Louis. Watching from a mattress on the balcony of the Little Stable was the Dauphin, patient and resigned. The great procession was the last occasion the *ancien régime* would be seen in all its magnificence. Louis XVI was in full robes and wearing the famous Regent diamond in his hat. At his side walked Marie Antoinette, and after them came Provence, Artois, Orléans and most of the Court and the ministers.

An American, Gouverneur Morris, was among the onlookers:

"The procession is very magnificent. Neither the King nor Queen appear too well pleased. The former is repeatedly saluted with the '*Vive le Roi*' as he passes along, but the latter receives not a single acclamation. She looks, however, with contempt on the scene in which she plays a part, and seems to say 'For the moment I submit, but I shall have my turn.' "

Not only did the crowds remain silent as she passed, but at that exact moment someone shouted "Long live the Duc d'Orléans!" Nor did the Bishop of Nancy spare her in his sermon. He called the French a martyred people, and attacked the squandering of money which went on at Court. The Third Estate, no longer overawed by their supposed superiors, disregarded the fact that they were in church and applauded.

The next day Gouverneur Morris was among those in the *Salle des Menus Plaisirs*, witnessing an event that really could be described as historic: the first meeting together of the Estates General for exactly one hundred and seventy-five years.

"Monsieur Necker," he wrote, "was applauded on his entry, and so was the Duc d'Orléans. On the other hand the Comte de Mirabeau (who soon would openly side with the Revolutionaries) was hissed. The King at length arrives and takes his seat, the Queen on his left, two steps lower than him. He makes a short speech, very proper and well spoken, or rather read. He is interrupted in the reading by acclamations so warm and of such lively affection that the tears start from my eyes in spite of myself. The Queen weeps or seems to weep, but not one voice is heard to wish her well."

Then Monsieur Necker read his financial statement in a flat droning voice, going on for more than three hours. He offered no sweeping tax reforms, nor even possible solutions to the financial crisis.

"After this speech is over, the King rises to depart and receives a long and affecting '*Vive le Roi!*' The Queen rises and to my great satisfaction she hears for the first time in several months the sound of '*Vive la Reine!*' She makes a low curtsy and this produces a louder acclamation, and that a lower curtsy."

While the Three Estates argued, discussed and considered trivial resolutions, the royal couple went to Meudon each day to be with the Dauphin, who had been moved there as his doctors considered the air might be beneficial. On June 4th he died, his title passing to his younger brother, Louis Charles.

Political action by the Third Estate came when, with the support of the clergy, they broke away from the whole body, and called themselves the National Assembly. According to them it would now be illegal to raise taxes without their consent. Necker was hastily summoned to the Palace, but his audience with Louis was interrupted by a message from Marie Antoinette who wished to speak to her husband in private. Louis left the room, and when he returned he would have none of Necker's conciliatory scheme or plans for constitutional reform.

The day following, June 20th, was pouring with rain, and when the members of the new National Assembly found the doors of the *Salle des Menus Plaisirs* locked (it was being prepared for a Royal Session of the Three Estates in the presence of the King), they crowded into the nearby *Jeu de Paume*, a covered tennis court. There all save one deputy took an oath to uphold the National Assembly, "and to go on meeting wherever circumstances might dictate, until the constitution of the kingdom and the regeneration of the state is firmly established."

For the last time, on June 23rd, 1789, the *ancien régime* met in all its magnificence at a Royal Session of the Estates. Louis chided them for having achieved nothing in two months, and added that if necessary he would act alone for the good of his people. Outside some four thousand troops waited, and when the Session was over they were ordered to clear the hall, but because of the mood of the crowd and their uncertain loyalty they never even entered the building. When this was reported back to Louis he merely exclaimed, "Oh well, devil take it, let them stay!"

On the surface it appeared that even the reactionary nobility was prepared to work alongside the clergy and—horror of horrors—the Third Estate, dressed in the simple clothes of ordinary townsmen and farmers. Secretly the King gave orders that six regiments should come to Versailles, while on July 1st ten more regiments, mostly Swiss and German mercenaries, were drafted into the Paris area.

When word of what was happening went round the National Assembly, their belief was that Louis intended to fall back on authoritarian rule, by armed force if necessary. When they objected, he told them, "Only the ill-disposed could mislead my people about the precautionary measures I am taking."

Already there was open unrest in Paris because of the price of bread, which was in short supply, costing the average workingman more than half a day's pay for a four pound loaf. What was more, the city was crowded with hungry and unemployed people who had flocked in in the vain hope of finding employment. Order was in the hands of the troops who formed the garrison, for the most part French Guards, whose sympathies were with the people, while the Champ-de-Mars (now overlooked by the Eiffel Tower) was nothing but a military camp.

Paris, on July 12th, was hot and sultry. In the gardens of the Palais

Royal a young lawyer, journalist and agitator named Camille Desmoulins jumped on a chair and shouted: "I have just come from Versailles. Monsieur Necker is dismissed. This is a signal for a St Bartholomew's Day massacre of the patriots. This evening the Swiss and German battalions will cut our throats. We have but one resource—to take arms!"

At Versailles the reactionary element had had their last triumph in engineering the King's dismissal of Necker. Baron de Breteuil now headed a new administration. The National Assembly waited to see what Louis would do, and as usual he hesitated.

Back in Paris cavalrymen were stoned in the Place Louis Quinze (de la Concorde), and there was a large demonstration by about six thousand in the Boulevard du Temple against the dismissal of Necker.

"They were armed," wrote an eye-witness, "some with guns, others with swords, lances and pitchforks. They were carrying in triumph the wax busts of the Duc d'Orléans and Monsieur Necker, which they had borrowed from Monsieur Curtius (the owner of a waxworks museum). Beside them they carried two standards in black and white as a sign of mourning for the disgrace of an idolised minister."

Baron de Besenval, once one of the closest of Marie Antoinette's associates at the Petit Trianon, was charged with maintaining order in Paris. He did not know how to handle the situation, and the horror of Frenchman killing Frenchman in a civil war made him determined to avoid shedding blood at all costs. Furthermore he doubted the loyalty of his troops. Versailles refused to believe the situation was really grave, and unwisely de Besenval decided to withdraw his forces and leave Paris to itself. His action meant that there was nothing to restrain the revolutionary elements. Barricades were set up, military posts looted for arms; and now the mobs were wearing cockades of red and blue, the city's colours.

Thirty-two thousand muskets and five cannons were commandeered from Les Invalides, then the mob surged across the bridges to the north bank, and eastwards towards the Bastille, a large heavy-looking fortress with massive walls about one hundred feet high, which stood not far from the present Gare de Lyon. For long it had been a symbol of oppression, real or imaginary, and the mob intended to storm it for the arms it was known to contain.

The Bastille should have been impregnable, but was in fact not properly garrisoned and quite unprepared for a siege. An ultimatum was passed out of the fortress through a loophole warning the rebels: "We have twenty thousand kilos of powder here, and we shall blow up the garrison and the whole quarter if you do not surrender."

As answer the cannon were drawn up opposite the entrance. The defenders lowered the smaller of the two drawbridges, and a moment or two later an old soldier opened the door beside the main one and asked what the besiegers wanted. "The surrender of the Bastille." So he let them in. The mob swarmed over the drawbridge, and the soldiers on the battlements, not knowing it was all over, fired down on them. Up till that moment the crowd had regarded the garrison as their brothers, but now they turned savage and attacked. De Launay, the humane Governor, was hurried through the streets towards the Hôtel de Ville. Within a few yards of the building, and safety, the mob closed in. On the steps he was lynched and his head was hacked off.

The Bastille and all it stood for had indeed fallen, but when the cells were opened all they contained were seven prisoners, none of them of any great consequence.

"Yesterday," wrote Gouverneur Morris, "it was the fashion at Versailles not to believe that there were any disturbances at Paris. I presume that this day's transactions will induce a conviction that all is not perfectly quiet."

Like Morris, the King was also keeping his diary up to date!

"July 13th. Nothing. July 14th. Nothing."

Late that evening of July 14th the Duc de La Rochefoucaud-Liancourt rode into Versailles from Paris and demanded to see the King, who was in bed and asleep.

"The Bastille has been taken by storm and the Governor has been murdered. His head, on the point of a pike, is being paraded in triumph through the streets."

"It is a revolt?" queried Louis.

"No, Sire, it is a revolution."

CHAPTER TWELVE

The Road to Versailles

No sooner had the Bastille fallen than its demolition began. It was a symbol of tyranny, and as such must be wiped off the face of the earth. Today all that remains to prove it ever existed are stones set in the paving of the Place de la Bastille, outlining the position of some of the walls; while daily thousands of Parisians and visitors pass over its masonry, re-used to complete the Pont de la Concorde over the Seine.

At Versailles, when the news from the capital had really sunk in, Louis' first reaction was to abdicate, while Marie Antoinette advised their immediate departure for the safety of Metz, the fortress-town in Lorraine not all that far from the German frontier. This was decided against, and instead Louis went to the National Assembly, together with his brothers Provence and Artois, where he told the deputies that the troops would be withdrawn from the Paris region. "I am one with the Nation," he declared emotionally. "I entrust myself to you." For a few hours at least the National Assembly, if not the Nation, was one with him.

To the crowd gathered in the Place d'Armes outside the Palace Louis was now something of a hero, and he and the royal family were to appear on the balcony. Marie Antoinette knew that there was one woman in France even more unpopular than herself, and she sent word by Madame Campan that Madame de Polignac must not accompany them, as it would surely provoke a demonstration. Then Madame Campan went and mingled with the crowd listening to their comments. Marie Antoinette was right, the people obviously hated her friend to a frightening degree. Back once again in the Palace she reported what she had overheard, and the Queen insisted that Madame de Polignac and her husband must leave at once, not only Versailles, but the country itself. Madame de Polignac refused, and when the King came in Marie Antoinette requested him to order the couple to depart for their own safety.

"I have just ordered the Comte d'Artois to leave, and I give you the same order," he said. "Pity me, but do not lose a single moment."

Artois, the youngest of the King's brothers, and the most arrogantly reactionary man at Court, had been ordered into exile, never to return to France.

At midnight, Madame de Polignac was handed a letter from Marie Antoinette just as she and her husband were preparing to leave Versailles.

"Goodbye, dearest of friends, it is a dreadful word. This is the order for the horses. Goodbye, I have only strength enough to embrace you."

Within hours they reached Bâsle and safety from the justified anger of the French. Now a new governess had to be appointed to look after the royal children, and the Duchesse de Tourzel was chosen. Belatedly Marie Antoinette was maturing, and showing she was capable of shrewd judgement. In a memorandum for Madame de Tourzel she wrote of the Dauphin:

"Like all robust and healthy children, he is very thoughtless, extremely absent-minded, and given to violent tempers: but he is a good boy, and most affectionate when he is not too thoughtless. He has an extremely good opinion of himself, but even so, in time even this may be turned to good account if he is carefully guided. When he has given his word he may be relied upon to keep it; but he is very indiscreet, and will always repeat anything he has heard. Quite often he will elaborate what he has heard, without meaning to tell lies. This is indeed his chief fault, and the one above all others which must be corrected. My son does not yet know how to read, and he is a slow learner, being too inattentive to think seriously about the task. He has no idea about the lofty station into which he has been born, and it is my strong desire that he should continue to be simple-minded in this respect, for our children learn all too soon into what rank they have been born."

Perhaps for the first time in her life, separation from Louis meant something to Marie Antoinette. On July 17th he would go to Paris to show himself to his "good people". But first he made his will, appointing Provence to take over the reins should the worst happen, and then set out for the capital. Marie Antoinette was almost in tears, convinced that she would never see him again, and during his absence the Palace was deathly quiet. In the event of his death she was even prepared to assume the role of sovereign and go and address the National Assembly.

Meanwhile, Louis was being both fêted and humiliated, almost in the same breath. Bailly, President of the National Assembly and also the new Mayor of Paris, greeted him with the remark, "Paris has achieved the reconquest of its King." At best it was a back-handed welcome, because "Louis XVI, father of the French, King of a free people", was made to put on that emblem of the Revolution, the cockade. But now there was white, the Bourbon colour, between the red and the blue, and the French tricolour was complete.

Not only was the municipal revolution recognised, but Lafayette assumed command of the National Guard, an army of the people. When Louis returned to Versailles in the evening, Marie Antoinette cried with relief at his safe return and flung her arms around him. She was learning to appreciate people for other qualities than their ability to amuse her; those who for so many years had filled that function were now fleeing the country as fast as their horses' legs could carry them. Esterhazy, Vaudreuil, Lazun—nearly all the Trianon set, in fact—vanished at the first sign of trouble. One of the few who remained loyal from the palmy days was Axel de Fersen. Seldom noticed, he was always hovering in the background in case his help was needed. Louis can have had no illusions. Saint-Priest, a not wholly amiable onlooker wrote: "She (Marie Antoinette) found ways and means of acquainting the King with the fact that she had a laison with the Comte de Fersen." That was honest, but hardly necessary, since in the summer of 1788 someone had sent Louis an anonymous letter. It reduced him to tears, but nothing changed. The situation was regrettable, but perhaps inevitable. In Louis XVI Marie Antoinette found affection but incomprehension, and in Fersen love and understanding.

July turned into August, and to an onlooker it might have seemed that the Revolution would achieve its aims without further violence. Throughout the country local volunteers formed a militia intended to protect the people from the power of the nobles, but the latter's influence had already been curtailed by the National Assembly, the only recognised authority in France. For many, particularly the more respectable citizens, the Revolution did not mean the abolition of the Monarchy, but the return of the King to Paris, the reform of the constitution, the curbing of privilege and the prevention of national bankruptcy.

The French Revolution was engineered and organised by such people as journalists and lawyers from the provinces, and not by malodorous peasants with scythes. At least in the early stages the mob committed all the atrocities and so stole all the headlines, but the exasperated and penurious sections of the middle classes did all the work.

At the time of the Fall of the Bastille, thirty-five per cent of arable land was in the hands of peasant landowners, but for several years the price of produce had been falling, while rents remained high. Then in 1788 the harvest failed, and was followed by a very severe winter. Now, in the summer of 1789, there was bitter disappointment that although the Estates General had been called, Louis had achieved nothing which really ameliorated the lot of the nation as a whole.

Bands of starving vagrants roamed the countryside like packs of dogs, ravaging the crops, and this was regarded as some deep and devilish plot by the aristocracy. Reforms were made in August. Even the Press was declared free, and tithes imposed by both the nobles and the clergy were abolished, as was the salt tax and the *corvée*. The *corvée* was a system of municipal press-gangs which could carry men to work on such projects as roadmaking or harbour-building, and resulted in as much hardship and misery as the Naval press-gangs in eighteenth- and early nineteenth-century England.

While Paris itself might be comparatively quiet, there was trouble in the countryside. August became the month of the Great Fear. Châteaux were attacked and burnt, ostensibly to destroy the Manorial Rolls which they contained, for these Rolls were records of the tenants and what they had to pay in rent. Exactly the same thing had happened in England over four hundred years earlier during the Peasants' Revolt of 1381. As a result, in September, 1789, the nobles started to emigrate in ever increasing numbers, many crossing the Channel, while others fled to Germany, and in particular to Turin where the Comte d'Artois had established himself.

Rapidly the feudal system in France, which dated from the days of the House of Capet, was breaking down, and its end was further hastened when the National Assembly declared that all men must be equal and without privilege.

"I will never consent to the spoliation of my clergy and my nobility," said Louis concerning the Declaration of the Rights of Man of August 3rd. "I will not sanction decrees by which they are despoiled." If he found that objectionable, there was something else: the National Assembly was discussing his power of veto, and one of the most vigorous opponents of the King's right of veto was Robespierre. Eventually a compromise solution was reached which left the King with some vestiges of authority; he should have the right to suspend legislation for the life of two legislatures – but that was all.

Now the King and Queen had new nicknames: Monsieur and Madame Véto.

By September there was a growing demand that the King should be brought to Paris, to live among his people, instead of being insulated from them, surrounded by pernicious reactionaries at Versailles.

"You have a hundred thousand, two hundred thousand fists; there are muskets and cannon in the arsenals; get them out ready for use: fetch the King and Queen from Versailles; take your destinies into your own hands!" Additional hardships were caused in Paris by the departure of so many of the aristocracy, leaving their employees not only jobless, but penniless. Bread was getting really short now, due to a long spell of completely windless days, which meant that the mills stood idle and could not grind the corn, Emotional temperature was starting to rise again, as it had done before the Storming of the Bastille; it would take very little to touch off an equally violent explosion.

On October 1st the Opera House in the Palace had once again been converted into a banqueting room, but the scene was very different from the occasion nearly twenty years before on the night of Marie Antoinette's wedding. Two weeks previously more than a thousand men of the Flemish Regiment had been posted to Versailles from Douai, and now they were the guests of their sovereigns at a social occasion. Two hundred and six were seated round a horseshoe-shaped table on the stage itself, while many more soldiers armed with wine glasses filled the pit. At first there were no plans for the Queen to attend, but after Louis returned from hunting he and Marie Antoinette went to the Opera House and showed themselves in the royal box. With them were their two children.

All had wined well that evening, and at the appearance of the royal couple the officers and men drew their swords, which they flourished in salute. Their shouts of welcome were nearly deafening, but particularly warming to Marie Antoinette, who had not heard such cries of "*Vive la Reine*" for many years. She responded with the charm of bearing and manner that was her special secret. Twice she walked around the horseshoe-shaped table on the stage, and every soldier in the Opera House would have given his life for her on the spot. An officer of the Swiss Guards lifted the four-year-old Dauphin on to the table, and to everybody's delight he walked from one end to the other. As the King and Queen moved among their guests, an orchestra played Grétry's "*O Richard, O mon roi,*" which, as it had strong royalist associations was to prove unfortunate when the news reached Paris.

Loyal toasts were drunk, and the evening became happier and noisier as the wine went to not a few heads—the last happy evening at Versailles which any of them would ever know. Harmless though it had all been, by the time the journalists and pamphleteers in Paris had finished, the evening was represented as a particularly foul orgy. Not only were the cockades of the Habsburgs and the Bourbons supposed to have been prominently displayed, but that emblem of the Revolution and all it stood for, the tricolour, was said to have been trodden underfoot, and even trampled on by Marie Antoinette herself.

The banquet provided the perfect occasion the agitators had been waiting for, and soon Paris was in a ferment of righteous indignation. Not only must there be luxury foods in plenty at Versailles, but rumour declared that there was also a great deal of bread and flour stored there, while in the capital it was no mere coincidence that the supplies were held up for two days, making the already hungry desperate.

Early on the morning of October 5th the tocsin rang out over Paris. A young woman broke into a guardroom and stole a drum. Beating it though the streets, she was soon at the head of an ever-growing mob. The women of Paris were rising in a carefully planned "spontaneous" demonstration. Among them were a number of men disguised as women, shepherding them towards the Hôtel de Ville. There they looted all the pikes and muskets they could lay their hands on, and dragged two cannon from the Châtelet nearby. Whoever engineered the rising knew the workings of the human mind: while the National Guard might have had no qualms about shooting down men, they would flinch at the idea of firing on unarmed women.

Maillard, a tall and thin young revolutionary who had played a prominent part in the events leading up to the storming of the Bastille, appeared from nowhere and exhorted the crowd to march to Versailles to demand bread—and to bring about the return of the King to Paris.

The day was cold and blustery as between six and seven thousand women, plus the agitators in disguise, turned to the west and set out along the twelve miles to Versailles. Fishwives, pedlars, vagrants, street-walkers, and the redoubtable *Dames des Halles*—the market women—were coming to visit their King and his hated Queen.

After a while it started to rain, and soon the drizzle turned into a steady downpour. As they marched the women threw their long skirts up over their heads to provide some protection, while their feet were up to the ankles in mud. Along the route wine shops were broken open and looted, and some paused to sharpen their long knives on the milestones. All the way they encouraged each other by telling what they would do when they laid hands on the Austrian Bitch. Cut her throat; cut off her head; rip up her belly; dismember her, make a cockade of her guts. There was no end to their bestial suggestions.

That morning Marie Antoinette had walked through the park to the Petit Trianon; to her perfectly proportioned little palace, her theatre and the charming Hameau nestling among the trees beside the lake. Now she was alone: no friends, most having fled abroad, and not even a lady-in-waiting with her. She went to the Grotto of Love and sat down on a stone bench to read a book. The rain was falling hard now, and after some while she was suddenly interrupted by a page sent by the Comte de Saint-Priest. He had scribbled a note telling her to come back to the Palace at once, as the women of Paris were reported to be marching on Versailles.

Quickly she hurried into the rain, away from the Petit Trianon and all that it and her life had meant so far. She would never see it again.

That day, as usual, Louis had gone hunting. A messenger was sent to Meudon to fetch him back, and at 3.00 in the afternoon he galloped in through the main gate of the Palace, scattering a handful of women who had already arrived from Paris. For the first time in seventy years or more the massive gilded gates were closed, in their very faces.

Confronting the insurgents in the Place d'Armes was the National Guard, of uncertain loyalty, and the men of the Flemish Regiment. In the Palace nobody knew what to do, and the place was in turmoil. The best advice came from Saint-Priest. He suggested that the main body of demonstrators should be prevented from reaching Versailles by stationing one battalion of the Flanders Regiment on the bridge at Sèvres, and another at St Cloud, while the Swiss Guards were to hold the bridge at Neuilly. Then, from a position of strength, the King could address them in person at Sèvres, and if necessary cavalry could then be used for their dispersal. Meanwhile, if she wished, Marie Antoinette could go to Rambouillet. She refused outright, saying that if her husband was in danger she wished to be near him, wherever that might happen to be.

"Sire," warned Saint-Priest, "if you let them take you to Paris tomorrow, you will lose your crown."

Meanwhile, as he vacillated, the hordes of women continued to pour into Versailles. Many, under the leadership of Maillard, went to the National Assembly. Emotionally he told the Deputies that Paris starved for want of bread, and he demanded the right to search houses in the town where it was suspected that flour might be hoarded. Bribes, he added, were being given to millers not to grind corn; according to him even the Archbishop of Paris had himself given two hundred livres to a miller to stop work.

"The Chamber had been invaded by the People of Paris and the arena was packed," recorded an eyewitness. "The galleries were full of women and men armed with scythes, sticks and pikes. The sitting had been suspended, but someone came on behalf of the King to request the President to send a deputation to the Château and to keep the Assembly in session."

The group chosen to go to the Palace consisted of five or six women together with a number of deputies. Among the latter was the Deputy for Paris, a professor of anatomy at the university, a large genial man called Dr Guillotin. Louis, usually so awkward in his movements and gauche in his manner, received them with such charm that one of the girls, Louison Chabry, was so overcome by the surroundings and the august company in which she found herself that she fainted on the spot. Louis ordered smelling salts to be brought, and put his arm round her shoulders in a paternal gesture. They should have bread, he ordered, and anything else they might require, and could borrow a coach from the royal stables for their return journey to Paris.

By then, however, other women from Paris had made their way into the courtyard of the Palace, and standing under the main windows were shouting for the head of the Queen. When the deputation came out they were abused and shouted at as traitors. The others declared they would not be seduced by words. Now Louis changed his mind; he and his family would all go to Rambouillet. Marie Antoinette agreed, and told the under-governess to pack up and be ready to leave with the children in a quarter of an hour. It was too late. The Stables (now barracks) were on the far side of the Place d'Armes from the Palace, and the crowd would not let carriages be brought out. If the royal family were to leave at all that night, and it was by then about 9.00 p.m., it would only be by force and probably with bloodshed. Again Louis changed his mind. They would stay at Versailles.

In tears Louis signed the Declaration of the Rights of Man, and ordered the Bodyguard to stand down. They were to camp in the Park, on the beautiful lawn called the *Tapis Vert*, between the Palace and the Grand Canal. At the same time the men of the Flemish Regiment marched off to spend an equally wet and uncomfortable night in the courtyard of the Little Stables. Now only the National Guard remained on duty in the Place d'Armes. The women of Paris slept where they could, trying to find shelter from the driving rain—on the floor of the National Assembly, in churches, in doorways, anywhere, even camped against the railings of the Palace itself. Some went soliciting among the soldiers.

At half past twelve General Lafayette arrived in Versailles at the head of his soaked French Guards, loyal but late. Instead of either stopping the demonstration before it left Paris, or at least keeping it under control, all he had been able to do was to form a shambling rearguard, following in the wake of the marching women. On October 5th, when events started to happen, he was late. The following morning, when great happenings were taking place, he overslept. Poor Lafayette, little wonder he was nicknamed "Général Morphée".

Theatrically he offered Louis his life: "Sire, I bring you my head, to save that of Your Majesty." He then asked that his French Guards should take over from the National Guard, and even from the Bodyguards in the Palace itself. That having been done he took himself off to the Hôtel de Noailles in the town for a good night's sleep.

It was 2.00 a.m. before Louis and Marie Antoinette got to bed in their separate apartments. Outside it was still raining, and few in either the waiting town or in the vast Palace could have slept for long, if at all. All was quiet, but beyond the railings it was as though Marianne was gathering her strength.

About 6.00 a.m., just as it was light, women forced their way into the courtyard and started demonstrating under Marie Antoinette's bedroom window, which faced on to the Place d'Armes. The noise woke the Queen, who rang to find out the cause of the disturbance. Women who had nowhere to sleep were walking to and fro, she was told. It was nothing to worry about. A few minutes later a drum started beating and a shot was fired. Hordes of women and men in disguise rallied round a blue and red flag, and then tried to get in by the main gate, but it was locked. The Chapel gate was conveniently open—unlocked by whom?—and they swarmed in. Nor were the doors of the Palace itself locked, but that was for the benefit of the sentries when being changed.

The mob pushed in and started to climb the great staircase, led by a guardsman of the Versailles Militia, who seemed to know the way. The Bodyguard formed up quickly as axes smashed in the doors of their hall. Already some of the revolutionaries were making for the Queen's apartments, shouting: "We are going to cut off her head, tear out heart, fry her liver, and that won't be the end of it."

Miromarde, an officer of the Bodyguard, called through an open door to a lady of the Queen's household: "Save the Queen, they mean to kill her. I am alone facing two hundred tigers. My comrades have been driven out of their own hall." Then he slammed the door and bravely faced the oncoming mob alone. He warded off a pike thrust, but another blow on the head felled him. Then the soldier from the Versailles Militia leading the insurgents brought down his musket on Miromarde's head with such force that he crushed his skull and killed him outright.

Now, according to some eyewitness accounts, the Duc d'Orléans appeared as though from nowhere in the courtyard below. Not only was he shaved and properly dressed, but he was even wearing a grey frock coat, a round hat and carrying a riding crop. The people made way before him, calling out, "Long live King Orléans," and "Our father is with us." Whether he was actually present or not is immaterial; beyond a shadow of doubt he was the brain behind the whole demonstration. Apparently he then made his way up the staircase, but at its head he stopped, pointed the way to Marie Antoinette's rooms, and disappeared in the direction of the King's apartments.

Two women were helping Marie Antoinette slip on a petticoat over her nightdress, and just as the mob started to break down her door she caught up a pair of stockings and left barefooted by another concealed door by her bed. It opened on to a corridor leading to the Oeil-de-Boeuf, but at the farther end the doors were locked from the other side, and as she banged frantically for someone to open them, she could hear the mob bursting into her bedroom. Again and again they stabbed the bed with their pikes, and started to smash up the furniture behind which some of the Bodyguard had taken refuge after getting into the room with the intention of protecting their Queen. Finally a boy heard Marie Antoinette calling for help, and opened the doors from the other side. The Queen ran into her husband's room crying: "My friends, my dear friends, save me!"

Louis was not there, having gone to look for the Dauphin, so Marie Antoinette went off to find Madame Royale. Five minutes later the family was reunited in the King's bedroom just as the mob started to break down the doors of the Oeil-de-Boeuf. That was as far as they were to get. The French Guards now counter-attacked, driving them down the staircase and out of the Palace, though not from the courtyard.

There an officer of the National Guard was handing out money and inciting the crowd to kill all except the Dauphin and the Duc d'Orléans.

"At these words a man with a frightful face, disguised as a woman, displayed a sort of sickle, and swore he would be the one to cut off the old bitch's head."

Now the mob was hunting the men of the Bodyguard. Two were caught under the walls of the Palace, brought to the King's Gate, thrown to the ground and beheaded by an enormous bearded man with an axe. Then their heads were paraded on pikes as trophies. About thirty more of the Bodyguard were rounded up and would have been similarly murdered but for the timely arrival on the scene of General Lafayette and a strong body of Grenadiers.

"Grenadiers, I have given my word to the King that none of the Gentlemen of the Bodyguard would be harmed. If you make me break my word of honour I shall not consider myself fit to command you and shall leave! Have at them!" So just in time the men of the Bodyguard were saved.

All this was witnessed by Marie Antoinette from a window of her private apartments. Beside her was Madame Royale and the Dauphin, standing on a chair. From time to time he repeated: "Mama, I'm so hungry," and ruffled his sister's hair.

Lafayette entered and told the Queen that the people were calling for her to appear on the balcony. It would be the only way to calm them.

"In that case, I'll do it. Even if it costs me my life."

Holding the hands of her children she started to go out on to the balcony.

"No children," shouted a voice in the crowd. She continued alone. A man raised his musket, hesitated, and then lowered it again. Marie Antoinette pulled a wrap more tightly about her shoulders, but otherwise remained motionless. For a full minute she and the mob stared at each other in profound silence. Then she curtsied.

"*Vive la Reine*," shouted the mob. It was incredible, but true. They were actually cheering the Austrian woman. Then she withdrew, and the chant started: "We want the King in Paris—the King in Paris."

Now Louis and General Lafayette came out on to the balcony, and after a while the King managed to make himself heard above the shouting: "My friends, I shall go to Paris with my wife and children. I trust all that is dear to me to the love of my good and faithful subjects."

Again Marie Antoinette appeared, this time with Lafayette. Gallantly he kissed her hand, and there were cries of "*Vive Lafayette! Vive la Reine!*"

Lafayette called down that the Queen had been deceived, but now she would love her people and be attached to them like Jesus Christ was to His Church. There was more cheering and applause.

After that the members of the Bodyguard appeared on the balcony together with members of the Paris Militia. The Bodyguard threw down their bandoliers as token of their peaceful intentions towards the crowd, and in an enthusiastically received gesture they exchanged their headgear with the men of the Paris Militia. There were even cries of "Long live the Bodyguard"—two of whose headless bodies were still lying in the courtyard.

It was all over. The demonstration had achieved its main object—the return of the King to his capital. Notes were thrown down from the windows telling the crowd that the royal family would be leaving shortly, and at 1.25 in the afternoon of October 6th the whole Court left Versailles in a huge procession, said to number some two thousand coaches. After all the rain of the last twenty-four hours it was now a beautiful calm autumn day: the Park, and especially the Petit Trianon, would have been looking its best, but now the Palace and its grounds were completely deserted.

"The heads of Monsieur des Hutes and Monsieur de Varicourt on two pikes led the procession," wrote the Marquis de Ferrières. "Following them were forty or fifty members of the Bodyguard on foot and unarmed, escorted by a body of men armed with sabres and pikes." Then in the exceedingly long procession came members of the Bodyguard, some wounded and with their shirts torn, held by National Guards. More of the Bodyguard were further back, some riding pillion or with National Guards sitting behind them on the horses. All around were men and women who forced them to shout "*Vive la Nation!*" and share their food and wine.

Immediately in front of the coach carrying Louis and his family went the cannon, with women astride their barrels. The noise must have been nearly deafening as muskets were let off at random, and the people kept chanting: "We are bringing back the Baker, the Baker's wife and the Baker's Boy!"

Marie Antoinette sat as far back in the coach as she could, almost out of sight, but she could not have failed to hear the insults shouted at her, many of them obscene. In the procession were a number of carts bringing flour to Paris, so the two objects of the demonstration really had been achieved.

In the capital the royal family was enthusiastically received at the Hôtel de Ville, and many believed that the Revolution had now run its course and was as good as over. The journey from Versailles had taken six hours, but it was not until 10.00 p.m. that the coach containing Louis, Marie Antoinette, the two children and their Governess (Madame de Tourzel) and the Comte et Comtesse de Provence turned into the courtyard of the Tuileries Palace. Not only had the old royal palace been empty since the days when Louis XV had been a small boy, but over the years it had been denuded of furniture. The Dauphin was not impressed with what he saw, and said so. Marie Antoinette told him it had been good enough for Louis XIV.

"You must not be more exacting than he was," she added.

All Louis wrote in his diary about the march of the women on Versailles was that his hunting had been "interrupted by events." Now he said: "Let us all shake down as best we can. For myself, I am content."

It had been a long day for all of them.

CHAPTER THIRTEEN

'Happiness is over and done with'

Bailly, the Mayor of Paris, quickly realised that of the royal couple it was Marie Antoinette who had the thinner skin and the quicker wit.

"The town is delighted to see you in the palace of our kings," he said pointedly. "It hopes that the King and Your Majesty will be so good as to make it their habitual residence."

Now that the King and Queen had come to live in their rightful home, the Tuileries, the satisfaction was widespread and genuine. The crowds who had shouted under the windows of Versailles for Marie Antoinette's head, now were calling "*Vive le Roi!*" and "*Vive la Reine!*" For days it was one deputation after another coming to express their loyalty, and more often it was Marie Antoinette and not her husband whom they really wanted to see. Among them were a deputation from the University, three representatives of the Parliament of Paris, the fishwives—who were told by the Queen that all hate must cease—and the whole of the National Assembly.

Marie Antoinette was doing what was required of her, but now her charm, that could hitherto have won over the most fervent anti-royalist, deserted her. She was an offended Habsburg Archduchess who had been made to do something against her will—namely, return to Paris from Versailles, and be obliged on sufferance to receive her objectionable subjects. It did not escape Lafayette's notice, and he wrote that if she wanted she could win the hearts of all Parisians, but since she could not really hide her arrogance or her temper she merely antagonised them. "I wish she could bring more goodwill to it."

Life was not as bad in the old palace as it might have been. Furniture was brought from Versailles, as well as most of the staff. In the

Tuileries, rambling and poky after the arrogant splendours of Louis XIV's creation, Marie Antoinette had her own apartments on the ground floor: a bedroom, dressing room, reception room, billiard room and dining room. Above were the apartments of Louis and the rooms occupied by Madame Élizabeth and the Dauphin. A private staircase led from the ground floor suite to that of her husband, but the only keys were kept by Marie Antoinette and Madame de Tourzel, the Dauphin's governess.

Even if there was not the same splendid ceremonial, Court life soon took on a more normal air. Madame Élizabeth left a description in a letter to the daughter of her governess.

"On Wednesday a crowd assembled beneath my windows calling for the King and Queen! I went to fetch them. The Queen spoke with the charm you know so well, and the way she behaved that morning made a good impression on the people. No one could have shown more grace and courage than the Queen has done in this last week. Everything is quiet here, and I must say I like the people more than at Versailles. The Court has been set up almost in the old style. People are received every day, and on Sunday, Tuesday and Thursday there is gaming. All of that, my love, does not displease me."

Certainly Madame Élizabeth's remarks about Marie Antoinette making herself charming are against other evidence, including that of Lafayette. But as her sister-in-law she was hardly likely to agree that the Queen was behaving in a manner less than perfect. Instead of going out and about among their genuinely well-wishing Parisian subjects the royal family kept themselves too much to themselves. Louis buried himself in the forge which was fitted up for him in order that he could spend his days making locks. Many locksmiths may have wished they were kings, but he was a king who wished himself a locksmith.

"As far as we are concerned personally," wrote Marie Antoinette, "happiness belongs to the past whatever the future may bring. I know that it is the duty for one king to suffer on behalf of all the others, and we are doing our duty well." And this was from the woman who only a few years before had said: "I am terrified of being bored." She had taken over what authority remained to the Crown. It was Marie Antoinette who interviewed the ministers and received the ambassadors, and for better or worse gave opinions and offered advice. This woman was changing so fast in character that her friends from the Petit Trianon days would hardly have known her for the same person. She was even learning to read and write dispatches in cypher.

For the first time she realised what a good friend Mercy had been, but now he was in Brussels and could only offer advice by letter. When not occupied by affairs of state the Queen busied herself educating her children, Madame Royale and her little *chou d'amour*, the Dauphin.

As ever Count Fersen was discreetly in the background, though that does not mean to say Louis was unaware of his frequent visits to the Tuileries. One of the minor tragedies of history must surely be the burning by Baron Klinckowström, Axel de Fersen's great-nephew, of some sixty letters from Marie Antoinette shortly before his death about 1900. Certainly, a version of them was published in 1878, but whole sentences were omitted and replaced by rows of dots. The creaking excuse for this old-maidish behaviour was that Fersen himself had blotted out parts of the letters where they contained unfavourable references to Gustav III before handing them on to his King for perusal! One letter did survive, because it was in cypher. It is the one which ends: "Farewell, most loved and loving of men. I kiss you with all my heart." Not only that, but part of Fersen's diary, letters to his father and sister and his correspondence book have come to light. When he was away from France after the mid-1770s he frequently wrote to "Josephine"—Josephine was one of Marie Antoinette's baptismal names.

After the isolation of Versailles the royal family were in the heart of revolutionary Paris. Just across the Tuileries Gardens, only a few hundred yards from the Palace, the National Assembly was now meeting in the Manège, a converted riding school. On the opposite side of the Rue Saint Honoré was the headquarters of the Jacobins, a club which met in a disused Dominican monastery, while on the south side of the Seine was the Cordeliers' Club, presided over by that bull of a man, Danton.

Once the idol of Paris, Monsieur Necker had become unpopular because of his failure to cure the country's financial ills. Lafayette now found himself between two fires: the people regarded him as a renegade in the pay of the Court, while the Court simply regarded him with distrust. Another man about whom there were reservations in Paris was the Comte de Mirabeau, the Deputy from Provence. Hideously pock-marked, yet an all-too-successful seducer of women, he was pamphleteer, orator, firebrand and politician all rolled into one. At the time of the march on Versailles by the women of Paris, the mob had affectionately called him "Little Mother Mirabeau", and he was also described as the mainspring of the National Assembly. But even so his fellow revolutionaries were not wholehearted in their admiration. As future events were to show, they were justified.

Mercy was the man who finally persuaded Marie Antoinette to accept Mirabeau as her intermediary with the National Assembly, though less than six months before the idea would have been quite unthinkable. Mirabeau, for his part, let it be known that his advice would be available in the Tuileries, at a price.

"Let it be known in the Palace that I am on their side rather than against them," he said. His loyalty varied with the amount of encouragement he received, but for six thousand livres a month, plus the payment of his debts amounting to two hundred and eight thousand livres, he was the King's, or rather the Queen's, man. For such a sum he would serve with "loyalty, zeal, activity and energy." Also, he would never advise in person, but only by letter. Small wonder that when all this came to light some two years after his death and burial in the Panthéon, his body was exhumed and thrown into a pit intended for offal from a knacker's yard.

In July, 1790, the royal family was allowed to go to St Cloud (the Château was destroyed during the Franco-Prussian War of 1870): this was the last experience of near-freedom they would ever know, and it was there at a secret meeting in the grounds that Marie Antoinette and Mirabeau met face to face. What they said is not known, but evidently Marie Antoinette went out of her way to charm him and afterwards he declared: "She is great, she is noble and unfortunate, but I shall save her. Nothing shall stop me, I would rather die than fail to fulfil my promises."

So, until April 2nd, 1791, Mirabeau ran his double course, haranguing the National Assembly as a good son of the Revolution, and at the same time advising the King. Then, worn out by his political and sexual excesses, he died and received the funeral due to a national hero.

Before then, in February, Marie Antoinette suffered a severe personal loss when her brother Joseph died after a long illness, and was succeeded by his younger brother Leopold II. Another link with Vienna had broken, just when she had most need of it.

Already July 14th had become a national day in France, and on the first anniversary the storming of the Bastille was celebrated with a *Fête de la Fédération* which combined both patriotism and religion in one extraordinary festival. For weeks beforehand thousands of labourers, assisted in the evenings by the Parisians themselves, had toiled to raise a huge earthwork on the Champ-de-Mars as an altar, surrounded by an amphitheatre, and with a triumphal arch at one end. In the presence of the royal family, representatives of the National Guard from all over the country and four hundred thousand spectators, Mass was celebrated by the more than usually cynical Talleyrand—the unlikely Bishop of Autun—and three hundred supporting clergy. On behalf of himself, the Army and the Militia, Lafayette swore to remain faithful to the nation. Then the Deputies followed suit, and finally Louis himself took an oath to maintain the Constitution. Marie Antoinette raised the Dauphin in her arms, banners were dipped in salute, cannon fired, and the acclamations resounded for several minutes. That evening there was dancing on the site of the Bastille.

Life for the Royal family at the start of the second year of the Revolution could not be described as unpleasant. There was more goodwill towards the King and Queen than there had been for many years; the Constitution was being reformed, privilege had been abolished, along with titles, and even if the millennium had not yet arrived France was no longer sick to the point of death. Then there was a revolt at Nancy in eastern France of soldiers supporting the extreme Jacobins. The Marquis de Bouillé, the officer commanding, put it down with a heavy hand, and when it was reported in Paris that Marie Antoinette had apparently expressed approval of the executions which took place, public feeling once again swung against her. She was even booed at the opera.

At first it looked as though the Church reforms being carried through might be entirely beneficial: the abolition of plurality, an end to aristocratic domination of the higher ranks of the clergy, and a sufficient living allowance for the average village *curé*. It became increasingly obvious that the Church was simply being manipulated by the National Assembly. In 1791 all priests were required to swear an oath to the constitution, but only Bishops Talleyrand and Gobel and half the *curés* did so, the others preferring to be guided by their consciences at the expense of being labelled "non-jurors". On March 10th the Oath to the Constitution was, in fact, condemned by the Pope. To Louis, a devout Roman Catholic, the situation was insupportable, and the idea of leaving France so that he could bargain with the leaders of the Revolution from a position of security abroad began to crystallise in his slow-working mind.

The scheme for leaving the country had first been mooted in November, 1790, when Breteuil began negotiations for foreign support, while Bouillé at Metz was told to prepare to receive the King. Now that the clergy was expected to take an oath of allegiance to the Constitution—thus making their first loyalty to the State and not to the Pope—Louis had become alienated from the Revolution. Even before then Louis was showing signs of restiveness. In October, 1790, he sent two documents to Spain in which he repudiated all acts forced upon him, declaring that he intended to abide by the programme of reforms set out by the National Assembly at Versailles in June, 1789.

"Little Mother Mirabeau" was even whispering that civil war might be the only answer to the King's problems, but to Marie Antoinette the whole scheme was "crazy from beginning to end." Escape abroad might well be the only solution, and when she made up her mind, Louis made up his. The decision was hastened by the unexpected death on April 2nd, 1791, of the volcanic Mirabeau, who had in fact been thinking (quite independently) along the same lines. Now that he was dead the royal family felt they had no one to whom they could turn. So on April 18th Louis decided on a public trial of strength. On Palm Sunday he ostentatiously refused Communion, though it was offered by a non-juring priest, and afterwards the National Guards refused to fall into line on his way back to the Tuileries from the chapel. Next he announced his intention to the National Assembly of going to St Cloud for Easter. At this there was an outcry in the Jacobin press, headed by Marat and his *Ami du Peuple*. Before the Revolution Marat had been in attendance at Versailles as physician to

I (*Previous page*) Marie Antoinette taking part in a Court ballet held at the Schoenbrunn Palace on 24 January 1765.
II (*Above*) The Schoenbrunn Palace, a painting by Bernardo Belloto.

III (*Above*) Maria Theresa and Francis I with their children, from a gouache painting by Marie Antoinette's sister, Maria Christina. This depicts the imperial family on St Nicholas' Day, 1762, and the children are shown with their gifts.

IV (*Left*) Marie Antoinette, aged twenty-eight, portrait by Lebrun.

v (*Previous page*) Detail from a portrait of Louis xv by C. Van Loo.
vi (*Above*) The gardens at Versailles, an oil painting by H. Robért.

VII Marie Antoinette in her bedroom at Versailles. This gouache was commissioned from Gauthier D'Agoty by Marie Antoinette, shortly after she became Queen of France.

the Bodyguard of the Comte d'Artois, and had become embittered because the French Academy ignored his experiments with electricity and optics. Now he was having his revenge on the whole of society. As a result of the articles in the press a huge crowd was waiting in the Place du Carrousel as the royal family got in to their carriages in the Cour Royale, within the railings of the Tuileries Palace. As they started to leave men seized the bridles and brought the horses to a stop. It was an impasse, and when Lafayette arrived he ordered a red flag to be raised—this was the equivalent to reading the Riot Act before using force to disperse a mob. The crowd took no notice; the National Guard would not clear a way and Bailly was not over co-operative when he was called.

Louis put his head out of the window and remarked loudly that while he had given the nation its freedom, he himself was not free. At this the air was thick with Gallic equivalents of four letter words, and he hastily withdrew his head.

Obviously they were not going to be allowed to leave, and for two and a half hours the royal family remained in the carriage, while the stature of the helpless, flustered Lafayette shrank before everyone's eyes. Excellent! It would demonstrate to everyone, and not only in France, that Louis was no longer a free man but merely the prisoner of his people. Once the point had been proved emphatically, the King got out of the carriage and asked those nearest if it was not possible for him to leave. On receiving no answer he added: "Very well, then I shall stay."

Now the crowd veered round and all were in his favour, and the National Guards promised to protect their sovereigns.

"Yes,"said Marie Antoinette in a carrying voice, "we count on your devotion. All the same, you must admit we aren't free any longer." Then she followed her husband up the steps and back into the Palace.

There was something else, for Marie Antoinette realised that if Louis was once again a free agent it would bring to nothing the schemes of his brother Artois, the Prince de Condé, and other scheming *émigré* royalists who felt they had everything to gain if the family was destroyed by the Revolution.

Marie Antoinette confided to Mercy that she thought the provinces were less republican in outlook than the capital, and if Louis could show himself in a fortified city the number of loyalists who would rally round would be amazing; but the troops were becoming more and more republican in outlook every day. If they were going to escape, they must do it quickly.

CHAPTER FOURTEEN

Varennes

If there was to be an escape, there was only one man that the Queen really cared to trust: Fersen. Such an undertaking was bound to be expensive, and after failing to raise substantial loans, he found himself having to mortgage his own estates in Sweden. The Marquis de Bouillé was contacted to arrange the posting of troops along the last part of the route to the frontier, and Louis sent him one million francs in paper money to cover such expenses as billeting and food. The plan was that the royal family should make for Montmédy, and from there cross into the Austrian Netherlands, a journey of about one hundred and ninety miles.

Bouillé and his officers planned the operation with the utmost care. An artillery train with sixteen guns was to wait at Montmédy, just on the French side of the frontier, while the Royal German Regiment would line the road to Stenay. A squadron of dragoons would be at Clermont-en-Argonne, and they were to send a detachment to Ste Menehould, while forty hussars under the command of the young Duc de Choiseul (a nephew of Louis XV's famous minister) would make for Pont-de-Somme-Vesle from a temporary base at Varennes. If possible, all troops would be foreigners in the service of France rather than Frenchmen who might be divided in their loyalties.

On May 27th Louis wrote to Bouillé telling him that everything was fixed for June 11th. For about a year now there had been rumours that the royal family might attempt to flee the country, long before Louis himself began to consider the idea seriously. Then almost at the last minute the date was put back because in the Tuileries they had become suspicious of Madame de Rochereul, the Dauphin's Waiting-Woman. The King and Queen knew perfectly well that she was the mistress of one of Lafayette's aides-de-camp, and since the General was responsible to the National Assembly for their safety, extreme caution was necessary. Madame de Rochereul's term of duty at the Palace ended on June 12th, but there was another and very good reason for postponing the date of departure for longer than that. After the 15th the Austrians would mass troops on their side of the frontier opposite Montmédy, which would give Bouillé an excellent excuse for manoeuvring troops in that region without causing undue suspicion.

All was now set for the escape to take place on June 14th. But no, it was postponed again. On the 20th Louis would receive his quarterly allowance, a sizeable sum, and he wanted to take it with him. So, for a third time, the date was changed, to the evening of June 20th.

Meanwhile, Fersen had been working round the clock making preparations for the actual escape from Paris. Passports were acquired, in the name of a Russian noblewoman, Baronne de Korff, en route for Frankfurt. Madame Royale and the Dauphin would be her children, and poor plebeian-looking Louis would become her steward. Madame Élizabeth would be a personal maid, and since Madame de Tourzel was taking the part of the Baronne, Marie Antoinette found herself cast as the governess.

If Marie Antoinette had been content to do a moonlight flit, the whole venture would undoubtedly have succeeded. When the Comte et Comtesse de Provence escaped at the same time, from the Luxembourg Palace, they travelled light and fast. Consequently they were in Brussels before the royal family had even reached Châlons-sur-Marne. But Marie Antoinette could not do things like that. The royal couple wished to arrive in some style in Montmédy, and not like two fugitives. So new clothes were made, which needed heavy trunks to hold them. Then the Queen must have a travelling-case; a magnificent one, which took two months to make, was ordered from the jewellers. Since a Queen of France should not be expected to look after herself, even for twenty-four or forty-eight hours, she must have two Ladies-in-Waiting. That meant a second coach would be necessary. Perhaps it would be as well if her hairdresser, Léonard, could make his own way to the frontier at the same time. The coach must be large, to take six, as Marie Antoinette dreaded the idea of the family being split up. Therefore Fersen ordered an enormous berlin, a travelling coach, for the actual escape. Of its kind it must have been magnificent, but extremely heavy, slow and as conspicuous as a double-decker bus in a country lane. In fact it was so large that it required six horses, and to crown everything was painted bright yellow. Fersen has been criticised for all this, but according to Madame de Tourzel, the real Baronne de Korff had just such a coach in which she had travelled part of the same route to Frankfurt.

This time it had to be June 20th, or nothing. Choiseul had definite orders that if they did not start that night the detachments of troops were to be withdrawn. At 9.00 p.m. he was at his house in the Rue d'Artois waiting, and wondering if anything had gone wrong, when Léonard arrived with his hat pulled down and his collar turned up, looking every inch a conspirator. Marie Antoinette had sent him a letter; also he had her diamonds. The Queen had not informed him of his ultimate destination; that was in the letter to Choiseul, who merely told him he must come on an important mission. Léonard said he couldn't possibly; for one thing, he had taken his brother's hat and coat without asking, and there would be a dreadful row. For another thing, he had left his keys behind, and then he was supposed to be going on to dress the hair of a certain Madame de Lage, and anyway his man was still waiting with his carriage outside the Tuileries. Choiseul hardly bothered to argue, but bundled the gesticulating Léonard into a light carriage and drove like a fury out of Paris.

For the royal family it was not just a question of walking out of the Tuileries and shutting the door behind them. To all intents and purposes they were under house-arrest. The Royal Bodyguard were no longer on duty, their function had been taken over by the National Guard commanded by Lafayette. Two mounted sentries were by the main gate, while foot sentries were set at all the garden doors and stationed a hundred yards apart along the terrace overlooking the Seine. Inside the Palace it was no better; they were everywhere, and if the King or Queen wanted to go out, even for a walk in the gardens, it was with an escort of two or three National Guardsmen. The royal family had seen the one chink in the armour, and to make use of it required the absence of Madame de Rochereul. Her room was on the ground floor at the south end of the Tuileries, in or adjoining the Pavillon de Flore (which still stands, now at the western extremity of the south arm of the Louvre). On one side was Madame Élizabeth's room, and on the other a suite of rooms which had been empty for six months. One of its doors opened into the Cour des Princes and the Place du Carrousel, but since the rooms had been empty for so long it had no sentry. That was the way the royal family would leave—across the Place du Carrousel to rendezvous with Fersen, who would be waiting with a fiacre in the Rue de l'Echelle (in what is now the Rue de Rivoli, which did not exist in 1791).

That afternoon, June 20th, Marie Antoinette, Madame Élizabeth and the children went for a walk in the Tivoli Garden and on their return the Queen ordered a carriage to go for a drive the following morning. Everything seemed like any other day, and she even jokingly asked a National Guard Officer if he had heard any new rumours about their supposed escape from Paris, which had been rumoured for months. Slightly embarrassed, he answered in the negative.

There was something of a family gathering in the drawing-room of the Tuileries that evening. In addition to Louis, Marie Antoinette and Madame Élizabeth, there were the Comte et Comtesse de Provence, also due to make their escape, but by a different route. Marie Antionette was particularly tense. At ten o'clock she got up casually and went to her daughter's room. There she told the under-governess to dress Madame Royale, adding that in a few minutes they would be making an escape, and that she, the under-governess, would be coming with them. For companion on the journey she would have Madame de Neuville, the Dauphin's Waiting-Woman. They would pick up a cab which would be expecting them by the Pont Royal, just outside the Palace, and join the main party on the outskirts of Paris.

Next Marie Antoinette went to the Dauphin's room. "We are going to a fortress where there will be lots of soldiers," she told him. The Dauphin jumped out of bed. "Quick, quick! Give me my sword and my boots and let's be off." Instead of a uniform the six-year-old was offered girl's clothing. Girl's clothing, at a time like that! Finally he was satisfied with the explanation that they were all dressing up for a play, and agreed to co-operate.

First to leave by way of the unguarded door were Madame Royale, the Dauphin and Madame de Tourzel. With them went Marie Antoinette and one of the boydguard. Across the Place du Carrousel to the Rue de l'Echelle where they found Fersen dressed as a cabby waiting with a fiacre. After seeing them safely into the cab Marie Antoinette returned the way she had come, and went back to the drawing room as though nothing untoward was going on.

To avoid suspicion Axel de Fersen drove the royal governess and the children round the streets and along the quais and finally back to the Rue de l'Echelle by way of the Rue St. Honoré. Then, after three quarters of an hour they were joined by Madame Élizabeth, the next to escape. Now a real cabby came along and started chatting to Fersen. The Swede played up magnificently, gossiping with him and taking snuff together. But it must have been an anxious few minutes for all of them.

The minutes dragged by. Although those in the cab could not know what it was, there had been a hitch. Every evening Lafayette had an audience with Louis last thing at night, just before the King retired. this night of all nights Lafayette held him up for nearly three quarters of an hour, but at last Louis got to his bedroom on the first floor, and was apparently preparing for the night. Escape for him was complicated by the fact that his valet, Lemoine, was not in the secret. By custom the man slept not only in the same room but had a cord round his wrist leading to the King's bed. This Louis could jerk in the night if he required anything. He climbed into bed and the curtains were pulled right round, completely concealing him; but no sooner had Lemoine gone into an adjoining room to undress, than he jumped out again and ran into the room recently vacated by the Dauphin. There a suit of clothes was waiting, similar to those worn by a man who regularly left the Palace each evening at 11.00 p.m. The plan was for Louis to walk out in an identical suit: grey coat, satin waistcoat, grey breeches and stockings, shoes with buckles and a small three-cornered hat.

After dressing Louis went down the private staircase and out into the Place du Carrousel, followed by the second bodyguard. Soon after he was in the fiacre with his children, his sister and Madame de Tourzel. At any moment they should be joined by Marie Antoinette, but now there was a half-hour delay. The Queen and her bodyguard were wandering round in the dark, lost.

For disguise Marie Antoinette put on a grey dress, with a hat of similar colour which had a veil to hide her face. Then she looked into the corridor outside her rooms. A sentry was pacing up and down, and it was ten minutes before she could get to the disused apartments. There the third bodyguard was waiting to escort her to the fiacre, but neither was sure where the Rue de l'Echelle was, and they got lost, crossed the Pont Royal and found themselves in the Rue de Bac on the south side of the Seine. They doubled back on their tracks, and got into the Place du Carrousel (by a wicket gate through the Galerie du Louvre), and at last found themselves going in the right direction, Just then a carriage came along, and Marie Antoinette had to flatten herself against a wall. It was Lafayette who had just completed his final inspection in the Tuileries and was now on his way back to the Hôtel de Ville, followed by Bailly, the Mayor. But after that she and Monsieur Malden, her bodyguard, found the waiting fiacre without further mishap. She climbed in, treading on the Dauphin's foot in the dark, and there were kisses for everyone.

A second fiacre was procured for the three bodyguards, and they all set off by a round-about route for the Barrière de Clichy, one of the gates on the north side of Paris. There a wedding was in progress, and so they passed through without attracting any attention. By now they were well behind schedule. Lafayette had detained Louis for three quarters of an hour longer than expected, and then Marie Antoinette was lost for half an hour. It was now 1.30 a.m., and there was further delay looking for the berlin, finally located in a side street with its lamps veiled.

Quickly the royal family climbed in, and by 2.00 a.m. they were driving hard for Bondy, the bodyguards travelling on the box. They reached Bondy, then well outside Paris, in under an hour, and found the two women of the household who had driven on there after failing to locate the coach at the agreed meeting place, Clichy.

Bondy was as far as Axel de Fersen would accompany the royal family. Midday should see them passing through Châlons-sur-Marne, and by about 4.00 p.m. they should meet the first of the troops under Choiseul at Pont-de-Somme-Vesle. Axel de Fersen would set out for Brussels, and then go on to join the fugitives in Austria. But now, still in his cabby's outfit, he must say goodbye to the royal family, or rather to Marie Antoinette. He opened the door of the berlin; Louis thanked him for all he had done, and embraced him warmly. Fersen asked permission to kiss hands; first it was that of the King, then Marie Antoinette. As he closed the door he touched his hat with his whip and said loudly:

"Goodbye, Madame de Korff!"

The berlin rolled away down the road to Châlons-sur-Marne, and Fersen made his way back to Paris. In a short while it would be dawn.

Inside the carriage identities were handed out along with papers and passports. Madame de Tourzel was the Baronne, and also the mother of the two children, while the Queen became the governess under the name of Madame Fochet. Louis was the Baronne's steward, and called Durand. In the lighter, smaller coach travelled the two Ladies-in-Waiting, as Madame de Korff's maids.

The tension relaxed, and the King's complacency started to return.

"Well, here I am," he said, "at last out of Paris where I have been saturated with so much bitterness. You can be sure that once I have got my backside in the saddle again I shall be a very different man to the one you have seen up to now."

He looked at his watch: it was just eight o'clock, and already they had been travelling for five hours.

"Lafayette must be feeling very embarrassed just now," he remarked. As their nervousness began to disappear, so their appetites returned. The hampers of food were brought out and some of the wine uncorked. With their fingers they ate cold chicken, veal and beef off silver plates. Then one by one the outriders flanking the coach rode up to the window to receive portions of chicken handed out by Marie Antoinette.

When the meal was over, out went the bones and the empty bottles on to the side of the road.

Louis studied their route on a map, and gave the Dauphin a geography lesson. Disregarding the fact they were escaping from revolutionary Paris, the journey was an event in the life of Marie Antoinette. Apart from coming from Vienna to Versailles it would be the furthest she had ever travelled.

Once at Versailles she never in nineteen years moved more than a few score miles: the greatest distance being to Fontainebleau or

Compiègne. The only idea she could have had of the sea was from a painting or a print in a book.

Behind them, Paris was in uproar. When Lemoine, the King's valet, drew back the curtains round his master's bed and found he had vanished in the night it was only a matter of minutes before the Tuileries was like an overturned anthill. The news was shouted over the whole city: "The King and Queen have escaped!"

Lafayette dressed hurriedly, came to the Palace, and then ordered men of the National Guard to fan out in all directions scouring the most likely roads for the King and his family. For most the surprise was not that Louis had actually escaped, but that he had not done so sooner. This was true not only in Paris, but above all along the roads which led to France's eastern frontier.

At Clermont-en-Argonne, the last little town before Varennes, the local inhabitants were already questioning each other about the arrival of one hundred and fifty dragoons. Waiting to escort treasure—the money to pay Bouillé's army. Waiting for the Queen more likely, whispered the people. Nearly all the way along the route from the frontier towards Châlons-sur-Marne the villagers had their doubts about these troops "waiting to escort treasure". At Ste Menehould the National Guard was issued with new muskets, and at Pont-de-Somme-Vesle curiosity would soon be aroused by the arrival of forty hussars from Varennes. They reached the hamlet at the same time as their commanding officer, Choiseul, drove into the street, accompanied by the over-wrought Léonard. The Court hairdresser was still worrying about taking his brother's hat and coat without asking, and about his appointment with Madame de Lage.

The berlin trundled on towards Châlons-sur-Marne, keeping up a steady pace, and stopping at regular intervals for the horses to be changed at posting-stations. On one occasion the over-confident Louis got out, "to go into an empty stable", as Madame de Tourze put it. But at Montmirail he again got out, against Marie Antoinette's wishes, to stretch his legs and to chat with the peasants about the harvest while a broken trace was being repaired. The job took longer than expected: two hours in fact. He did the same thing at Fromontières, where a small group had gathered to stare at the huge coach and its smartly dressed outriders. This time Monsieur de Moustier tried to stop him, but Louis brushed aside his warnings with:

"Don't bother. I don't think these precautions are necessary. I feel nothing can go wrong with my journey."

He was wrong many times over of course. Already a National Guard was galloping down the road to Metz. The royal family had a ten-hour start, but he was a single rider against the slow moving berlin, weighing several tons.

The day was beautiful and the countryside must have shimmered in the heat, though ahead, over Châlons, there were the makings of a thunderstorm. Before Etoges, not far from Châlons, there was a long uphill incline, and to spare the horses they all got out of the coach, and the bodyguard climbed off the box. The King, the Queen, their two children, Madame Élizabeth and the royal governess walked up the hill in the sunshine. The children chased after butterflies. Within four years all except Madame Royale and Madame de Tourzel would be dead: the three adults guillotined and the ten-year-old Dauphin mysteriously vanished.

But now as they wandered up the dusty road beside the coach it seemed that there could only be freedom ahead. Beyond Châlons they would meet the first hussars, and once in their care nothing could go wrong.

Pleasant though the walk must have been, as for the first time in about twenty months their every step was not dogged by a National Guard, it cost another half hour. Châlons should have been reached about midday, but it was 4.30 p.m. before they drove into the city.

Louis looked out of one window and Marie Antoinette out of the other. The King was recognised first by the posting-master and then by an onlooker.

"Sire," said the royalist posting-master, "don't show yourself like this, or you are lost!" The onlooker ran off and disappeared. In his anxiety to see the coach on its way the posting-master helped the postillions to change the horses. Then just as the berlin started to move again the leading horses fell, then the next pair, trapping a postillion as they came down. There was more delay as they were helped up, and to Marie Antoinette it seemed a bad omen.

Behind them Commissary Bayon, sent by the National Assembly, was galloping along the route they had just taken. Some distance further back was Romeuf, an aide-de-camp to Lafayette, and a royalist at heart. He hoped to overtake Bayon, and either delay him or else throw him off the scent while the royal family made their escape.

At last the berlin was on its way again, and it rattled out of Châlons as fast as the horses could go. They were hardly through the gateway when a man rode past the open window shouting: "Your plans are discovered. You will be stopped."

Surely they could not be stopped now. Just down the road was the village of Pont-de-Somme-Vesle, where Choiseul would meet them with forty hussars. Choiseul and Léonard had passed through Châlons on their drive from Paris at about 10.00 a.m., reaching Pont-de-Somme-Vesle about an hour later. There the young Duke explained to Léonard that he had been entrusted with a most important mission: to go to the frontier and collect a letter for the Queen which he would bring back. Now Léonard was verging on the hysterical, but he agreed to do it. At that point the forty hussars under Monsieur de Goguelet arrived. De Goguelet reported that the countryside was in a state of excitement because of the rumours of the escape, inspired by all the troop movements.

Choiseul was expecting the royal family at 1.00 p.m., but one o'clock came, then two o'clock and three. Léonard was sent on his way in a *cabriolet*, and the last he saw of Pont-de-Somme-Vesle was a growing crowd of suspicious peasants, and no sign of the King.

Now the local inhabitants were becoming thoroughly suspicious of the hussars. Recently there had been trouble in the district because of non-payment of dues by the peasants, and they thought this was connected with the presence of the soldiers. At 3.00 p.m. they became openly hostile, and the tocsin was sounded. By 4.15 p.m. the hussars found themselves menaced by three hundred peasants, and soon after their numbers had grown to six hundred. To quiet them Choiseul said that they were waiting to act as escort for money being taken to Metz. At this the posting-master spoke up and said a diligence with one hundred thousand crowns in it had been escorted through that morning by two gendarmes. It was pure coincidence, but it gave the hussars a valid excuse to withdraw from the hamlet. At 5.00 p.m. they all mounted their horses and left.

Less than an hour later the berlin, preceded by the smaller coach, rumbled into Pont-de-Somme-Vesle, and the royal family were shaken to find the escort had already left.

Behind them Bayon was gaining ground. At Chaintrix he changed horses for the tenth time since setting out from Paris, and now he was only three hours behind the fugitives. Acting in his capacity as a Commissary he wrote: "On behalf of the National Assembly, all good citizens are ordered to stop the berlin with six horses in which the King and Queen are suspected of travelling."

Ahead, on the route to the frontier at Montmédy, was Léonard, spreading rumours to the troops he encountered that the royal family was not coming. Then, about twenty miles behind was the berlin itself, which in its turn was followed by Bayon and the unwilling Romeuf.

The next small town along the route was Ste Menehould. All day its inhabitants had been thoroughly suspicious of the troops standing about, waiting for what, or whom? Now de Goguelet and his forty hussars were back from Pont-de-Somme-Vesle. At 7.00 p.m. a courier arrived to order Drouet, the posting-master, to have fresh horses ready. Soon after the two coaches appeared.

When Marie Antoinette was recognised by the troops, they saluted, and she graciously acknowledged the gesture. An onlooker asked Monsieur Malden, one of the bodyguard who had accompanied the royal family out of the Tuileries, who were the important people.

"The Baronne de Korff!" said Malden.

Another *émigré* leaving the country, and taking money out with her, conjectured the local inhabitants. Then Monsieur de Andouinis, the commanding officer of the dragoons at Ste Menehould, did a very unwise thing. He stood by the open coach door, cap in hand, talking deferentially to a man who looked like the Baronne's steward. Drouet came for a closer look, and at that moment someone came up to him with money for the relay of horses. The man handed over assignats, paper money. One, for fifty francs, had the King's head on it. Drouet looked at the note and then at the so-called steward. A municipal officer rushed off to the Hôtel de Ville, where the Town Council decided on the spot that the coaches, which had just left, must be stopped. It was now well after 8.00 p.m.

Behind the royal family Ste Menehould was in uproar. The tocsin sounded and Bayon's message, ordering the berlin to be stopped, had just arrived. Drouet and a friend called Guillaume mounted horses and rode off after the coaches.

Meanwhile, ahead of the royal carriages, Léonard had reached Clermont-en-Argonne, where Monsieur de Damas was waiting with more troops. The excited Court hairdresser told him of the threatening attitude of the peasants at Pont-de-Somme-Vesle, who had in fact dispersed quietly after the hussars had left before the arrival of the King. Now it was the turn of the people of Clermont to become restive. The soldiers were told to stand down and go to their billets, but to be prepared for immediate action. Then along came the berlin. The horses were changed though ten minutes were lost arguing over the cost of the relay. Then they were once more on their way. Next was Varennes, after that Stenay and Montmédy and safety. Another forty miles or so, and it would all be over. But the fateful Léonard was still tearing along ahead of them, saying they were not coming.

Varennes perhaps deserved the description of a one-horse town, for it had no posting-station. But General Bouillé's son was waiting there with a fresh team, stabled in one of the two hotels. Now Léonard was coming down the hill into the town. He stopped by the soldiers, and without getting out of the carriage pushed his head through the window and said:

"I am Léonard. I know all! The King has left Paris, but there is no sign of him having continued his journey." Then he was on his way again, towards Stenay and safety.

About 9.45 p.m. Drouet and Guillaume galloped into Clermont. Monsieur de Damas ordered loyal dragoons to come forward. Only three did so: the others had been fraternising and drinking with the local inhabitants, and were half-mutinous. One of the loyal dragoons, named Lagache, was told to ride after the horsemen, and if necessary, not hesitate to kill.

Beyond Clermont the road goes straight on eastwards, towards Verdun, while a sharp turning to the left leads to Varennes. While Guillaume turned off towards Varennes, Drouet kept to the main road. After going only a little way he met a postillion coming back from Verdun. Had he seen two coaches, asked Drouet. The man said no. Drouet decided to cut across the open country to reach Varennes, jumped a ditch and rode on. In the distance Lagache saw him start down the Verdun road, and did not follow. When he saw him suddenly change direction it was too late to catch up.

Now it was about ten o'clock, and the dusk was warm and peaceful, that time of day the French call "between dog and wolf". The carriage lamps were lit, and in the berlin the royal family felt secure, thinking that the dragoons were following a little way behind. Marie Antoinette fell asleep.

The town of Varennes is divided into two parts by the river Aire. To the west on a hill is the upper town centred around the Place de Latry, from which a narrow street runs down to the bridge leading to the lower town.

About 10.30 p.m. the berlin, with the smaller coach still leading the way, reached the first houses of the upper town. There should have been horses waiting, but because Léonard had told General Bouillé's son the King was not coming, the dragoons had been dismissed to their quarters in the old Convent of the Cordeliers at the further end of the upper town; and Bouillé and his fellow officers, Röhrig and Raigencourt, had gone to their billets for the night.

Darkness had fallen when the carriages stopped. The King and Queen got out, and apparently Marie Antoinette and one of the bodyguard knocked at a house, only to be told to go away. They climbed back into the carriage to wait while one of the party went into the town to search for the missing horses and the escort of dragoons.

About 10.45 p.m. Drouet and Guillaume caught up, and as they passed the berlin one of them remarked to the other that they would be very late getting to a neighbouring village where there was a fair, so as to avoid arousing any suspicions. They went on down the hill into the town, and found that people were still up and about at the Hôtel Bras d'Or (no longer an hotel) in the Place de Latry. Drouet took the landlord aside and asked if he was a good patriot, and on being assured that he was, added:

"The King is at the top of the hill. He'll be passing through soon. Go at once and get all the good citizens you know to stop him getting away."

Then they went on further into the town, and by the river they came across a cart full of furniture. The very thing they needed.

Quickly it and other carts were man-handled on to the centre of the bridge, where they formed a complete road block. Then the men went to Monsieur Sauce, the Procurator of Varennes, and the Commandant of the National Guard. When there were about eight or ten of them they marched up the hill, and met the coach coming down. Already it had reached the Place de Latry and was starting to come round the church of St Gengulph, which nearly divided the square in two. On its further side was the Hôtel Bras d'Or and Monsieur Sauce's house.

A vaulted passageway formed a short cut by which small vehicles could pass right under the church, but the berlin was far too large to make use of it.

Monsieur Sauce, who was a grocer, stopped the first of the two coaches and asked for papers. The ladies of the household said they were in the other vehicle, and when Monsieur Sauce asked the identity of the travellers Madame de Tourzel said: "I am the Baronne de Korff, and I am going to Frankfurt."

M. Sauce pointed out that in that case she was on the wrong road, and asked for her passport. Then he raised his lantern, and recognised Louis.

"Madame," he said to Madame de Tourzel, "it is too late to visa your passport at this time of night; it is my duty to forbid you to continue your journey."

"Why?" asked Marie Antoinette.

"It is dangerous, because of the rumours."

"What rumours?"

"People talk about the flight of the King and the royal family."

The two women brought the passport to the Hôtel Bras d'Or, where it was carefully scrutinised. Monsieur Sauce was impressed by the fact it bore the King's signature, but suddenly Drouet noticed it was not countersigned by the President of the National Assembly. Monsieur Sauce went back to the berlin and very politely, almost obsequiously, asked Louis to descend and come to his house. The others followed him across to his shop, a few yards down the Rue de la Basse Cour from the Hôtel Bras d'Or.

Perhaps it was the first time in her life that Marie Antoinette had ever been into a grocer's shop; the only other times she may have set foot in the house of an ordinary citizen was when she and friends entered a merchant's house after their coach had broken down on its way to the Opera Ball in 1779.

Now she was nearly at the end of her tether, and tired of pretence: "Well, if he is your King and I am your Queen, treat us with the respect due to us."

Politely the overawed Monsieur Sauce asked the party to come upstairs to the two rooms on the first floor. There were eight of them, including Mesdames Neuville, and Brunier, the Ladies-in-Waiting. Two peasants stood guard with pitchforks at the door.

Immediately the Dauphin fell asleep on a bed, and the others sat down to wait. The Queen lowered the veil on her hat as though to hide her expression from the others. Outside the tocsin had been ringing for a quarter of an hour, and it was probably the first Bouillé and the other officers knew of what was going on. Their dragoons were none too reliable and had been drinking, so the three made off hell-for-leather to advise General Bouillé, about twenty-five miles distant at Stenay.

Suddenly there was a clattering of horses' hooves in the street, followed by shouts. It was Choiseul and the hussars from Pont-de-Somme-Vesle. In an attempt to take a shortcut, avoiding Ste Menehould, they had cut across country and become hopelessly lost in the Argonne Forest. The ground was bad and one of the hussars fell into a deep hole; the others stopped to search for him and by the time he was once again conscious and able to continue, three-quarters of an hour had been lost. Now, at half past midnight they had reached Varennes. The mob was forced back from the front of Monsieur Sauce's house, leaving a way clear for the coaches.

De Choiseul went upstairs, informed the King quietly that he had seven horses, and if they were prepared to ride they could escape. Although the bridge was blocked there was a ford close by, and they would have the hussars as escort.

Once again, at a critical moment, Louis hesitated. What if one of them should get hit by a stray bullet? As he dithered, the crowd grew, and now the hussars were beginning to fraternise with the inhabitants. Also Marie Antoinette's nerve was beginning to break; she was dead tired, and felt defeated by the course of events.

"Speak to the King, gentlemen," she said. "It is the King who decided to make this attempt; it is for the King to order. My duty is to follow him."

If only someone had been there of sufficient stature to order them about the royal couple would have obeyed without hesitation—if only because they were too tired to argue. Now the mob was stopping the outriders and the bodyguard from harnessing fresh horses to the berlin.

The night had nearly gone, and at 5.00 a.m. Romeuf and Bayon drove up to the door. Romeuf had tears in his eyes as he went upstairs holding the decree from the National Assembly which ordered the detention of the fugitives.

"What, Monsieur? You?" said Marie Antoinette. "I should not have expected it of you."

From their casual encounters in the Tuileries the Queen and the young officer had grown to like one another . . . and now this. Louis read the document, and remarked dully:

"There is no longer a King in France," and dropped the decree on the bed where the children were asleep. Marie Antoinette snatched it up and threw it on the floor.

"I will not have my children soiled by contact with this document," she exclaimed with a flash of temper. There was an agonised silence from everyone else in the room. At last Choiseul stooped down and picked it up.

Now Louis started to play for time. He asked if the children could sleep on for another two or three hours. Bayon saw what was in the King's mind: to wait until General Bouillé could march from Stenay to Varennes. He agreed and went downstairs. Outside he told the still waiting crowd:

"They don't want to start yet. Bouillé will be here soon, and they want to wait for him."

"To Paris, to Paris!" shouted the mob, as he knew it would.

Upstairs went the Town Councillors and Monsieur Sauce to urge the King to return to his capital. Marie Antoinette turned to Madame Sauce, imploring her aid: but all she replied was, "Madame, you are in a very unpleasant position, but my husband is responsible. I don't want any trouble to come to him."

Louis then tried another delaying tactic. He asked for food. The meal was soon over, and there was no further excuse for delay. Then

Madame de Neuville simulated an epileptic fit, and the King refused to move until she had been seen by a doctor. One was found with unwelcome speed, and all too soon Louis walked out of the shabby little room, down the stairs and into the street. He was followed by Marie Antoinette, on the arm of Choiseul, and the rest of the royal party.

In front of the house the crowd now numbered about six thousand, for many had flocked in from the neighbouring villages to see this extraordinary sight: a runaway King and Queen being sent back where they belonged. The family climbed up into the berlin, and to cheers, boos and the singing of revolutionary songs the coach was helped on its way up the street and out of the town. It was 7.30 a.m. and going to be another hot, fine summer day: the day before was the longest. A non-commissioned officer stationed at the entrance to Varennes watched them pass:

"I saw the royal carriages coming surrounded by a troop of armed men. It passed close to me and moved so slowly that I could see the Queen returning my salute. The King made a gesture which revealed his deep grief and prostration. The Queen appeared even more distressed."

Across the valley General Bouillé and the Royal German Regiment could just see the great coach trundling down the road towards Clermont and Paris. Thinking that the river was too deep to ford he ordered his men to withdraw towards Stenay. Had he but known, about half a mile further on the Clermont road crossed the Aire back on to his side of the river, and if his troops had galloped across the fields they could have cut off the berlin, overpowered the escort, and taken the royal family in safety to Montmédy, not thirty miles away, before anything could be done to stop them. Fortune had long since turned its back on Marie Antoinette and her family.

CHAPTER FIFTEEN

The Long Road Back

The flight to Varennes had taken twenty-four hours, while the return to Paris was prolonged over four days. In sweltering heat the journey must have been a nightmare in the berlin, and Louis even had to borrow a clean shirt from one of the escorting soldiers. But it was Marie Antoinette who must have suffered the most. How little real impression the escape from the Tuileries as far as Varennes made on Louis can be gleaned from his diary, a most revealing document. The day the Bastille fell he wrote "nothing"; the day the women of Paris marched on Versailles his only comment was that his hunting had been "interrupted by events". All he could find to say about the escape was: "June 21st, Tuesday. Left Paris, reached Varennes in Argonne and were arrested there at 11.00 p.m. 22nd: Left Varennes at five or six in the morning; lunched at Saint-Menehoul [*sic*]; reached Châlons at ten at night; had supper and slept in the old governorate."

Nothing untoward happened on the road between Varennes and Ste Menehould, and the two coaches went slowly along, surrounded by National Guards and a huge crowd of peasants armed with pitchforks and scythes. At least for the first part of the journey their reception was a strange mixture: insults from many of the country people, and respect from the town worthies wherever they stopped. After only four or five hours in the coach they reached the outskirts of Ste Menehould where the Mayor was waiting. A municipal officer harangued Louis on the trouble and upset his attempted flight had caused to the people of France. Although National Guards from Châlons lined the way to the Hôtel de Ville the crowd was so dense that it took half an hour to reach it. At about 11.30 a.m. they entered the building, where they were to dine, and while they waited a gendarme brought Madame Royale some cherries in his hat.

The Mayor suggested that it might be a good idea if they showed themselves on the balcony to the crowd filling the street. Because it was so small Louis stepped out first, then Marie Antoinette carrying the Dauphin. Originally it was intended that the royal family should rest at Ste Menehould—the Mayor had offered his house—but the National Guard would not hear of the idea as they considered a daring rescue by Bouillé not beyond the bounds of possibility. "Traitors!" shouted the crowd, so Louis agreed to leave.

At 2.00 p.m. they were on their way again, making for Châlons-sur-Marne, and as they drove away the only cries were of "*Vive la Nation!*" For the first time since the market-women invaded the Palace at Versailles, the royal family were to see the Revolution in its ugliest mood. A certain Monsieur Dampierre, Comte de Hans and an over-zealous royalist, was in Ste Menehould that day. Finely dressed with a great deal of gold braid he must have looked aggressively aristocratic for such a day as this, on horseback and carrying a small shotgun. As the berlin passed he presented arms, and Louis returned the salute. Then he raced through sidestreets and re-emerged ahead of the coaches. He repeated the performance. Then he did it a third time, and pushed up to the carriage window and told the King who he was. The National Guard thrust him away, but instead of disappearing from the scene before they were all thoroughly antagonised, he rode alongside making gestures to the occupants of the berlin. Not altogether unnaturally the local inhabitants and the National Guard thought this was some plot to carry off the King, and closed ranks to keep Monsieur Dampierre at a distance. He rode off, halted, cried "*Vive le Roi!*" and fired his shotgun in the air. Then he started off towards a wood, where the crowd thought soldiers must be hiding. Men of the National Guard fired, but he was out of range. He turned to wave as he jumped a ditch, fell and was rolled on by his horse. He remounted, but a peasant fired one well-aimed shot. Monsieur Dampierre fell again, and the peasant together with forty others caught up and literally shot him to pieces at close range.

After that the ride to Châlons continued at a walking pace, and surrounded by a huge mob. Some of the civic dignitaries who rode out to meet the royal family took fright at the mob they saw advancing towards them across the flat countryside of Champagne, and retreated back to the city.

Nearly twenty-one years before, when Marie Antoinette first came to France, Châlons had erected a triumphal arch to welcome the fifteen-year-old Dauphine: it still stands, the Porte Ste-Croix, and now late on the evening of June 22nd, 1791, she was once again passing through it. Here in a royalist city the family was received as honoured guests. They dined in public, presentations were made, and bouquets given to Marie Antoinette.

Next day the plan was that they should make a late start, after hearing Mass and having a main meal, but during the service the National Guard from Rheims arrived and even entered the chapel, interrupting the Mass. Louis and Marie Antoinette left, and showed themselves on a balcony, but now the crowd had dragged the coaches from the stables and was insisting that the party must go on its way. So, after a hurried meal, they left Châlons at about 11.00 a.m.

Up to this point the royal family had been retracing the route they had taken as far as Varennes, but now they departed from it, travelling towards Épernay and Dormans. Then they passed through Château-Thierry and rejoined the old route at La Ferté-sous-Jouarre. Now the general mood was openly hostile. When the coaches stopped at Chouilly so that the National Guard could slake their thirsts, the berlin was surrounded by a hooting fist-shaking mob, and one man climbed up, leant in and spat straight into the King's face. At Épernay when they descended to go into a hotel for a meal, Marie Antoinette had her dress torn, which the innkeeper's daughter tried to sew together on the spot. Then, as she was climbing back into the berlin a woman exclaimed: "Take care, little one, you will soon look on other steps than those!"

Not far short of Dormans the procession, now swollen to three or four thousand people, stopped. Three Deputies of the National Assembly were waiting to escort Louis along the last stage of the journey back to Paris. They were Latour-Mauborg, a royalist sympathiser, and Barnave and Pétion, centre and left-wing Deputies. Pétion carried a decree from the National Assembly commanding them to watch over Louis' safety, but also to ensure that he was treated with respect.

Barnave and Pétion insisted on travelling in the berlin, which must have been crowded to suffocation, while Monsieur de Latour-Mauborg had to travel in the smaller coach with the two Ladies-in-Waiting.

Pétion, an insufferable man, left an account of the drive to Paris, and while it gives an interesting picture of the royal family, it sheds even more light on the workings of his own mind. He started having erotic fantasies first about Madame Élizabeth, and then about the Queen herself.

Louis, Barnave, the Queen and the Dauphin sat facing the horses, and opposite were Madame Élizabeth, Pétion, and Madame de Tourzel with Madame Royale on her lap. At first the atmosphere was tense, and apart from the Queen asking for assurance that the three bodyguards would not be harmed, neither side intended to make conversation.

One of the first remarks, made by Barnave, was calculated to offend. Casually he said it was believed in Paris that the fiacre in which the royal family escaped from the Tuileries had been driven by a Swede. Turning directly to Marie Antoinette he asked what was his name.

"Do you think I am likely to know the name of a hackney coachman?" she in her turn questioned.

Not unnaturally the Dauphin became thoroughly fidgety, and in desperation Barnave took him on his own knees. The six-year-old boy twisted round and started playing with the buttons on the deputy's jacket, and spelled out the words they bore: "Live free or die." After that the conversation became general, and to the deputies' surprise they found the royal family were flesh and blood, and almost likeable.

Wrote Pétion: "After the first bout of cackling was over, I noticed an air of simplicity and family feeling which gratified me. There was no longer any royal showing-off—just easy manners and good-tempered domesticity. The Queen called Madame Élizabeth her little sister and Madame Élizabeth replied in similar terms. Madame Élizabeth called the King, 'my brother'. The King watched his family with a satisfied air, though he seemed unemotional and obtuse.

"I also had a look at the travellers' clothes. They could not have been more shabby. The King was wearing a brown plush suit and his linen was very shabby. The women wore very common day dresses."

Louis said little, so Marie Antoinette and Madame Élizabeth made themselves pleasant to the deputies sitting at their sides. Now it was dark, and Pétion recorded his thoughts with remarkable candour: "Madame Élizabeth gazed at me with soft eyes and with that languid air which unhappiness causes. Our eyes met from time to time with a kind of understanding and mutual attraction. Madame Élizabeth took Madame (Royale) on her knee, half on mine. Her head was supported by my hand and she fell asleep. I reached out my arm and Madame Élizabeth stretched out hers over mine. They were interlaced and mine touched her armpit. I felt a rapid heartbeat and warmth through her clothing. Madame Élizabeth's glance grew more and more touching. I noticed a certain abandonment in her attitude. Perhaps I was wrong, because it is easy to mistake feelings caused by sorrow with those caused by pleasure. All the same I believe that if we had been alone, if by some magic all the others had disappeared, she would have fallen into my arms and abandoned herself to the promptings of nature."

Not content with an affair of the mind with Madame Élizabeth, Pétion even started imagining the Queen liked the look of him. He believed ". . . she might find me attractive and realising as well that she was of an age when passions are powerful, I persuaded myself—and it gave me pleasure to do so—that she felt strong emotions and would not have been averse to those gentle advances and delicate caresses, and that she would have surrendered without offence, and that her defeat would be accomplished without shock to her feelings, with passion and nature alone to blame." His amorous feelings do not seem to have been aroused by Madame de Tourzel, sitting on his right hand.

About one in the morning Pétion had to jerk himself out of his reverie when they reached Dormans. All went into an inn, dined and then went upstairs to rooms guarded by sentries. Louis preferred to spend the night in an armchair rather than sleep on an old iron bedstead, though sleep must have been almost impossible for everyone because of the singing and dancing which the National Guard kept up for the rest of the night.

Pétion could write of Louis: "His face remained painfully expressionless and impassive and I came to the conclusion that this mass of flesh was devoid of feeling." Then a few lines further on he remarked: "Those who did not know him would mistake this shyness for stupidity, but they would be wrong. He very seldom speaks away from the point and I have never heard him say anything downright stupid."

Marie Antoinette he considered superficial, but agreed that she talked as the mother of a family and a well-educated woman. However: "She possessed in no way either the bearing or the attitude of mind which should go with her position."

The afternoon, June 23rd, they reached La Ferté-sous-Jouarre, where they all went to the Mayor's house, and walked about enjoying his well-kept garden which ran down to the Meuse. Then, to speed up the rate at which they travelled, the deputies decided to do without the escort on foot, and that meant they were also free of the accompanying mob. Once they were under way again Marie Antoinette brought up the subject of a republic with Pétion. Whilst telling her that kings everywhere had brought misfortune to their peoples, he added that the desire for a republic was not all that general in France, and was chiefly favoured by those who wanted to form another political party, non-constitutional-royalist, which could then overthrow the Constitution.

Now they had reached Meaux, the last overnight stop before Paris, and there Louis slept in a nightshirt borrowed from an usher. The next day was as uncomfortable in the berlin as the other two had been.

"The heat was extreme," wrote Pétion, "and we were enveloped in a cloud of dust. Several times the King offered me something to drink and poured it out for me. We spent twelve whole hours in the carriage without getting out for a moment. What surprised me in particular was that the Queen, Madame Élizabeth and Madame de Tourzel showed no desire to get out." But the Dauphin was only a small boy, and several times the silver chamber pot came out, held either by Louis or by Barnave.

Near Pantin there was a quarrel between the Grenadiers and the National Guards as to who should escort the carriages. The soldiers became really angry with one another, and one turned and shouted at Marie Antoinette:

"Look at the bitch. It's no good her showing us her child. Everyone knows it isn't his." Louis heard the remark clearly.

Now Barnave showed remarkable consideration. There was a very real risk from an assassin, and he insisted on occupying the seat of honour in the carriage, which was now one of danger. To lessen the likelihood of a shooting incident the Grenadiers with their tall plumed headgear walked on either side, almost hiding the windows. More Grenadiers, on horses, rode beside the berlin, while two more stood on a plank fixed below the box on the front. The three bodyguards were still on the box, a target for abuse if nothing worse. They had been there for the whole journey, enveloped in dust.

More than once Marie Antoinette was nearly overcome by the heat as they drove towards Paris, and at Le Bourget they stopped so Louis could have a drink.

The coaches did not drive straight on into Paris, but circled round the northern outskirts and entered via the Champs Elysées, to be met by a vast and silent crowd. National Guards, their muskets reversed as for a funeral, lined the way, and huge placards had been set up: "Whoever applauds the King will be beaten. Whoever insults him will be hanged."

Eventually they reached the Tuileries, and pulled up at the foot of the steps. At once Marie Antoinette spoke to a somewhat triumphant General Lafayette:

"Monsieur de Lafayette, save the bodyguard before everything. They have done nothing but obey."

The three men were got down, and although slightly manhandled by the crowd, were hustled to safety without there being an ugly scene. First the Dauphin and Madame Royale entered the Palace, then Marie Antoinette and finally Louis. A meal had been prepared, and Louis at least enjoyed his chicken.

The whole family was white with dust and their faces streaked with sweat and grime. Marie Antoinette's first need was a bath:

"She bore herself with spirit towards the officers appointed to her particular guard, and called it ridiculous and indecent that she should be required to leave the doors of her bathroom and of her bedroom open."

Louis wrote up his dairy:

"Saturday 25th: Left Meaux at 6.30, reached Paris at 8.00 without a stop."

"26th: Nothing of interest. Attended Mass in the Gallery. Commissioners of the Assembly met in conference."

And what happened to the luxuriously equipped coach? When last heard of it was carrying the mails between Paris and Lyon.

CHAPTER SIXTEEN

The Betrayal

"Will Heaven allow this letter to reach you?" wrote Marie Antoinette to Axel de Fersen, immediately after her return to the Tuileries. "Do not write to me, for that would expose us to unnecessary risks; and above all, do not come back here on any pretext. It is known that you were chiefly responsible for getting us away, so all would be lost if you returned. We are kept under watch day and night, but care nothing about that. Do not be troubled in your mind, I shall get on all right. The Assembly wants to treat us gently."

Then within twenty-four hours Marie Antoinette, like a woman truly in love, contradicted herself and in another letter begged Fersen to write, if only to tell her that he was safe, and asking what address she should use in future. Then she ended with the most overt declaration of her feelings that has survived: "Farewell most loved and loving of men." Not only were the authorities aware of his part in the escape, but a warrant had been issued for his arrest.

Marie Antoinette was correct in saying that the royal family was kept under day and night surveillance. At every door and in every room and corridor there seemed to be sentries, even on the roof, while officers entered the Queen's bedroom regularly during the night to see she had not managed to give them the slip once more.

The attempted escape had put the authorities in a very awkward position. Before making off into the night Louis had left behind a document condemning the National Assembly for placing him outside the Constitution and for reducing the Crown to a cypher. Now the Assembly found itself between two fires: if it abolished the monarchy, foreign powers might invade, and half France rise in a civil war. Equally, if the monarchy remained, Paris might itself become the centre of a savage revolt.

Louis now sank into a state of torpor, perhaps a reaction to the failure of the escape, and occupied his mind with such trivia as recording in his diary the number of occasions he had been out since 1775. The result of that piece of addition, he found, was two thousand six hundred and thirty-six times. So it was Marie Antoinette who took over his tasks, and assumed what should have been his responsibilities.

The Revolution had lasted two years, and there was no longer the same unifying drive and zeal among its political leaders. On July 15th the Cordeliers joined with the Jacobins in demanding the abolition of the monarchy, but many of the latter felt that this measure was too extreme, and broke away to form the Feuillants, so named because of their meeting-place near the Rue St. Honoré. Since these right-wing deputies refused to work in the Assembly, the political scene was directed by the centre group headed by Barnave and by the left-wing Jacobins.

Marie Antoinette contacted Barnave, flattered him by saying how much he had impressed her during their two days together in the coach on the return from Varennes, and said she wished to ask his advice:

"Things cannot be left as they are. Something must be done. But what? I do not know. It is to you that I address myself in the hope of finding an answer."

Her overtures were accepted, and Barnave offered to help, if only to counter the threat of republicanism, born after the flight to Varennes. Robespierre and republicanism went together, and both were feared by moderate men like Barnave. Meanwhile Louis was suspended as far as his authority was concerned, until the new Constitution was ready, which he would then have to accept.

Provence had long been a thorn in the flesh of the royal family, but now he was a thorn in the flesh of all who supported Louis and Marie Antoinette. From the safety of Koblenz he barked loudly at the Revolution, and made menacing gestures, while Fersen described him as being "positively radiant" because Louis had been caught. He called himself Regent of the Kingdom, and talked about invading France. Barnave told Marie Antoinette that both Provence and Artois must return to France, and that Austria must be prepared to accept the new Constitution when it was ready, and that above all Leopold II must not try to interfere in internal affairs. Barnave wrote that Marie Antoinette "could neither adopt other ideas nor leave that path without being ruined."

On July 9th the National Assembly ordered the seizure of *émigrés'* property if they did not return, which prompted the Queen to tell Barnave that the Assembly could hardly expect co-operation from people who had left the country two years previously and who were threatened with losing their property. Also, she said, while she had no influence with her brother Leopold II, she would not refuse to write to him. At this hint of arrogance Barnave warned her that the Triumvirs—the centre group—would turn against her if she did not co-operate.

At this time the entire European political scene was one of cold-blooded self-interest and double dealing. The remaining crowned heads were not worried about the ultimate fate of Louis and Marie Antoinette, merely about preventing the spread of republican ideas to their own kingdoms. Frederick William II of Prussia was negotiating in secret with the French revolutionaries, while Leopold II was more concerned in bargaining with Prussia and Russia over a second partition of Poland than in worrying about his sister in Paris.

Three things had happened to Marie Antoinette in the last few months. She had felt let down by Europe's other sovereigns; she had been badly frightened by some of the incidents on the return from Varennes; and her Habsburg pride had been hurt. She therefore felt no qualms in becoming almost unbelievably double-faced herself. She would make herself civil to the *factieux*, the rabble, and appear to be working alongside them when in reality she was merely biding her time till they could all be swept into the limbo where she considered they belonged. Politics are seldom clean, and before it was all over just a year later, Marie Antoinette's hands would be extremely dirty.

At the request of the Triumvirs she wrote to Leopold II. "The Revolution must be ended," said Barnave, adding that it was not too late for her to win the esteem of the French people. In her letter to her brother she asked him to recognise the new Constitution, but immediately after she dispatched another to Mercy in Brussels explaining that she was merely doing what was asked of her. "This fraud would be humiliating to me if it were not that I have good reason to hope my brother will realise that in my present position I have no alternative but to do and to write whatever they demand." She went on to admit: "It would be unjust to deny that, although they hold fast to their opinions, I have always found them very open, strongwilled, and motivated by a genuine desire to restore order."

Next the Queen made it clear to Fersen that not for one moment did she mean all that she had written in her official letter to Austria. She explained that if she had interviews with the leaders of the Revolution, it was only so that she could make use of them. There could never be a common bond between the woman in the Tuileries and the political leaders in the Manège; the loathing on her part was too great. Her conduct was necessary, Marie Antoinette explained to Fersen, because if she had not taken the line she did, the royal family would have been in an even worse situation.

The Cordeliers, headed by Danton, were openly calling for the abolition of the monarchy, and on July 17th, 1791, six thousand would-be republicans signed a petition laid on the Altar of the Nation in the Champ-de-Mars. That morning two peeping-toms had concealed themselves under the wooden platform on which the altar stood, with the intention of spying up the skirts of the women. They were soon discovered, taken for real spies, lynched and their heads paraded on pikes. Martial law was declared, Lafayette and Bailly appeared, the National Guard was called out and the red flag displayed, the sign that the crowd must disperse at once. Then there was firing and some fifty people were killed.

"The Massacre of the Champ-de-Mars" precipitated a rift between the right wing constitutionalists and the ultra-progressives, headed by Desmoulins, Danton, Couthon, Robespierre and Santerre. Several went into hiding, Danton coming to England for a while.

If Marie Antoinette was tormented in her political actions, her private thoughts concerning Fersen were no happier. In fact she heard nothing from him till the end of September, by which time she had sent him two rings with *fleurs-de-lys* and the motto "Faint-heart he who forsakes her." One she wore for two days before sending it off. But most of her waking hours were occupied with playing for time with the National Assembly, worrying about the activities of the *émigrés* and trying to stir Austria to come to her aid. For her the Constitution could be nothing more than a means of diminishing the Crown's authority, and in August she wrote to Barnave:

"It is not words that are needed, but the preservation of the monarch's real rights, giving him the necessary dignity, in a word, giving him the means to govern." To her the Constitution would be a moral death, but Barnave, Duport and Lameth were hurt by her tone, for they had been fighting not only to preserve the monarchy itself, but to see it retained some semblance of authority.

Thanks to those men the Constitution was accepted by the National Assembly, and as a result Louis was to have far more power than is wielded by any constitutional monarch today. He would have the right to veto decrees if he so desired, and the right to nominate ministers, ambassadors and army chiefs; but the National Assembly alone would have the right to declare war. Louis would have the title of Representative of the Nation.

Robespierre and Pétion promptly attacked Barnave, accusing him of selling out to the "Austrian Committee", while Marie Antoinette wrote confidentially to Mercy that she considered the new Constitution "a tissue of insolence and impractical absurdities". She could not relinquish the idea that a sovereign's rule must be absolute, and she went on to declare that it was impossible to go on existing as they did at that moment. All they had to do was to hoodwink the National Assembly and make them "trust us the better to defeat them afterwards".

Certainly she was an isolated, proud woman playing a lone hand in a very difficult situation; but even so her comment leaves an unpleasant taste in the mouth; the more so when one knows that in the end Barnave and others were sent to the guillotine for having tried to help her at this time.

On September 14th Louis went to the Manège, and before the National Assembly—which ostentatiously remained seated—he took the oath to the new Constitution, and was formally reinstated as King. Many now thought that the Revolution was over, and those who had been involved in the royal family's escape were freed. On September 18th Marie Antoinette went to the opera, and there were cries of "*Vive le Roi!*" and "*Vive la Reine!*" But it would be for the last time.

VIII Portrait of Louis XVI by Duplessis.

IX-XI Water-colours of the Petit Trianon at Versailles.
IX (*Above left*) The Hameau, a miniature village, built for Marie Antoinette beside a lake. It included a farm house, cowsheds, dovecotes and barns. X (*Left*) The Belvedere.
XI (*Above*) The Temple of Love, a Corinthian rotunda completed for the Queen in 1777.

XII (*Left*) Marie Antoinette and her four children, from a portrait by Madame Vigée Lebrun. Marie Therèse Charlotte (Madame Royale) stands on the left, the Dauphin Louis Joseph on the right, Louis Charles (the future Louis XVII) sits on the Queen's knees, and in the cot lies Sophie Hélène Beatrice, who died as a baby.
XIII (*Above*) A *sans-culotte* with his wife. He is shown wearing trousers like jeans, rather than the breeches of the well-to-do.
XIV (*Below*) The return of the royal family to Paris, following their unsuccessful flight to Varennes in June 1791. From an anonymous engraving.

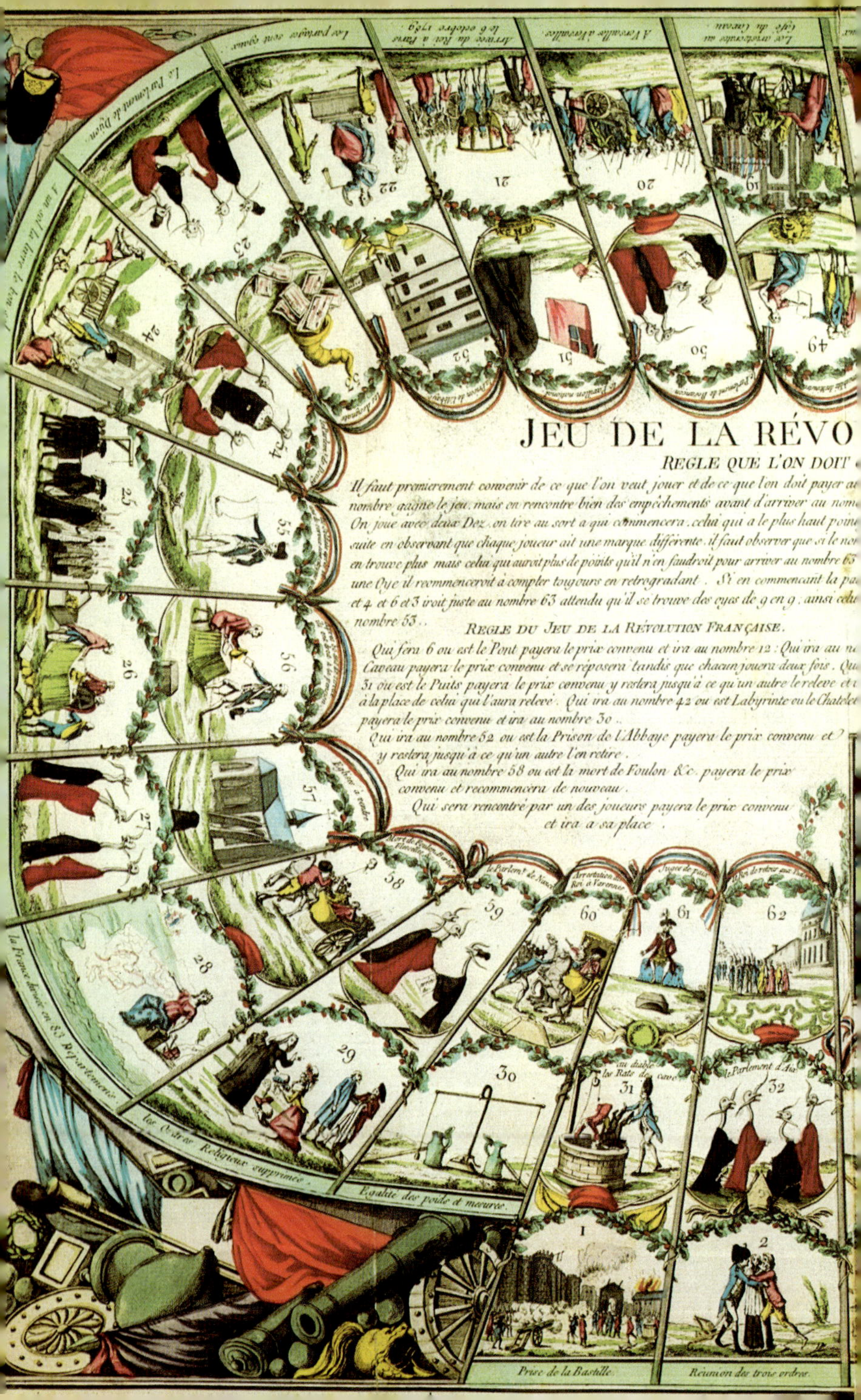
JEU DE LA RÉVO
REGLE QUE L'ON DOIT
Il faut premierement convenir de ce que l'on veut jouer et de ce que l'on doit payer a
nombre gagne le jeu, mais on rencontre bien des empêchements avant d'arriver au nom
On joue avec deux Dez, on tire au sort a qui commencera, celui qui a le plus haut poin
suite en observant que chaque joueur ait une marque différente. il faut observer que si le no
en trouve plus mais celui qui auroit plus de points qu'il n'en faudroit pour arriver au nombre 63
une Oye il recommenceroit à compter toujours en retrogradant. Si en commencant la pa
et 4 et 6 et 3 iroit juste au nombre 63 attendu qu'il se trouve des oyes de 9 en 9; ainsi celu
nombre 53..
REGLE DU JEU DE LA RÉVOLUTION FRANÇAISE.
Qui fera 6 ou est le Pont payera le prix convenu et ira au nombre 12: Qui ira au n
Caveau payera le prix convenu et se reposera tandis que chacun jouera deux fois. Qu
31 ou est le Puits payera le prix convenu y restera jusqu'à ce qu'un autre le releve et
à la place de celui qui l'aura relevé. Qui ira au nombre 42 ou est Labyrinte ou le Chatele
payera le prix convenu et ira au nombre 30..
Qui ira au nombre 52 ou est la Prison de l'Abbaye payera le prix convenu et
y restera jusqu'à ce qu'un autre l'en retire.
Qui ira au nombre 58 ou est la mort de Foulon &c. payera le prix
convenu et recommencera de nouveau.
Qui sera rencontré par un des joueurs payera le prix convenu
et ira a sa place.
Prise de la Bastille
Réunion des trois ordres
Egalité des poids et mesures
les Ordres Religieux supprimés
la France divisée en 83 Départements
le Parlement d'Aix
le Parlem.t de Nancy
Arrestation du Roi à Varennes
Juges de paix
Le Parlement de Dijon
Les partages sont égaux
Arrivée du Roi à Paris le 6 octobre 1789
A Versailles
1
2
30
31
32
58
59
60
61
62
57
56
55
54
53
52
51
50
49
19
20
21
22
23
24
25
26
27
28
29

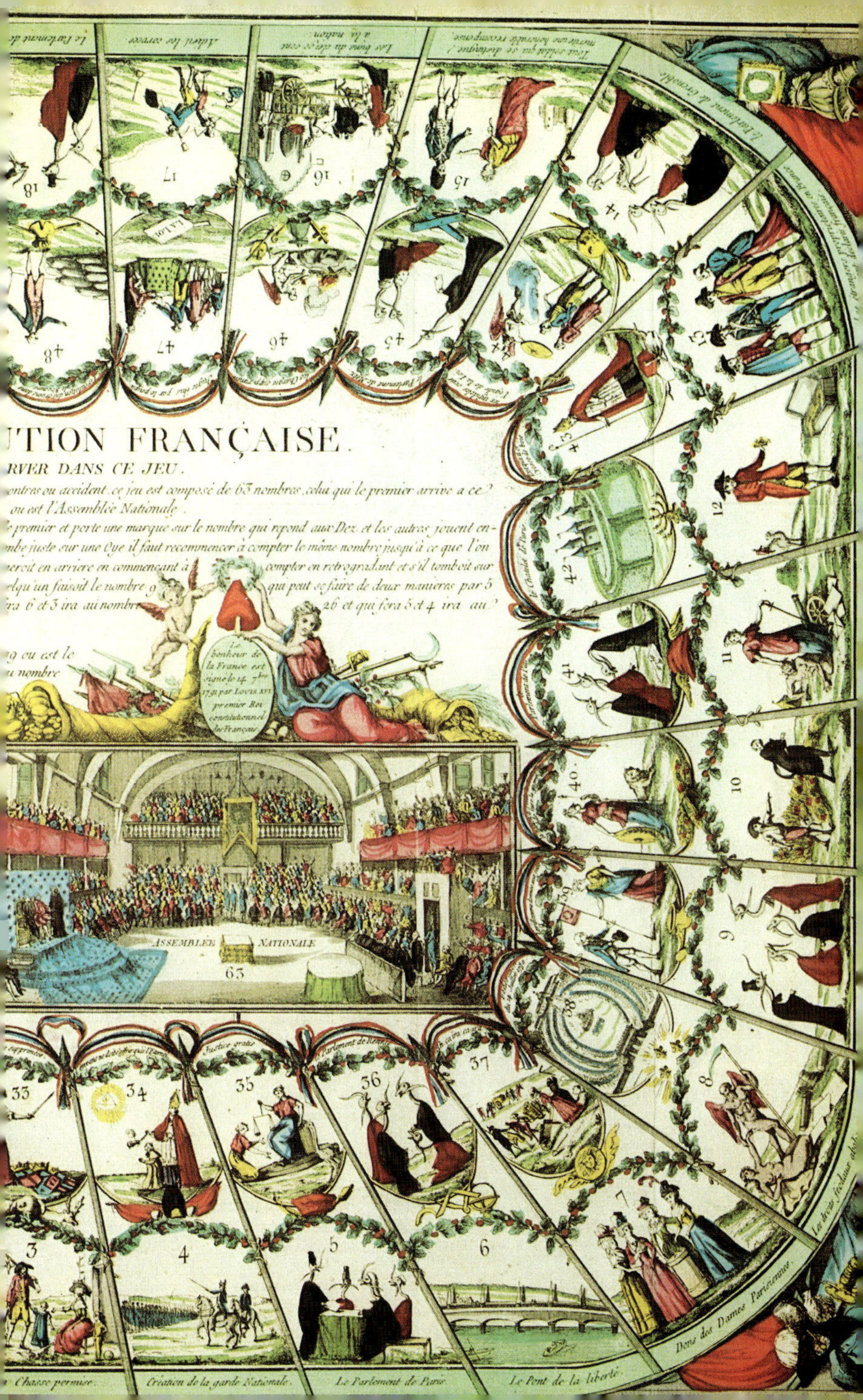
UTION FRANÇAISE.
RVER DANS CE JEU.
ontras ou accident. ce jeu est composé de 63 nombres, celui qui le premier arrive a ce
ou est l'Assemblée Nationale.
premier et porte une marque sur le nombre qui repond aux Dez et les autres jeuent en-
mbe juste sur une Oye il faut recommencer à compter le même nombre jusqu'à ce que l'on
eroit en arriere en commencant à
compter en retrogradant et s'il tomboit sur
elqu'un faisoit le nombre 9
qui peut se faire de deux manieres par 5
ra 6 et 3 ira au nombre
26 et qui fera 5 et 4 ira au
9 ou est le
u nombre
Le bonheur de la France est signé le 14 7bre 1791 par Louis XVI premier Roi constitutionnel des François
ASSEMBLÉE NATIONALE
63
Chasse permise.
Création de la garde Nationale.
Le Parlement de Paris
Le Pont de la liberté.
Dons des Dames Parisiennes.

XVI (*Above*) The taking of the Tuileries Palace on the night of 8–9 August 1792. This scene from a painting by Bertaux, shows the Swiss guards being cut to pieces by the Marseillais.
XV (*Previous pages*) Game of the French Revolution.

"You would never believe how much it costs me to do all I have to at present!" she wrote to Fersen. "If I have relations with some of them it is merely to do all to make use of them. They revolt me too much for me ever to go over to their side." Try as she might she could never quell her innate arrogance, even towards those who wished her well. It would be wonderful, she wrote, if one day she would again be powerful enough to show them that she was never fooled.

At the end of September the old National Assembly ceased to exist, and was replaced by a Legislative Assembly, of which Barnave was no longer a member. On September 29th non-juring clergy were ordered to take the oath of civic allegiance or be deported, and also it was decreed that after the end of the year all Frenchmen still beyond the frontiers would be regarded as traitors liable to the death penalty.

Louis vetoed both decrees. "I do what everyone wants often enough for them to do what I want for once," he exclaimed stubbornly. As might be expected all the rancour against the monarchy revived, and matters were not improved when the Duc d'Orléans offered to help Louis in his predicament, only to be insulted in Marie Antoinette's drawing room.

The royal family must indeed have felt isolated as the other sovereigns turned their backs. A letter from Louis to Gustav III explaining his acceptance of the Constitution was returned unopened, while Leopold II told his sister: "There can be no question of using our gold or our blood in order to re-establish France in its former powerful state."

Madame Élizabeth was making herself heard in family discussions, and proving very reactionary. Distractedly Marie Antoinette wrote:

"My sister (-in-law) is so indiscreet, surrounded by schemers, and held in leading-strings by her brothers across the frontier, that we find it impossible to converse with one another except at the risk of quarrelling from morning to night." Candidly she admitted: "Our family life is hell."

Fersen decided that the Gordian Knot must be cut by another escape attempt, and in February, 1792, he returned to Paris disguised as a courier and with papers bearing his forgery of the King of

Sweden's signature. On the evening of the 13th, he slipped into Marie Antoinette's apartments in the Tuileries by "the usual route", and remained there for twenty-four hours before the Queen made his presence known to Louis. At six that evening he had a long interview with the King, but the latter refused to consider the idea of escaping. "I know I have missed the right moment," he said, but once before he had broken his word, and that was something he was not prepared to do again. "Louis is, in truth, a man of honour," wrote Fersen admiringly in his diary. So the Swede prepared to leave, by the way he had entered the Tuileries. Marie Antoinette went with him as far as she dared, but before they could say goodbye a sentry was heard approaching, and Fersen had to slip away quickly: away from the Palace, Paris and France itself. They never did say a real goodbye, and they never saw each other again.

Just a week after Fersen's departure, the unloving Leopold II of Austria died suddenly, and was succeeded by his son, Francis II. Now conflict between France and Austria was not just a possibility, but a certainty. Francis II was far more bellicose than his father, while in Paris Jacques Brissot and the Girondins were demanding war. The Girondins forced General Dumouriez on Louis as his principal minister, but Marie Antoinette antagonised him from the start with her remarks, "Your existence depends on your conduct," and "Neither the King nor I can bear all these innovations in the constitution." Dumouriez could have served the Queen as well as Mirabeau or Barnave, but she would have none of him, even though he was one of the few men left who wished to help her.

War was only a matter of days, because Francis II had allowed the Prince de Condé to assemble an *émigré* army in the Austrian Netherlands. Marie Antoinette now put her loyalty to her fatherland before her duty to her adopted country, and sent Mercy details of the plans for the French advance.

Dumouriez, the French General, was in no doubt that the Allies were going to act in concert, because of all the troop movements which had been going on, and he planned to be the first to attack in Savoy and also near Liège. He would himself be in charge of the operations in the latter sector.

Hostilities began on April 20th when Louis had to rise in the Legislative Assembly and declare war on Austria, or rather on the "King of Hungary and Bohemia", to give Francis II of Austria his lesser title. French troops advanced in the Netherlands, and were routed; General Dillon was murdered by mutinous troops in the streets of Lille, and by the end of the month Lafayette was suing for peace. While nothing could be proved against Marie Antoinette, all Paris knew on which side her sympathies lay during the campaign. Old hates were revived, and more pornographic pamphlets and books found their way into circulation.

In the Manège, a few hundred yards from the garden front of the Tuileries, the Girondin Pierre Vergniaud declared that he could "see the home of false counsellors who misled the King, and who forged chains for the French people, and who schemed to hand over the country to the Austrians."

"I can see the windows of the palace where they are planning a counter-revolution, and where they scheme to make slaves of us once again. Those who live in that palace should realise that our Constitution only guarantees inviolability to the King. Let them know that our laws can reach them without distinction, and that not a single guilty head can hope to escape the axe."

Already shaken by the humiliating defeats of the war, France was now in a precarious position. Financially the situation was as grave as it had ever been. The paper assignats, which were backed by confiscated Church lands, were now only worth fifty-seven per cent of their face value. Hoarding and speculation increased, and the cost of living soared. As a result the Revolution entered a new and more intense phase. Marat, Desmoulins, Couthon and Robespierre united against Brissot, one-time advocate of war against Austria. The red cap of liberty made its appearance, and the *Ça Ira*—the most stirring and at the same time the most chilling of the songs of the French Revolution—was given more savage words. Now it was the *Enragés*, the Wild Men, who ran the country.

On May 27th a decree was passed for the deportation of any non-juring priests who had been denounced by twenty 'active' citizens, and on the 29th the King's recently formed Constitutional Guard of one thousand two hundred men was to be dissolved. Then on June 8th the Minister of War brought Louis a plan for the establishment of a camp for twenty thousand National Guards just outside Paris. Louis would only agree to the dissolution of the Constitutional Guard. Monsieur Roland sent him a letter, largely written by his more celebrated wife, warning that by opposing measures for the public safety he was risking another revolution.

Louis replied by dismissing Roland, and formed a new ministry of Feuillant nonentities. Then, on June 19th, he formally banned the decrees issued by the Legislative Assembly; Paris seethed, and everyone demanded the suppression of the vetoes. Assemblies were declared illegal, and it was obvious that in a matter of hours there would be an explosion.

All night the crowds gathered in the centre of the city, but Pétion, now Mayor, chose to stay out of the way in the Hôtel de Ville. At 8.00 a.m. the Minister of the Interior considered that there was no cause for alarm, but only an hour later he sent a message to the Directory, the governing body of Paris, requesting troops to defend the Tuileries, where the gates were closed. At 10.00 am the vast crowd marched towards the Manège, where their leader asked the Legislative Assembly why the Army was idle, and if it was on the King's orders, then he must go. "The blood of patriots must not be shed for the pride and ambition of the Tuileries." At 2.00 p.m. the crowd, now about twenty thousand strong and armed with every imaginable offensive weapon, surged the few hundred yards to the Tuileries, led by the left-wing brewer Santerre. First, they got into the grounds on the garden side, but then moved round to the Place du Carrousel. By then it was 4.00 p.m. and Santerre was standing on the steps urging the people to enter the Palace. A cannon was dragged up, Santerre ordered the main doors to be opened, and the mob flooded in, dragging the cannon with them up the stairs to the first floor. There was a gallery, called the Oeil-de-Boeuf after the one at Versailles, which looked on to both the Place and the gardens, where they installed the cannon, which started to sink through the floorboards.

Marie Antoinette's apartments were still those on the ground floor which she had occupied before the escape, while those of Louis and the children were above, overlooking the gardens. With Marie Antoinette was Madame de Lamballe, who had returned from the safety of England to be near the Queen in her time of trouble. They hurried up the private staircase leading to the Dauphin's rooms, but already the boy had been taken to his sister. A few minutes later the mother was reunited with her children, and they all went to hide in the corridor at the top of the private staircase. With them was Madame de Lamballe and one or two women of the household. A few feet away they could hear the mob breaking into the adjoining rooms, and for the Queen it was October 6th at Versailles all over again. She could not stifle her sobs. For fifteen minutes they hid, not knowing what had happened to Louis and Madame Élizabeth. Finally word was brought that the brother was in the Oeil-de-Boeuf, hemmed in by the crowd, but otherwise all right. A Chevalier de St-Louis was holding one of the King's hands, and Monsieur de Farre, a theatrical producer, the other.

The mob forced their way into the Dauphin's rooms, and in tears Marie Antoinette felt that she would rather face them, instead of hiding terror-stricken in the narrow corridor. But Chevalier de Rougeville, a frequent visitor to the Tuileries, stopped her and led the whole party to the Council Room, which had not yet been entered by the mob. He made them sit behind a large table which was dragged into a corner, with three rows of Grenadiers stationed in front of it.

Meanwhile the mob was shouting into the King's face, demanding that he withdraw his vetoes. Someone handed him a red cap of liberty, which he put on himself. A butcher shouted: "Monsieur, listen to me. It is your business to listen to us. You are a traitor. You have always deceived us and you are still deceiving us. But take care; the measure is full to overflowing and the people are tired of being your plaything."

At 6.00 p.m. Pétion arrived from the Hôtel de Ville, saying that he had only just heard of the King's plight. Without heat Louis pointed out that his "plight" had already lasted two hours. Pétion told the mob they had behaved as they should, with the pride and dignity of free men, but now it was time for them to leave.

Louis then said that since the crowd was in the Palace they had better satisfy their curiosity, and see the state apartments. The door of the Council Room was opened, and there to everyone's surprise was Marie Antoinette, the children and the rest of the party, still sitting behind the table. Santerre ordered the Grenadiers to divide so the people could see the Queen.

A red cap of liberty was put on her head, but Marie Antoinette promptly snatched it off and set it on the Dauphin. Santerre leant across the table and told her that she was in the wrong, but that he would make himself responsible for the good behaviour of the people. Then he shouted: "See the Queen and the Royal Prince." Royalty was on display for whoever came to gape, and that must have seemed like half Paris late that afternoon, June 20th, on the first anniversary of the Flight to Varennes.

Slowly the dirty, ragged queue moved through the Council Room, gazing at Marie Antoinette who by now was quite drained of emotion and expressionless. Some carried slogans such as *A la Lanterne!* while one man held a doll dangling from a gallows. An old harridan exclaimed: "You're a vile woman!"

"Have I ever done you any harm?" asked Marie Antoinette through almost closed lips. One woman burst into tears as she passed, and Santerre hastily explained this away by saying she was drunk. But at last there was a familiar face coming towards the Queen. Madame Élizabeth had joined the slow-moving queue as the only means of reaching her sister-in-law to tell her that Louis was unharmed.

By 8.00 p.m. the last of the rioters had left the Tuileries, behind them was a trail of smashed doors and wrecked furniture in most of the elegant state apartments. Then Louis entered looking for Marie Antoinette. He was still wearing the red cap of liberty.

CHAPTER SEVENTEEN

Point of No Return

From the time of her arrival in France in 1770 until the royal family was taken to the Tuileries by the revolutionary mob, Marie Antoinette's appearance had hardly changed. The twenty years which separated the fifteen-year-old schoolgirl from the woman of thirty-five hardly showed in her face. In all the official portraits painted by Madame Vigée-Lebrun, the Queen's face is curiously expressionless, and perhaps there really was very little going on behind those large but unsparkling eyes beneath arched brows, separated by an exceptionally wide bridge to her nose.

The Polish artist Kucharski started a pastel, which remained unfinished because of the flight to Varennes; but even so it shows a completely different woman to the one depicted in earlier state portraits. The eyebrows and the bridge of the nose remain the same, but the face itself is thinner and with much more character, while for the first time the eyes are those of someone who has suffered; one might say they are the eyes of someone who has lived and understood. Gone is the voluptuous figure with the flaunting half exposed breasts, measuring no less than forty-three and a half inches, if her dressmaker's notebook is to be believed. Now she dressed simply, and her hair was no longer elaborately styled. After October 6th, 1789 it started to go white, and though it did not turn in the course of a single night, as legend has it, by the summer of 1792 she must have looked more than her thirty-seven years.

Beyond a shadow of doubt Marie Antoinette and the rest of the royal family now knew who were the real rulers of Paris. Not the Legislative Assembly, the Directory or even the Army, but the people. Not all those who marched and demonstrated deserved the epithet *canaille*—the scum only interested in what they could loot. The *sans-culottes* formed a distinct strata in the social structure of the Revolution, and were not simply an amorphous mass of "have-nots". Their nickname, "without breeches", referred to the fact that they wore trousers somewhat like jeans, and not the breeches with knee-buckles of the well-to-do. Their ranks were composed of small shopkeepers, and skilled and semi-skilled workers who had a vested interest in the retention of private property and of law and order. "Brothers" or "Comrades" they may have been, but not anarchists.

Such men as Marat, Robespierre, Danton, Santerre and Pétion found they had raised up a monster they could not control, but only appease, and the monster wanted the abolition of the monarchy.

After vacillating nearly as much as the King himself, Lafayette decided it was his duty to try to help the royal family. This made Marie Antoinette remark:

"I see that Monsieur de Lafayette wants to save us, but who will save us from Monsieur de Lafayette?"

Songs were sung within earshot of the Palace windows about Madame Véto (Marie Antoinette) having promised to cut the throats of all Parisians, and obscene prints of her and her reputed lovers were sold in the gardens of the Tuileries. Only more violence could end the tension building up in a city already on edge with the heat of an excessively hot summer.

For the last time Louis and Marie Antoinette left the Tuileries to attend a function, the July 14th celebrations on the Champ-de-Mars. Louis wore a waistcoat that was supposed to be bullet or dagger-proof, but Marie Antoinette refused to follow his example. Not that she had become entirely fatalistic about the future.

"Your friend is in the utmost danger," she wrote to Fersen in Brussels on July 23rd. "His illness advances in a most alarming fashion. The doctors no longer know what to do. If you want to see him again you must be quick. See that his relations are kept informed of his critical condition." Three days later another letter was sent: "Only an immediate crisis can save him, and as yet there is no sign of one, and as a result we are in despair. Let those who deal with him know of the situation, so that they may be able to take such precautions as are necessary. Time is short."

On August 1st the Queen wrote what was to be her last letter to Fersen: like the others it was in code and in the third person.

"It is obvious that for some time there has been a threat to the King's life, and also to the Queen's. The arrival from Marseilles of some six hundred men, together with a number of deputies from the Jacobin Clubs has increased our well-founded anxiety. All kinds of precautions are taken for Their Majesties' safety, but assassins wander through the Palace; the people are being stirred up, some of the National Guard are disloyal, while the remainder have neither strength nor bravery. An earlier letter will have made it clear how vital it is to gain even twenty-four hours. Now I only repeat that statement, while adding that unless help arrives promptly, only Providence can save the King and his family."

Before then, however, the cumulative effect of her letters had been disastrous for Fersen. Any day, he felt, she might be murdered by another mob breaking into the Tuileries, and the thought was more than he could stand. Certainly the Duke of Brunswick was making plans for an invasion, but with elephantine deliberation and slowness; it could not be launched before mid-August at the earliest. Most unwisely, Fersen drew up a manifesto, prepared with the best intentions in the world, which was meant to make the revolutionaries in Paris pause for reflection before doing anything rash. The effect was the opposite to that intended: they became enraged to the point of losing self-control. The final draft approved by the Duke of Brunswick—a man with a bull-necked mind—and the *émigrés*, was aggressive and tantamount to a declaration of war. According to this ill-timed document it was the aim of the allied sovereigns to put an end to anarchy (i.e., the Revolution) in France; National Guardsmen and civilians alike would be executed if they opposed Brunswick's invading army, and Paris would be totally destroyed if the Tuileries should be stormed. The manifesto was issued in Koblenz on July 25th, and published in Paris a week later. After that, all the leaders of the left-wing Jacobins waited for hourly was the arrival of the "reds" from Marseilles. Even by the standards of the French Revolution they were a tough body of fanatics.

A few weeks earlier, in May, a young captain in the Engineers, called Rouget de Lisle, wrote the words and music for a marching song, which was first sung by Monsieur Dietrich, the Mayor of Strasbourg, at a gathering in his house. "It is like Gluck, only better—more lively and spirited," wrote Madame Dietrich. Now it had been adopted by the men marching from Marseilles. "*Allons, enfants de la patrie!*" they sang, galvanising the inhabitants of the towns and villages through which they passed. On August 6th, for the first time, the *Marseillaise* was heard in the streets of Paris.

No one could describe the reds from Marseilles as a simple band of brothers united only by thoughts of Liberty, Fraternity and Equality. "One cannot imagine anything more horrifying than these five hundred fanatics, three-quarters of them drunk, almost all wearing the red bonnet, marching bare-armed and dishevelled."

At the Hôtel de Ville, Pétion, Mayor of Paris, refused to believe their arrival would increase the danger to the lives of the royal family. Any day, or night, an attack on the Tuileries was expected, and as night fell on August 9th the Palace was like an armed camp. Nine hundred men of the loyal Swiss Regiment had been summoned from Courbevoie to guard the Palace, and there were also about one thousand five hundred men of the Battalion of the Filles Saint-Thomas, National Guardsmen, the majority of whom were royalist in sympathy. No one went to bed, and the royal family gathered in the drawing-room of the state apartments. The heat was brassy, and everything was quiet, unnaturally quiet in a city where few were sleeping. In the distant suburbs side-drums rattled calling the people to rallying points. Both Pétion and Roederer, the Procureur of the Paris Directory, were at the Tuileries, and at 12.30 a.m. the latter was brought a letter advising him of activity in the Faubourg St Antoine.

At the Hôtel de Ville delegates from the different sectors into which Paris was divided started to collect at about midnight. They called themselves a Commune, and intended to replace the authority of the Municipality. In the small hours they sent an order to National Guardsmen with a cannon stationed on the Pont Neuf to withdraw. That meant there was nothing to stop a mob crossing from the South Bank via the Ile de la Cité, and gathering near the Hôtel de Ville.

At a quarter to one a single bell belonging to the Cordeliers Church started to toll. Some two hundred and twenty years before the bell of St Germain l'Auxerrois had signalled the start of the St Bartholomew Massacre, and now another of Paris' churches was signalling the beginning of the end for the French Monarchy. One by one other churches started to sound the tocsin. In the Tuileries the courtiers crowded to the open windows, trying to identify them by their bells.

The man in charge of the defence of the Palace was the Marquis de Mandat, commanding officer of the National Guard, and a capable soldier. If the Commune feared any man, it was de Mandat, and an order was sent commanding his presence at the Hôtel de Ville. Louis was undecided, but reluctantly Roederer advised that the Marquis should obey. Outside the Hôtel de Ville Mandat was shot by a youth, and his body thrown into the Seine. His death meant there was no one to take charge of the defence of the Tuileries.

Meanwhile Louis lay down, fully dressed, and slept. Marie Antoinette and Madame de Lamballe wandered about, from room to room, and all the time the bells of Paris were booming and clanging as an ever increasing number of people converged on the Hôtel de Ville. Between four and five o'clock dawn broke, and the whole sky was red. Madame Élizabeth called to Marie Antoinette: "Come here, my sister, and see the sunrise."

About five the tocsin stopped. As on occasions in the past Marie Antoinette took the lead. She asked Roederer to come to her, and he found the Queen sitting near the fireplace in the room normally occupied by her husband's valet. What should they do, she asked. Go to the National Assembly, advised Roederer.

"Monsieur," said Marie Antoinette, "this is a conflict of forces. We have come to the point where we must know which is going to prevail—the King and the Constitution or the rebels."

"In that case Madame, let us see what measures have been taken for the defence."

Monsieur Lachesnaye, who had taken command in the Palace since the departure of the Marquis de Mandat, was sent for, and the three discussed plans for the defence of the Tuileries. Later Roederer said of Marie Antoinette: "During this fatal night the Queen made no show of masculinity or heroics, was neither affected nor romantic: I did not see rage or despair, nor any spirit of revenge. She was a woman, a mother and a wife in danger. She feared, hoped, sorrowed and was reassured."

Louis, with his wig askew, wandered like a lost dog through the rooms on the first floor of the Tuileries. Ever since the Revolution began he had shrunk from the thought of shedding the blood of Frenchmen, and as danger grew with every minute his moral haema-phobia increased his sense of indecision. This soon communicated itself to the Switzers and also to the National Guardsmen, who were of uncertain loyalty. As best they could, they prepared for a pitched battle; three cannons faced the Place du Carrousel, while two more had been set up on the terrace overlooking the gardens.

Somewhere about six o'clock Marie Antoinette, her eyes red with weeping, advised Louis to go out and review the soldiers and try to stiffen their morale. With his hat tucked under his arm Louis descended the steps into the Cour Royale and addressed the defenders:

"My cause is that of all good citizens," he began. "We have been told they are coming, and we should make a good fight, don't you think?"

It was worse than useless. The Switzers and the loyal members of the National Guard—the ranks of the latter thinning rapidly—applauded, at which a great cry went up of "*Vive la Nation!*" Louis walked on, to the iron railings which separated the Cour Royale from the Place du Carrousel itself. "Down with the Veto!" yelled the crowd. "Down with the fat pig!"

A minister, Monsieur Duboucharge, heard the commotion and put his head out of a window. "Good God," he exclaimed, "it's the King they are booing. What the devil is going on down there? Come quickly and let us go to him." Among those who hurried downstairs and out into the courtyard was Roederer. He and the others formed a ring round the well-meaning but bewildered King and hurried him to safety.

Marie Antoinette had seen and heard what happened. From time to time she wiped her eyes.

"All is lost. This review of the troops has done more harm than good." Then she went into the King's bedroom to await his return. "Half her face was flushed with tears," wrote Roederer. "Soon after, the ministers returned with the King, who was quite out of breath and very hot from the effort of running. He sat down at once, but seemed hardly upset by his experience."

A police officer entered with alarming news; it was the first time those in the Tuileries heard that Marquis de Mandat had been murdered on his way to the Hôtel de Ville, and that Paris seethed as the people surged in from the suburbs. Also, the "reds" from Marseilles as well as the men of the Cordeliers battalion were marching towards the Palace, bringing cannon with them. Roederer urged the ministers to insist on the royal family going to the Manège, where they would be the responsibility of the Legislative Assembly.

"No, he must not go to the Assembly," said another minister. "It is not safe for him to go. He must stay here." But Roederer decided to go across the gardens to advise the Assembly that the King would be coming shortly, only to be informed that there were insufficient deputies in the Chamber to issue a decree summoning him.

Roederer walked back straight through the Palace and out the other side into the Cour Royale. Immediately ahead were the cannon facing the Royal Gate and the Place du Carrousel. On the south side, nearest the Seine, was a battalion of National Guards, while on the north another battalion was drawn up, that of the Switzers. At that moment the battalions of the Cordeliers and the Marseillais marched into the Place du Carrousel. The two forces confronted one another through the railings, and a deputy went over to the Swiss begging them not to fire on the "patriots". Roederer had seen enough. He went back into the Tuileries, and with his colleagues ran up the great staircase and pushed his way through the crowd to the King's room. "They made way and we entered. The King was sitting at a table by the door leading into his cabinet. His hands were resting on his knees. The Queen, Madame Élizabeth and the ministers were between the window and the King." Roederer went on: "Your Majesty has not five minutes to lose. There is no safety for you except in the National Assembly. There are not enough men in the courtyards of the Palace to defend the building, and what is more, they are ill-disposed. As soon as the gunners were warned to remain at the ready, they unloaded their pieces."

"But I did not see many people in the Carrousel," insisted Louis.

"But Monsieur, we have troops," added Marie Antoinette.

"Madame, all Paris is marching," came the chilling reply.

"Are we alone?" she asked. "Can no one do anything?"

"There are vast crowds coming from the suburbs with a dozen pieces of artillery."

Monsieur Gerdret, a civic official, and in other days the supplier of lace to the Queen, backed up Roederer's insistence that they should go at once to the Assembly. Even at such a time Marie Antoinette could not forget who she was, and the Austrian Archduchess came to the fore once again as she rapped:

"It is not for you to raise your voice here, Sir, and don't take the words out of the mouth of Monsieur le Procureur General." It was not only useless to stay, it was dangerous. Louis would do as Roederer wished. "The King raised his head, looked at me fixedly for some seconds and then, turning towards the Queen, said, 'Let us go', and got to his feet."

Roederer insisted that only members of the royal family and the ministers should to go the Manège, but at Marie Antoinette's request the Princesse de Lamballe and Madame de Tourzel were allowed to accompany them. Roederer opened the door and called for the commanding officer of the National Guard.

"You must bring up some men of the National Guard to march on either side of the King's party. This is the King's wish."

The royal family entered the Council Room, where most of what remained of the Court was assembled, about fifty in all. Louis walked round the circles into which they had formed themselves saying: "I am going to the National Assembly." The detachment of National Guards arrived and the party filed out into the Oeil-de-Boeuf at the head of the great staircase. Reaching over, Louis exchanged headgear with the National Guard on his right. Somewhat surprised the soldier whipped off the King's hat and kept it tucked under his arm. As they trooped out of the Tuileries Marie Antoinette turned and called to a minister, "We shall soon be back."

Between two lines of soldiers the French royal family walked on its way to the Assembly in the Manège, mourners in its own funeral procession. First went Roederer, as he had said he would, to protect the King from an assassin's bullet. Next came Marie Antoinette supporting herself on the arm of the Navy Minister and leading the Dauphin by the hand. After her followed Madame Royale, Madame Élizabeth, the Princesse de Lamballe and Madame de Tourzel.

It was just after 7.00 a.m. on Friday, August 10th, and the day promised to be fine and very hot. "We walked over the leaves which had fallen in the night and which the gardeners had piled up in heaps across the path followed by the King," wrote Roederer. "We sank up to our knees in them. 'What a lot of leaves!' said the King. 'They have begun to fall very early this year.' One of my colleagues told me that the Dauphin was amusing himself by kicking the leaves at the legs of the persons walking in front of him."

A little further on they were met by the President of the Assembly:

"The Assembly is anxious to contribute to your safety and offers a refuge in its precincts for you and your family."

The Manége itself was surrounded by an excited mob on the edge of violence, while within the deputies were tense and afraid at the centre of a storm they could no longer control. Suddenly National Guards with fixed bayonets appeared in the entrance below the tiers of seats, trying to thrust their way through the wedge of people in the narrow passage. Down scrambled the deputies from their benches to drive them back. "No soldiers! No arms!" The thought that crossed their minds was that perhaps the King was trying to stage a *coup d'état* and seize the Assembly. Suddenly Louis himself emerged into the Chamber, followed by Marie Antoinette, Madame Élizabeth holding Madame Royale's hand and followed by a Grenadier bearing the Dauphin high over everyone's heads. Vergniaud, the President, addressed the King:

"You can count, Sire, upon the loyalty of the National Assembly. We have all pledged ourselves to give even our lives to maintain the rights of the people and constituted authority."

The whole family now came right into the Chamber, and sat down in the seats at an oval table usually reserved for the secretaries, while Louis took a chair beside the President. The Monarchy had indeed come to its subjects for protection. But now one of the deputies rose to point out that under the rules of the Constitution no debates could take place in the presence of the sovereign, and the Assembly was actually in session. They had in fact been debating the gradual abolition of slavery. A compromise was quickly reached when the royal family were invited to go into the room normally occupied by the reporters, which was immediately behind the President's desk. Less than twelve feet square, its ceiling was so low that a full-grown adult could not stand upright. Here the royal party would be confined in unbearable heat until ten in the evening, to return on the two succeeding days. Because of fear of an attack by the mob, the grille dividing the box from the Chamber was broken down, so that if the worst came to the worst the deputies could bring the royal family to safety through the opening.

Now an officer of the National Guard hurried to the bar of the Chamber to tell the President that the mob had passed from the Place du Carrousel into the courtyard of the Tuileries, and it looked as though they were about to storm the Palace. Twelve commissioners were sent to try to calm them, but soon afterwards firing was clearly audible in the Assembly through the open doors and windows. A defender had fired the first shot from an upper window, which brought immediate replies from the attackers. When Louis left the Tuileries he never gave the order to the Swiss to stand down, and after his departure the eighty-four-year-old Maréchal de Mailly assumed command, and decided to defend the place to the death. The loyal troops, among whom were comparatively few National Guards by now, fired on the mob, and succeeded in driving them out of the courtyard. For three hours the shooting went on, until about eleven o'clock when Louis suddenly remembered he had never given the order to stand to, and hastily scribbled a cease-fire note. By then the Swiss had been driven back into the Palace itself by the shooting directed at them from the top of the Long Gallery which connected the Palace to the Louvre. When the order came they were making a stand at the foot of the great staircase. A drum sounded the retreat, and the Swiss fell back through the Palace to the gardens beyond.

Perhaps only the September Massacres that same year exceeded the storming of the Tuileries and its aftermath for sheer horror, and by the time the fighting was over eight hundred of the defenders had been killed, including five to six hundred Swiss and some seven hundred revolutionaries and ordinary Parisians. Many of the Swiss were cornered and butchered in the Tuileries itself, while most of the remainder were bayoneted and clubbed to death near the Round Pond in the gardens. A few got as far as the Place Louis Quinze (de la Concorde) before being cut down, murdered and their bodies obscenely mutilated by the women of Paris. All the streets in the area were filled with milling crowds, heads stuck on pikes, while in the Place Vendôme workmen passed ropes round the equestrian statue of Louis XIV and tried to pull it to the ground. Only twenty-four hours later, after they had filed through the horse's legs, it came crashing down, smashing to pieces on the cobblestones.

Meanwhile, in the stuffy atmosphere of the Manège, the debate on the future of the monarchy commenced. Louis had quickly recovered his composure; Marie Antoinette sat expressionless, and for part of the time with her face to the wall. Fitfully the children slept, worn out by a sleepless night. In the distance the staccato rattle of muskets and the duller boom of cannon was followed by silence; then by the cries of the Swiss being hunted through the Tuileries Gardens. Some ran into the Assembly itself, covered in blood and blackened by powder. Later they were taken to the Prison de l'Abbaye, while a group of sixty others were massacred on their way to the Hôtel de Ville.

The mood of the deputies changed; now the Swiss were accused of treachery in firing on "patriots", and the instant deposition of Louis was demanded. More interruptions followed—about midday—when the mob started bringing over loot from the Tuileries. From her place in the press-box Marie Antoinette could see her jewellery, letters and personal possessions being heaped on the table in front of the President. She showed no emotion; only from time to time she wiped her face with a handkerchief wet with tears and perspiration.

For thirteen hours that day they were cooped up in the tiny room, and all Marie Antoinette had was a glass of cold water. During the course of the afternoon the monarchy was whittled away to vanishing point. The King's power of veto was abolished; the Assembly declared itself the sole and supreme legislative authority. A National Convention would be formed, and finally Louis was "provisionally suspended from his functions". France no longer had a King.

During the day four of the cells in the one-time Convent of the Feuillants, adjoining the Manège, had been furnished for the royal family, and at 10.00 p.m., after nearly fourteen hours in the press-box, they were escorted the few yards to where they would spend the night. Clean underclothes had been procured for them, and with great difficulty shirts small enough for the Dauphin, but there was nothing to eat and only water to drink.

All through the night the mob literally howled and raged outside the Feuillants, even trying to break down the grating at the end of the corridor which led to the cells where the royal family were resting if not sleeping. They were not completely cut off from the outside world though; somehow several sympathisers managed to visit them during the night. Choiseul and Goguelet, who had been involved in the Flight to Varennes, Madame de Tourzel's son and Messieurs Nantouillet and d'Aubier. When Marie Antoinette remarked: "My handkerchief is soaked with tears," d'Aubier handed over his own, together with twenty-five louis, and in return received "a painful smile" which wrung his heart. "I think she is doomed," said Madame de Lamballe to Madame de Tourzel in the adjoining cell. Within three weeks the Princess would herself be murdered during the September Massacres.

Early the next morning, Saturday, August 11th, the royal family was up early, and after sitting down to a breakfast none could eat, at 7.00 a.m. they were taken back to the press-box. Another interminable day dragged on as deputy after deputy rose to his feet to denounce the monarchy and praise a republic. It was the same on the 12th, though by then M. Thiéri, the King's *valet de chambre*, had arranged for proper meals, cooked in his own kitchen, to be taken to the Feuillants.

One man, Dufour by name, but otherwise anonymous in history, did all he could to soften the harshness of the royal family's stay in the one-time convent. "I did my best to be always with their Majesties in order to take precautions against the unpleasantness to which they were exposed, day and night. When their Majesties had dined they returned to their rooms, and there allowed their tears to flow freely; then they returned to the Assembly."

On top of everything else Marie Antoinette lost her locket containing portraits of herself, Louis and their children. "This seemed to distress her very much, and I (Dufour) promised her to look for it with the greatest care. I was fortunate enough to find it, and I had it returned to her without delay, which seemed to give her much pleasure."

When Louis first sought the protection of the Assembly, that body agreed he and his family should go to the Luxembourg Palace when order was restored; but on August 11th, the Commune sent word asking the Assembly to think again—the Luxembourg was difficult to guard, and they suggested a move to the Temple. There were two parts to the Temple: a fine, comparatively modern house, once the home of the Comte d'Artois, and an old castle keep built in the Middle Ages by the Knights Templar. They did not specify to which building the royal family should be consigned, but the Assembly guessed what was in their minds. Then someone suggested the Archbishop's Palace, while another voice spoke in favour of using the house of the Minister of Justice on the Place Vendôme. Bewildered and unsure of itself, the Assembly decided to leave the choice to the Commune, a tacit admission of the identity of the real rulers.

On August 13th the royal family remained in the cells, and at about 6.00 p.m. a large coach drawn by two horses appeared at the entrance of the Feuillants. The whole party, including the Princesse de Lamballe, Madame de Tourzel and the Mayor Pétion climbed in. Inside it must have been even more crowded than on the return journey from Varennes. First they drove through the Place Vendôme, so that Louis could gaze shortsightedly on the overthrown statue of Louis XIV and then by a roundabout way to the Temple in the north-east corner of the old city. The journey through crowded streets took two hours, and for the royal family it was a progress towards oblivion.

CHAPTER EIGHTEEN

The Temple

While Paris has had the good fortune to keep so many of its old buildings, one cannot help regretting the loss of three so closely associated with Marie Antoinette and the royal family. The Tuileries, the Riding School (Manège) and the Temple only exist today in old illustrations, and, in the case of the first and last, the loss is unfortunate from an architectural point of view.

Founded in the Middle Ages by the Knights Templar as their headquarters in France, the Temple was matched by a similar establishment in London, now the centre of the legal world. Today nothing remains of the Temple in Paris except the name of a long street and a square, but at the time of the outbreak of the Revolution it was like a small town within its own high wall. There was a large church, demolished in 1796 for the building material it contained, and a palace once occuped by Marie Antoinette's brother-in-law the Comte d'Artois, who was the unsuitable Grand Prior of this religious and military order founded during the Crusades. To the south of the church, and almost adjoining a complex of small buildings, stood the keep. Square in plan with four enormous turrets at each corner, it was about sixty feet high to the parapets, and capped with a pyramid-shaped roof in the centre, and candle-snuffer roofs to the turrets. Inside, the walls were up to six feet thick, with vaulted stone ceilings. On the north side was an outbuilding several stories high which was occupied by Monsieur Berthélemy, the archivist to the Templars. As the years passed much of the land had been leased for building purposes, and by 1789 there were no less than four thousand people living within the Temple precincts.

Darkness had fallen by the time the royal family turned under the archway from the street after their long and roundabout journey from the Feuillants. Once in the Palace they were taken to the Salle des Quatre Glaces where eighteen years before Mozart and his sister Nannerl had played before an illustrious company. Food was waiting, ample and well-cooked, though served by men who must have looked more like vagrants than servants, and the royal family was almost too tired to eat. The meal dragged on, but no one had the courage to tell the unfortunates where they would sleep that night, and for many more to come. Pétion even went back to the Hôtel de Ville to say he had authorised them to stay in the Palace itself, only to be overridden by the Commune. Back he went to the Temple and to the little outbuilding which adjoined the keep. Without ceremony or warning, the archivist was expelled, and the rooms hastily prepared for the royal family. There they would stay until the main rooms could be made ready in the keep itself.

The first to arrive was Madame de Tourzel, who came by way of a long tunnel-like passage connecting the Palace with the keep. In her arms she carried the Dauphin who had fallen asleep over his supper. About one o'clock Louis, Marie Antoinette and the remainder of the royal party crossed the grounds, their way lit by torches. All evening the guards had been singing a song which included the refrain—

Madame monte à sa tour,
Ne sait quand descendra.

Madame is climbing to her tower,
Don't know when she'll descend.

For Marie Antoinette, whose face showed no feeling, it would be nearly a year before she descended to make her penultimate journey through Paris to the prison of the Conciergerie on the Ile de la Cité.

Two days after the arrival of the royal family in the Temple, work started in earnest to make either rescue or escape impossible. Furniture was brought from the Tuileries for the rooms they occupied in the little outbuilding, whilst all the remaining houses between the keep and the church were demolished. Soon it stood completely isolated in the midst of a bare patch of ground which by the end of September was enclosed within a high brick wall. The only way in was through two guard-houses, and then there was the outer wall which completely surrounded the Temple and its precincts. In all there were some three hundred National Guards to watch over the handful of prisoners, including gunners who set up their pieces in the main courtyard of the Palace.

Since the Little Tower, as it was called, consisted of only five rooms, space must have been cramped, but on the evening of August 19th the first blow fell. Two muncipal officers came from the Commune with orders that only Louis, Marie Antoinette, the children and Madame Élizabeth were to remain in the Temple. Madame de Lamballe, Madame de Tourzel and her daughter, three waiting women and one or two valets were to be removed elsewhere. Only two valets were left, Cléry and Hue, though the latter also would soon be removed.

Some six months earlier Marie Antoinette had said goodbye for the last time to Axel de Fersen, now for the last time she was saying farewell to Madame de Lamballe. Perhaps this was the occasion when the Queen gave her a ring containing some of her hair, "made white by misfortune".

They were quite alone now, the three adults and two children, at all times under the surveillance of the guards. The first few days were the worst. One of the commissioners of the Commune, an artist called Daujon, left an account of what it was like in the Temple. Each evening the four commissioners who had just come on duty drew lots to decide which two should spend the night with the men already on duty, in the actual rooms which the prisoners were sleeping. One went with Louis, others with the women and children. Then all the doors were locked and the keys placed in a cupboard in the Council Room, which itself was locked and the key kept by the oldest commissary on duty. Quite apart from the fact the royal family was crowded together in the most uncomfortable manner, some of those in charge found additional ways of twisting the knife in the wound. One such was Goret, a municipal officer often on duty at the Temple.

"I was told to address the King simply as Monsieur," he wrote, I had heard that this did not disturb him in the least, but that he was obviously annoyed when addressed as Capet (the family name adopted by the kings of France). This name therefore never left my lips in his presence. At this time he was still wearing his orders, of which he was deprived later on."

Goret was soon to discover that they were not bloodthirsty, mannerless tyrants, but an average family in difficult circumstances. The first time he came on duty, which consisted of staying with them in what passed for a living room, he was ill at ease. To hide his embarrassment he sat in the darkest corner, pretending to read a book, and well away from the royal family who were by the window. Louis and Madame Élizabeth were playing chess, watched by Marie Antoinette and the children.

"Come over here, Monsieur," Marie Antoinette said to Goret, "You will see better to read where we are," but he dared not accept her offer because he knew the National Guards were watching his every move through the keyhole.

Soon it was time for the prisoners to go for their daily walk in the garden, and Louis explained that first they must have permission from the Council at the Temple. It soon arrived.

"Madame Élizabeth came up to me, saying: 'As this is the first time you have been here, Monsieur, perhaps you do not know the correct rules of precedence. I will teach them to you. You lead the way, and we will follow you.' " And off they went out into the garden where Louis and his valet Cléry played ball with the Dauphin. After about an hour they all returned to the Little Tower. "The Queen was left alone with me. She took from a little cabinet a handful of twists of paper, which she came and unfolded before me, saying, 'This is my children's hair—at such-and-such an age' I noticed that all the pieces of hair were more or less fair."

In Goret's opinion the dinner eaten by the royal family that day was "sumptuous", with two different roast meats, puddings and entrées and dessert, plus champagne and red and white wines, though only Louis drank them, the others preferring water. When it was time for bed Goret accompanied Louis to his room, even following him into a little turret where he had gone to say his prayers. "He undressed with Cléry's help, and went to bed. Without undressing I threw myself on a sofa, in the hope of obtaining a little rest, but I found this impossible, for no sooner had the King laid down than he fell into a sleep that not only appeared to be profound, but was accompanied by continuous and truly remarkable snoring."

Had it not been for the continual surveillance under which they were kept, and that even included breaking open the rolls and prodding the insides with either a fork or a finger to see they contained no secret messages, life in the Temple during the second half of August would have seemed almost tranquil after what had gone before.

In the past a library had been installed in the Petit Trianon for Marie Antoinette, but apart from some of the plays and books about the theatre it had remained unread. Now all the family became avid readers: Louis asked for books, and was given over two hundred and fifty, many of them Latin authors, which he read in the original. Marie Antoinette and Madame Élizabeth preferred romances and novels such as *A Thousand and One Nights*, and Fanny Burney's *Evelina*.

Life formed itself into a pattern: the mornings passed with Louis teaching the Dauphin, while Marie Antoinette took Madame Royale's education in hand. After lunch, eaten beneath a poster giving the Declaration of the Rights of Man, the adults played chess or backgammon, and then went down to the garden for air and exercise. Sometimes the National Guards watched the overthrown tyrant at his satanic pleasures—the portly Louis running to and fro trying to make the Dauphin's kite fly.

Although life might seem placid within the Temple itself, perhaps the most repellent figure in the whole history of the Revolution was continually trying to inflame public opinion against the royal family in his journal, *Père Duchesne*. He was Hébert, the Deputy Public Prosecutor, who paid deferential weekly visits to the prisoners in the temple, and then returned to his desk to further blacken their reputations. Continually he demanded that, as he euphemistically called it, "the national razor" should be used on "the boozer and his whore".

Almost on the same day that the royal family were moved to the Temple, the humane killer advocated by the well-meaning Dr. Guillotin was moved from the courtyard of the Conciergerie to the Place du Carrousel, opposite the main entrance of the now deserted Tuileries Palace. Before long "the national razor" would be well and truly installed in the most public place of all, the Place de la Révolution.

The work of demolishing the houses between the keep and the church continued steadily, though the enclosing brick wall had hardly begun to rise. On September 2nd Daujon, the Commissioner of the Commune, was standing beside Louis at the window of his room watching the demolition of a house close by. "He called my attention to the pieces of stone and wood that were on the point of falling; as each piece fell he broke into a roar of the hearty laughter that indicates simple, good-humoured enjoyment. His pleasure was brief. The loud report of a gun checked it; a second report quenched it; a third replaced it with terror. It was the alarm-gun."

Although the royal family did not know it, the Republic was fighting for its life. The Duke of Brunswick had at last invaded France, and already Verdun had capitulated. Paris must prepare its defences, and what Louis and Daujon heard were warning guns, soon to be joined by the tocsin rung from the church towers on the orders of the Commune. It would be a life or death struggle and there must be no risk of a stab in the back from traitors in the capital itself. So, before going off to confront Brunswick's advancing army, there was a job to be done. Notices were posted up: "The people must themselves execute justice. Before we hurry to the frontier, let us put bad citizens to death." The prisons of Paris were filled with "bad citizens", among them non-juring priests, aristocrats and relatives of *émigrés*. Soon the carnage of the September Massacres was under way, and by the time it was over between eleven hundred and fourteen hundred helpless people had been murdered in cold blood.

Whatever speculations the royal family may have been indulging in, they were soon interrupted by the arrival of two commissaries with an order. Monsieur Hue, Louis's valet, was to be removed from the Temple. Louis complained bitterly, but "the women far surpassed him in acrimony, especially Élizabeth, who strode up and down the room, giving vent to her anger in a loud voice, and darting menacing glances at us all. Marie Antoinette seemed deeply affected by this separation: 'It is plain,' she said, 'that the object is to part us from all the people who are most attached to us, and in whom we have placed our confidence.' " (Daujon) To silence the royal family, one of the Commissioners said brutally:

"The alarm-gun has been fired, the tocsin is ringing, and the call to arms is still being beaten; the enemy is at our doors, they are asking for blood; they are demanding heads. Well, it will be yours that they take first!"

Now pleas for their own safety were added to those that Hue should be allowed to stay in the Temple, but the valet had to leave, and was taken to the lockup of the Commune. However he was lucky, and outlived the Revolution.

The killing in the prisons went on all night, but shut away in the Temple the royal family knew nothing of what was going on. All too soon they would find out though. Among those in the Prison de la Force (not far from the Place des Vosges) was Madame de Lamballe. A number of men brought the "little woman dressed in white" out of the entrance, stabbed her to death, and then in the open street perpetrated one obscene outrage after another upon her body. Afterwards more than one "patriot" was proud to claim that he had been the one who ate her heart then and there in the Rue St. Antoine.

Surrounded by a huge and filthy mob the headless and eviscerated body of the Princess was dragged through the streets. Leading the maniacs was a man who had stuck the wretched woman's head on a pike, which was to be taken to the Temple for Marie Antoinette to kiss. At the prison those in charge had warning that a huge crowd was coming up the Rue du Temple, and that it would reach the entrance within five minutes. The authorities knew they were outnumbered and could not control the mob by force, so guile would have to be used. That day Daujon was on duty, and it was he who did most to try to protect Marie Antoinette and the other prisoners from the horrible sight.

Both halves of the main gate were opened, so that the crowd could come as far as the courtyard, but Daujon hung a tricolour sash across the entrance through which anyone must pass to reach the keep on the far side of the Palace. A table was placed in front, and Daujon climbed up, ready to harangue the mob, and make them change their minds about breaking into the keep where the Queen was held.

"At the sight of the honoured symbol the murderous frenzy in the hearts of these men, drunk with blood and wine, seemed to yield to a feeling of respect for the national badge."

The body was dragged right up to the table, and Daujon needed all the courage he could find as they waved their ghastly trophies in his face. He began by telling them that he had heard some wanted to kill the prisoners, but he thought it would be most unwise to destroy such valuable hostages, especially as the enemy was crossing the frontiers. Also, he said, it would look as though they had chosen that way out rather than bring them to trial. His argument worked; the mob thought he had a good point and calmed down. As a compromise a few of them would be allowed to march round the garden.

"These we led towards the tower, and were able to keep them fairly in check till they were joined by the workmen, after which it was more difficult to restrain them." By then it was about three o'clock, and Cléry and the man and wife, by name Tison, appointed by the Commune to wait on the royal family, were sitting down to a meal when the mob gathered outside. Suddenly Madame Tison screamed—she had caught sight of Madame de Lamballe's head being thrust against the window. The revolutionaries laughed wildly, thinking it was Marie Antoinette herself. Cléry and a municipal officer ran upstairs to the room occupied by the royal family. The officer pulled the curtains, saying to the Queen, "They are spreading a rumour that you and your family are no longer in the tower. They want you to appear at the window, but we won't allow it."

Below the window the mob was now calling out that as Marie Antoinette would not show herself they would have to come up to make her kiss the head of her whore. Anxiously the Queen asked what was being hidden from her, and another National Guard bluntly told her it was the head of the Lamballe, "which has been brought here to show you how the people revenge themselves on tyrants". Marie Antoinette fainted away without a sound.

Meanwhile the demonstrators were attempting to force their way into the little tower which adjoined the main keep. Again the quick-witted Daujon saved the situation:

"I praised their courage and their exploits, and made heroes of them. I told them the trophies they were carrying were common property. 'By what right,' I added, 'do you alone enjoy the fruits of your victory? Do they not belong to the whole of Paris? Night is coming on. It is in the Palais Royal or in the Garden of the Tuileries, where the sovereignty of the people has so often been trodden under foot, that you should plant this trophy as an everlasting memorial of the victory you have just won!' "

The bestial mob swallowed his words whole, and streamed out of the precincts of the Temple, back towards the centre of the city, still waving the remains of the wretched Princess.

Quiet returned to the Temple, though the afternoon's events were something none would forget. "My aunt and I heard them beating the call to arms all night," wrote the fifteen-year-old Madame Royale. "My poor mother could not sleep all night. It was only later that we learnt that the massacre had lasted for three days. Another evening at supper-time the call to arms was heard several times. The guards thought the foreigners had come and that horrible Rocher (a turnkey) took his great sabre and said to my father, 'If they come here I shall kill you." It turned out to be nothing but a misunderstanding between patrols."

As the Duke of Brunswick advanced there was talk of abandoning Paris and preparing a line of defence along the Loire. At this Danton showed his contempt for such defeatist talk by having his children and aged mother brought into the capital. Then on September 20th the picture changed. At Valmy, only a few miles from where the royal family had been recognised during their escape as far as Varennes, fifty thousand French confronted thirty-five thousand Prussians. In addition to superior artillery, the French were fighting for their very existence, and the result was an overwhelming defeat for the invaders. Brunswick had to sue for terms, and Dumouriez allowed him to withdraw back over the frontier. Now it was the French who were on the attack. Savoy and Nice were occupied, and along the Rhine the cities of Spier, Worms and Mainz fell to the revolutionary armies. On November 6th the Austrians were defeated at Jemappes in Flanders, and the following week Brussels was captured.

Two days after Valmy, Louis was formally deposed, and the monarchy in France ceased to exist. From being Louis XVI of France and Navarre he became simply Louis Capet, and life for him and his family became harsher day by day.

"They took the newspapers from us," wrote Madame Royale, "fearing we should learn the news from abroad. But one day, full of glee, they brought one to my father, saying it contained something interesting. What a horror! It said that they would put his head inside a red-hot cannon-ball." The girl went on to describe her parents' routine. Louis rose at 7.00 a.m., prayed for an hour, and then he and the Dauphin dressed and went upstairs to join the others for breakfast. After that the father and son came down again for lessons, which lasted until eleven, when they all went for a walk in the Temple gardens. At two they dined, and then the adults played chess, backgammon or picquet. At 4.00 p.m. Marie Antoinette and her sister-in-law and the children returned to their own rooms so that Louis could sleep undisturbed, but two hours later the Dauphin returned for more lessons until supper. At 9.00 p.m. he was settled down for the night by his mother, before she had to go back upstairs, leaving Louis on his own.

"My mother's life was more or less the same as my father's. She worked a lot at her embroidery. My aunt often said prayers during the daytime; she always went through the service of the day, reading many religious books and spending much time in meditation. Like my father, she fasted on the days ordained by the Church."

Rocher, the turnkey who had threatened to kill Louis, was particularly objectionable: "Sometimes he sang the *Carmagnole* and other horrid songs and sometimes, knowing that my father did not like the smell of a pipe, would puff smoke at him as he passed."

None of the royal family met rudeness with rudeness. On one occasion Marie Antoinette called the Dauphin back into the room after he had left without greeting Goret, who entered at that moment.

"My boy, come back, and say good morning to the gentleman as you pass him." The Dauphin did as he was told.

Though cut off from the world outside, news of what was happening filtered its way into the Temple from time to time. One way of passing messages was on the paper used to stop up the necks of the decanters brought into the dining-room, while a woman held up a card for a few seconds at a window in view of the Little Tower with the words "Verdun is taken" written on it. The information was spotted by Madame Élizabeth. Quite openly she asked Goret if he had any newspapers they could borrow, but he dared not let her have any. Thwarted in that direction, she devised an elaborate sign language with Turgy, a royalist servant, who had made his sympathies known.

"For the English, place the right thumb upon the right eye; if they are landing near Nantes, place it on the right ear; if near Calais, on the left ear." There was a sign for nearly every battle front and possible situation. "If the Powers should concern themselves with the royal family, touch the hair with the fingers of the right hand." Turgy never had reason to touch his hair: the other European sovereigns had washed their hands of the French royal family, and that even included Marie Antoinette's relatives in Vienna.

On September 26th Louis was moved from the Little Tower into the rooms prepared for him on the third floor. According to Goret they had been newly decorated, but wooden shutters had been fitted on the outside, set at an angle so light could enter from the top, but making it impossible for anyone to see in or out.

Exactly a month later Marie Antoinette was transferred to her rooms, passing through no less than twelve wicket gates on the newel stair which were so low and so small that a person had to stoop to enter. Also there were massive doors with bolts and chains from the stairs to the rooms themselves. Naturally, all this had a most depressing effect on the spirits of the royal family:

"The father, wife, and sister were together less frequently," wrote Goret. "It seemed they feared to increase their misfortunes by talking about them. The children had lost their playfulness they had maintained till then. The King walked to and fro, and wandered from his room into the outer one where we were sitting. The Queen sat in her room more quietly, but Madame Élizabeth walked to and fro like the King, and often had a book in her hand."

Another of those who came to the Temple was Lepitre, a young professor who became a member of the provisional Commune on December 2nd. With him on duty one morning was Toulan, a man who did all he could to make life more bearable for the royal family. There was a harpsichord by the door of Madame Élizabeth's room, which he tried to play, only to find it was badly out of tune. Marie Antoinette came up to him: "I should be glad to use that instrument, so I can continue my daughter's lessons, but it is impossible in its present condition, and I have not yet succeeded in getting it tuned." Lepitre and Toulan sent out a message, and the harpsichord was tuned the same evening.

"As we were looking through the small collection of music that lay upon the instrument we found a piece called *La Reine de France.*

'Times have changed!' said her Majesty, and we could not restrain our tears."

A day or two later, December 11th, the Dauphin was moved up to his mother's room. Soon enough Louis would discover the reason. He was to be brought to trial.

CHAPTER NINETEEN

Death of a King

Beyond the walls of the Temple much had happened unknown to the prisoners. The Legislative Assembly had been succeeded by a Convention elected in the weeks after the suspension of Louis on August 10th. On September 21st the Convention met for the first time in the Tuileries itself. There it was dominated by a small but vociferous minority, the Montagnards or Men of the Mountain, so called from the seats they occupied high up in the chamber. Politically they were extreme left-wing, and had the backing of the *sans-culottes*. According to them it was Louis himself who engineered the attack on the Tuileries, and with ever increasing vigour they demanded his trial. All who opposed the idea, said the Montagnards, were royalists and not republicans.

A preliminary report of November 8th asserted that the Convention was empowered to try Louis, but the majority of the members were not anxious to see their former king at the bar of the house. Royalist uprisings were feared, and even Danton thought his trial might upset peace negotiations and even lead to the outbreak of further wars. But the Montagnards were relentless. According to them the patriotism of the centre party was suspect because on August 10th they did not abolish the monarchy outright, but merely suspended it; that in itself looked like an attempt to ensure its preservation.

Louis was indicted, and charged with crimes committed before his deposition. On November 13th the debates began in the Convention, but made little progress. Then on November 20th the King's private papers were discovered in a secret cupboard in the Tuileries. Mirabeau's double-dealings, and their price, came to light, as did Lafayette's obvious royalist sympathies. By that time he had defected to the Allies, which was as well for him. Had the Montagnards believed in God, they would undoubtedly have considered the discovery heaven-sent. As it was, from being a hero of the Revolution, Mirabeau was branded an arch-traitor, and was dragged from his grave in the Panthéon.

A new figure was emerging on the political scene—St Just, only twenty-five, clever, good-looking but as cold as ice, a disciple of Robespierre.

The Convention should not consider bringing Louis to trial, he declared, as there was no question of his guilt. Kingship was itself a crime, and Louis should be executed forthwith according to the laws of war. On the 3rd and 4th of December Robespierre elaborated on St Just's statements. Louis had already been tried, by the people who rose against him, and now it was merely a matter of carrying out the sentence.

Opposition was easily silenced, since to object was to risk being labelled a traitor. On December 8th the Convention ordered an indictment to be prepared, and Marat declared that decisions would be reached by *appel nominal*—each must give his reasons for the way he voted, "so that traitors in this Assembly may be known".

Three days later Louis, who had been separated from his family in the Temple, was brought to the bar of the Assembly and charged with encouraging counter-revolution. He behaved with dignity and only showed feeling when he was accused of shedding the blood of Frenchmen. Had he done just that on October 6th, 1789, in order to leave Versailles when the market-women stopped the carriages being taken out of the stables or had he forced a way through the crowd in the small hours of the morning at Varennes on June 22nd, 1791, he would not have been in his present position. All listened in silence to his defence, but considered him guilty.

Among those in the hall at the northern end of the Tuileries was the King's own cousin, the one-time Duc d'Orléans, now Citoyen Egalité, sitting as a deputy for Paris. Two other deputies, Buzot and Salle, suggested there should be a national referendum to decide the King's future, but this, it goes without saying, was opposed by the Montagnards, while Robespierre said such an action might lead to civil war.

Voting began on January 14th. Each deputy had to get up in his turn and give his decisions on four questions. This took several days, and the referendum was rejected by a vote of one hundred and thirty nine. Sentence of death was approved by a majority of fifty-three not, as sometimes stated, by one vote, that of Orléans. Finally, a stay of execution was rejected by seventy votes.

Cléry was with his master on the third floor of the Temple when Monsieur de Malesherbes came from the Assembly. "All is lost," said Louis' counsel to Cléry. "The King has been sentenced to death." When told, Louis showed no emotion, but only gave Monsieur de Malesherbes a warm hug. Later Cléry tried to offer what consolation he could: "Oh, Sire, you must hope for a reprieve. Monsieur de Malesherbes thinks they could not refuse it." But Louis was pessimistic.

"I don't see any hope of that. But it really hurts me to see that Monsieur d'Orléans, my relation, voted for my death."

"The people are disgusted by the infamous behaviour of the Duc d'Orléans. A rumour is going around that the ambassadors of the foreign powers are going to meet and go to the Assembly. In fact, many think the Convention is afraid of a popular uprising."

"I should be truly sorry if that happened," said Louis. "It would mean fresh victims. I am not afraid of death, but it makes me shudder to think of the cruel destiny which awaits my family—the Queen and our poor children."

Then he asked Cléry to look through the books for the volume of a history of England which contained an account of the death of Charles I.

The following day a Municipal Guard came, ostensibly to make an inventory of the King's effects and furniture, but in fact to search for any knife or sharp instrument with which Louis might try to circumvent the last act in the Place de la Révolution.

It was Sunday, January 20th, and Louis was worried because Monsieur de Malesherbes was not allowed to visit him. At two o'clock the door opened and the Executive Council, twelve to fifteen strong, trooped in.

"The King heard the sound of many footsteps outside and, rising to his feet, walked a few paces towards the entrance, but on seeing this large body of people he remained between the door of his room and that of the antechamber, in a noble and imposing attitude."

Garat, the Minister of Justice, who kept his hat on, addressed the King.

"Louis, the National Convention has instructed the Executive Council to inform you of its decrees of the 15th, 16th, 17th, 19th and 20th January."

Gronville, the Secretary of the Council, then read out the decrees in a "weak and trembling voice". Under the first article Louis was declared guilty of conspiracy against the liberty of the nation and of attempting to undermine the safety of the state. Article II declared that he should suffer the death penalty, while the third declared that the document calling for a referendum was null and void. Finally, under Article IV the Executive Council were to inform Louis of the decrees, take the necessary police and security measures and have the sentence carried out within twenty-four hours. Louis was prepared for this, and took out a letter he had written to the National convention asking for a respite of three days, and not to be under continual surveillance, and to be allowed to see his family without the presence of witnesses whenever he wished. He also asked that the National Convention should take care of his family and remove them from the Temple. Finally, he gave Garat a letter with the address of the Abbé Edgeworth de Firmont, asking if he could come to him.

Santerre, who had organised the demonstration at the Tuileries on June 20th the previous year, returned at six in the evening to tell him he could send for the Abbé and be visited in private by his family. With the self-righteousness so common to dictatorships of either left or right, he announced: "The Nation, invariably generous and just, would see to the future of his family. Just payments would be made to his creditors." But a respite of three days was out of the question.

Although she had not been told, Marie Antoinette already knew her husband had been sentenced to death. Toulan, the sympathetic guard, had bribed a paper-seller to shout the latest news within earshot of the Temple keep. That day, January 20th, he cried: "The National Convention decrees that Louis Capet shall undergo the death penalty. The execution shall take place within twenty-four hours of its notification to the prisoner." All day Marie Antoinette wept.

"At seven in the evening they came to inform us that an order from the Convention authorised us to go down to my father," wrote Madame Royale. "We ran to his room and found him very much changed. He wept for our grief, but not on account of his own death."

The whole family then went into the dining-room, which had a glass panel in the door. When it was shut their conversation was inaudible, though the guards could see all that went on. Louis sat down with Marie Antoinette on his left, Madame Élizabeth on his right, Madame Royale facing him and the Dauphin standing between his knees.

"They all leaned towards him," wrote Cléry, "and often embraced him. This sad scene lasted for an hour and three-quarters. One could only see that after each sentence spoken by the King, the princesses started to sob once more and after an interval of minutes the King began to speak again."

According to the Abbé Edgeworth, another of those in the Temple at the time, for the first quarter of an hour no one could speak for tears, and their cries could be heard outside the building itself.

"My son," said Louis, "promise me never to think of avenging my death. You heard what I said? Lift your hand and swear that you will fulfil your father's last request."

At a quarter past ten Louis rose, and they all came out of the dining-room, "groaning and sobbing painfully".

"I assure you," said Louis, "that I shall see you tomorrow at eight o'clock."

"Why not seven o'clock?" asked Marie Antoinette. Louis agreed. It was only a lie to make the situation more bearable. He would never see them again, and he knew it. Urgently the Dauphin begged to be allowed to accompany his father to the scaffold so that he could beg the people to forgive him. Madame Royale fainted, clasping her father round the legs. She was helped up by Madame Élizabeth and Cléry. After embracing each of them in turn Louis said *Adieu*, and went back into his room. "Although the two doors of the King's apartments were closed, one still could hear the cries and lamentations of the princesses on the staircase." (Cléry)

That night Louis slept soundly until he was awakened at 5.00 a.m.

by Cléry lighting the fire. Above, Marie Antoinette had spent a sleepless night, lying dressed on her bed, "trembling with cold and grief". At six o'clock an officer came up to borrow Madame Élizabeth's missal. Louis was to hear Mass and receive Communion. A chest was dragged into the middle of the room to serve as an altar. Watched through the half open door by the guards, Cléry acted as server while the Abbé Edgeworth celebrated Mass for Louis, who knelt on a horsehair cushion.

Paris had been astir since 5.00 a.m., drums beating the call to arms and troops marching to take up their positions along the route from the Temple to the Place de la Révolution. At nine o'clock Santerre almost burst into the King's apartments, accompanied by seven or eight officials and ten gendarmes. The latter formed up in two lines across the room. Louis appeared, handed his will to one of the officials, a constitutional priest. "None of my business," said the man. "I am here to take you to the scaffold . . ." Louis gave it to Gobeau, who was less callous. Then he asked for his hat, shook hands with Cléry and said, "Gentlemen, I would like Cléry to remain with my son who is accustomed to his ministrations. I hope the Commune will grant this request. Let us go now." And with that he walked out of the room towards the stairs.

Above Marie Antoinette, Madame Élizabeth and the children could hear trumpets and then the sound of departing footsteps, but because of the shutters they could not see Louis walking across the courtyard, now surrounded by a high wall. Twice he paused to turn and look up at those blind windows. Then he entered the guardhouse, passed through the Palace and out into the courtyard on the far side where a closed carriage was waiting. A moment later he was gone, away into the morning mist. The day would probably be fine when it cleared later.

"At about ten o'clock," wrote the servant Turgy, "the Queen tried to persuade her children to take some food, but they refused. Soon we heard the report of firearms. Madame Élizabeth raised her eyes to heaven, cried: 'The monsters—now they are content!' The Queen was speechless with grief; the young prince burst into tears; Madame Royale shrieked aloud. Picture the scene! And all the time the drums were rolling and the maniacs who guarded the Temple were shouting their applause."

Though quite unfitted for the role of king, and in many ways inadequate in his everyday life, the man whose last words to the crowd had been drowned by drums on Santerre's orders was none the less good, and there are worse epitaphs than that. On occasions so insensitive and so unimaginative, he yet found time that morning only an hour before he left the Temple to write a note for Cléry:

"I charge you to tell Turgy how greatly I have been pleased with his faithful attachment to me, and with his zeal in carrying out his duties. I give him my blessing, and beg him to continue caring, with equal devotion, for my family, to whom I commend him."

CHAPTER TWENTY

Last Hopes

A wave of horror passed through London, as it did through most of Europe, when news of the death of Louis reached the English capital. In the theatres people stood in silent tribute, shocked and tearful. But in Vienna still no reactions, in spite of goadings by the now quite elderly Mercy. The Widow Capet, as the Revolutionaries contemptuously referred to Marie Antoinette, was an embarrassment to be ignored if not forgotten.

No doubt congratulating itself on its magnanimity, the Commune allowed a seamstress to visit Marie Antoinette to take measurements for mourning clothes, including dresses, a petticoat, fichu, stockings and gloves, all in black. Day after day she sat in an armchair by the window, out of which she could not see, endlessly knitting.

"I remarked how greatly it (the King's death) had affected the whole family," wrote Goret, "and especially the Queen, who had become exceedingly emaciated and was quite unrecognisable. Like her, Madame Élizabeth preserved a melancholy silence; the children, too, were speechless."

Goret, who had done so much to try to soften their existence in the Temple, now suggested the royal family should go out into the courtyard for fresh air.

"We do not want to pass the door of the place which my husband left only to die," said Marie Antoinette without rancour. So Goret suggested they should go up to the top of the keep. The prisoners agreed, and Goret had seats taken on to the roof for their use.

"The princesses remained on this narrow promenade as long as they wished, and returned to it every day when the weather was fine enough. One thing I noticed up to the very last time I was with the princesses, was that their meals were perhaps less sumptuous than in the King's time, though there was nothing lacking. They gave the young prince the same position and precedence they used to give to the King. Everything they wanted was procured by the man Simon." This man was a member of the General Council of the Commune—a shoemaker, uneducated and coarse in both speech and habits. "The princesses summoned him fairly often to bring them anything they might require. His behaviour in their presence was rather free and easy. 'What do you wish for, ladies?' he would say, and then he would try to do what they wanted. If they asked for something that was not in the stores of the Temple, he would run out to the shops. I have heard the Queen say: 'We are lucky to have that Monsieur Simon, who gets us everything we ask for.' "

"Good Monsieur Simon" was to become the man who completely ruined her son's character after his separation from Marie Antoinette. For the present the unofficial Louis XVII was still receiving his education from his mother and his aunt.

"It is impossible not to be touched by the sight of the little king," wrote Lepitre, "bending over his little table, reading the history of France with the greatest attention, then repeating what he had read, and listening eagerly to the observations of his mother or aunt."

By degrees the one-time Queen and her sister-in-law realised they had well-wishers within the Temple who were prepared to do more than look sympathetic. Not only that, but General Jarjays had left the safety of Koblenz to return in secret to Paris. At the beginning of February he was approached by Toulan, the out-and-out republican guard who was now prepared to risk his life for Marie Antoinette.

"You can trust the man who brings this message to you from me. I know his feelings towards me, and they have not altered during the last five months." Toulan did not lack either courage or audacity; he told Marie Antoinette that he would arrange the escape of them all. First it would be as well for General Jarjays to pay her a visit, though Marie Antoinette warned him for God's sake to be careful to avoid recognition, especially by the servant, Madame Tison, who was with them continually.

How would Jarjays be smuggled into the Temple, and into the very rooms occupied by Marie Antoinette? The ingenious Toulan had found a way. Every evening a lamplighter came to the Temple not only to light the lamps which had been set up round the keep to make escape after dark almost impossible, but to clean and trim those in the keep itself. Toulan made himself affable to the man, who was probaby awed by this municipal officer with his tricolour sash, and told him a story that he had a rabidly anti-royalist friend who was longing to get into the Temple simply to have a gloating look at Marie Antoinette in confinement. Money changed hands, the man lent Toulan his clothes and lamplighting equipment for one evening, and in that disguise Jarjays had his interview with Marie Antoinette. Lepitre was drawn into the scheme, at a price of two hundred thousand francs.

"We had obtained some men's clothes for the Queen and Madame Élizabeth, and we brought them in one at a time, either in our pockets or about our persons, hidden under our capes. We also got hold of two padded cloaks to hide their figures from too close scrutiny, and also to hide their walk. Also, we provided two hats specially made, along with scarves and tickets of admission such as those used by the Commissioners of the Commune."

Again the unwitting lamplighter had his use: frequently he was accompanied by his two children, who helped their father with his work. Lepitre and Toulan noted their clothes, and had similar ones made for Madame Royale and her brother. Dirty trousers. a coarse jacket—the carmagnole—thick shoes and shabby hats. The plan was for Madame Royale to walk out through the gate, while the young Louis was smuggled away in a basket full of dirty linen which left the Temple every week. This time there would be no travelling in a slow cumbersome coach drawn by a large number of horses. Three cabriolets would take them to Dieppe, insisted Marie Antoinette, with painful memories of Varennes. The lamplighter came in at about 5.30 p.m. and left before 7.00 p.m., so that if Marie Antoinette asked for her supper not to be served before 9.30 p.m., the discovery of the escape would not be made for several hours; what was more it would take the guards some time to break down the massive ironbound doors leading to her rooms.

Everything was ready. Toulan would offer Tison and his wife Spanish snuff containing a drug that would leave them unconscious for seven or eight hours. Then disaster came: General Dumouriez defected to the Allies (for some months now France had been at war with England), and as a result no more passports were to be issued.

This was Lepitre's province, since he was president of the commission in charge of their issue. Now he had cold feet, and would not hand them over. The whole plan was in jeopardy, and all that could be salvaged was the escape of the Queen herself. Desolately she wrote to Jarjays:

"We have dreamed a pleasant dream, nothing more; but we have gained much by discovering fresh proof of your wholehearted devotion to me. There is no limit to my confidence in you. But whatever may befall, you will always find I am full of character and courage; but my son's interests must be my sole guide. However happy I should have been to escape from this place, I could never agree to leave him. Nothing could bring me joy if I abandoned my children, and so I do not regret giving up the idea."

Even if Marie Antoinette and her children and sister-in-law must remain in the Temple, at least General Jarjays could take the few possessions given by Louis to Cléry on the morning of his execution to Provence and Artois. There was a seal from the King's watch, the wedding ring used at the marriage by proxy April 19th, 1770, in Vienna, and locks of hair from all his family. Cléry had not been allowed by the Commune to give them to Marie Antoinette; instead they were kept under seal in the Council Room. That was too much for Toulan, who stole them for his Queen. Now these few treasures were on their way to the frontier in the General's care.

"Adieu," Marie Antoinette wrote to him. "If you have made up your mind to leave, I think that the sooner you go the better. I am so sorry for your poor wife! What happiness if we can meet again before long. I shall never be able to show all the gratitude I feel for all you have done for me. Adieu—how cruel is the word!"

Although neither Marie Antoinette nor General Jarjays knew of it, yet another escape plan was reaching maturity. In pre-revolutionary France the Baron de Batz had been a financier, and now from a place of hiding he was preparing to use his wealth to help the Widow Capet. Michonis, a one-time lemonade-seller turned inspector of prisons, was only too willing to be bribed. Cortey, the military governor of the section in which the Temple was located, was no better, and before long Baron de Batz was actually on guard at the prison. Day by day the sentries were replaced by men chosen by the

Baron, with the connivance of Cortey, until they were strong enough to take over the building from its appointed guardians. All was set for the night of June 21st, and Michonis was already in the Queen's rooms, waiting to play his part. Cortey marched into the precincts with a detachment of soldiers. Later they were to march out again with the young Louis and the three women, wearing military cloaks, in their midst. But at 11.00 p.m. Simon returned hot foot from the Commune to see if all was well. Earlier, he had been sent an anonymous letter betraying the plan by warning him not to trust Michonis that night.

It was no use going through with the escape. The guards who were not in the plot were now on the alert. So, as the shoemaker hurried up the stairs to the Queen's rooms to assure himself she was still there, Cortey, together with Batz, marched away into the darkness. Michonis went with Simon to the Commune, where he succeeded in making the shoemaker look at best a zealous patriot and at worst a fool who had been hoaxed by an anonymous letter. Acting on the principle that there could be no smoke without fire, a number of commissaries were dismissed, among them Toulan and Lepitre; both had been denounced by Madame Tison. In November of that year Lepitre was charged with having had an understanding with Marie Antoinette, but was acquitted and set free. The faithful Toulan was less fortunate; he fled to Bordeaux, where he lived under an assumed name, but was arrested, tried and condemned to death.

As if Marie Antoinette, Madame Élizabeth and the children had not enough to bear in the darkened rooms, their constant and unwelcome companion, Madame Tison, was obviously going out of her mind.

"After a time," wrote Madame Royale, "she would not go out into the air and then she began to talk to herself, Madame Tison kept talking about her sins and the ruin of her family, as well as about the prison and the scaffold. She thought that the people she had denounced had been put to death. Every evening she waited to see whether the municipal guards she had denounced would come or not. When she did not see them, she went to bed and had terrible dreams which made her worse."

Finally it took eight men to remove her from the keep, first into the old palace, and then to the Hôtel Dieu.

Marie Antoinette really was a prisoner under strict surveillance, and from now until the end, her life became a dialogue with Hébert, the man who would finally send her to the Place de la Révolution. Born into a comfortable home at Alençon in 1757, Hébert was an unruly youth who drifted away to Paris where he worked in the box-office of the Théâtre des Variétés. With the Revolution he discovered his métier as a scurrilous journalist. From editing *Père Duchesne*, the foulest rag in the city, he became assistant prosecutor of the Commune. Then in 1793 he headed an anti-Christian campaign in France, and his fate is one that can be contemplated with equanimity: guillotined during the height of the Terror in March, 1794.

At eleven o'clock one night he appeared in Marie Antoinette's room, and for five hours ransacked her possessions and the furniture. Even an old hat which had belonged to Louis and was found under a bed was regarded as an object of the gravest suspicion, as was a stick of sealing wax and an empty pencil-holder. Other similar late-night searches followed, and on July 3rd six officials of the Commune tramped up the stairs and into the apartment on the top floor. They came with a decree from the Committee of Public Safety ordering mother and son to be separated. Henceforth the young Louis would be kept in the rooms below, once occupied by his father, with Citizen Simon as his "tutor".

"When my brother heard this he started screaming and threw himself into my mother's arms begging not to be taken from her." And Marie Antoinette stood by his bed and refused to let him go. An hour passed in argument and insults which reduced the prisoners to tears. Madame Royale continues:

"At last my mother agreed to part with her son. We got him up and when he was dressed my mother handed him over to the municipals after bathing him in tears, as if she realised she would never see him again."

From now on the Queen, Madame Élizabeth and Madame Royale were locked in their rooms alone; the guards had been withdrawn, and the only time they saw them was when their meals were brought up three times a day. Again and again Marie Antoinette begged to be allowed to see her son, but the request was never granted. Sometimes Tison gave her scraps of news, but now her only consolation was to stand for hours by a small barred window near the stairs. Sometimes, if she were lucky, she could just glimpse her son playing in the courtyard. To make matters worse, when he was in the rooms below, she could hear him singing the *Ça Ira*, the *Carmagnole* and the *Marseillaise* at the top of his voice. Already Simon had begun the transformation of the eight-year-old Louis XVII into a foul-mouthed gutter-snipe.

CHAPTER TWENTY-ONE

Seventy-six Days

Few happenings concerning the royal family during the Revolution are more horrifying than the speed with which the ruination of the Dauphin's character was achieved by Simon and his associates in the Temple. At the beginning of February, Moëlle, a member of the Commune, wrote of the eight-year-old he helped to guard: "This royal child had the most noble and most lovable face. His figure was perfect, and at that time he enjoyed the most excellent health. His bright, intelligent remarks, and his habitual merriment, bore witness to a charming character."

Yet within a month of being separated from his mother he had turned into a cold-blooded monster. Daujon, who prevented the mob carrying the head of Madame de Lamballe from reaching the royal family, recorded one of the child's remarks.

"One day I was having a little game of bowls with him: it was after his father's death, and he was separated from his mother and aunt by order of the Committee of Public Safety. The room we were in was beneath that occupied by his family, and we heard sounds as though someone were jumping and dragging chairs about, which made quite a noise over our heads. With an impatient gesture the child said, 'Haven't those damned whores been guillotined yet,' " Only a month before, at the very latest, he had cried for two days at being separated from his mother.

On two occasions an English spy in Paris talked with Simon after the latter had given up his duties as "tutor" at the Temple. According to him the child was taught to swear, blaspheme, curse his family, encouraged to drink and instead of being educated was given obscene books. From time to time the boy became aware of the situation in which he found himself, and started to cry. When that happened the commissaries distracted his attention with brandy and billiards, while the infamous Hébert on several occasions threatened to have him guillotined. That so terrified him that he fainted outright. What is more, Hébert would have had no compunction about carrying out the threat. In *Père Duchesne* he wrote: "Sooner or later this brat will bring disaster on you; for the more amusing he is the more he is to be feared. The best thing would be to maroon the young snake and his sister on a desert island, for we must be rid of them whatever the price. Anyway, what does one child more or less matter when the safety of the Republic is at stake?"

All too well Simon succeeded in obliterating the child's royal background, and before long he had turned the young Louis into a thorough-going *sans-culotte*, clad in a carmagnole jacket and wearing a red bonnet. His health deteriorated rapidly: according to his sister he put on weight, but did not grow in stature. Soon the boy withdrew into himself, and the last picture we have of the child who was technically King of France and Navarre is horrifying. Again it is drawn by Madame Royale. She tells how his bed was not made for six months, that both it and he were alive with bugs and fleas, chamber-pots remained unemptied and since the windows were never opened the smell was unbearable. Two years later, on June 8th 1795, Louis is reputed to have died, still in his stinking room in the Temple.

On the top floor the two women and the fifteen-year-old girl knew nothing of what was going on in the city beyond the Temple precincts. Much had happened, and was still happening, since the execution of Louis. The Revolution had entered its most extreme phase: the Terror had begun and as Madame Roland would one day exclaim at the foot of the scaffold, it was consuming its own children. Danton and Robespierre still towered over all others, but one figure had already vanished from the scene: Marat, the editor of *L'Ami du Peuple*, had been stabbed by Charlotte Corday as he sat writing in his medicinal bath. In the Vendée, in western France, the royalists had risen and captured the town of Saumur, while Brittany and Normandy were of doubtful loyalty. Worse still was the news from the Belgian and eastern frontiers. The French in Mainz were isolated, and on July 28th the great fortress of Valenciennes fell to the Allies.

"It is time to root out every trace of the monarchy," exclaimed the deputy for the Hautes-Pyrénées at the bar of the Convention. Unanimously it was agreed that Marie Antoinette must be brought to trial, if only in the hope that such an action might make the Allies more cautious and slow the pace of their advance. The infamous Revolutionary Tribunal had been set up in March that year with Fouquier-Tinville as the Public Prosecutor. "Let us be terrible, to spare the people being terrible," declared Danton. Marie Antoinette must appear before the Tribunal, a pawn in the game of international politics. The revolutionaries were overestimating the importance of the Widow Capet; to the rest of Europe she was of no consequence. The monarchs of Europe were only really interested in saving their own skins; that is, in preventing the spread of republicanism to their countries.

Once again Marie Antoinette was awakened in the middle of the night. At 2.00 a.m., August 2nd, Michonis together with a number of officers and gendarmes entered the room where the prisoners were sleeping. A decree from the Convention was read out ordering the Widow Capet's removal to the Conciergerie to stand trial. Promptly Madame Élizabeth and Madame Royale asked to be allowed to accompany her, but the decree was specific—only Marie Antoinette was to be moved.

Quickly the Queen gathered together her clothes and made them into a bundle. Then, with the men still watching, she had to dress. Now she was searched, and only allowed to keep her watch, a handkerchief and a bottle of smelling salts. Other personal possessions were made into a packet, which would be opened in the presence of the Tribunal. Goodbyes were brief to her daughter and sister-in-law. None was under any illusions about the implications of a transfer to the Conciergerie, and they knew it was goodbye forever.

For the first time since his execution Marie Antoinette passed her husband's door, as she descended the winding stair. At the bottom she forgot to stoop as she passed through the last of the wicket gates, and hit her forehead a hard blow.

"Have you hurt yourself?" asked Michonis anxiously.

"No, nothing can hurt me now," replied Marie Antoinette.

Surrounded by mounted gendarmes, the Queen drove away from the Temple in a small carriage. Down the Rue du Temple to the square in front of the Hôtel de Ville, over the Pont au Change, and into the Cour de Mai, surrounded on three sides by the Palais de Justice. Three massive towers, César, d'Argent and Bonbec, look on to the northern arm of the Seine flowing past the Ile de la Cité. Once part of the old palace of the French Kings, the Palais de Justice was now the nerve centre of the Revolution, and in the Tour Bonbec the ruthless Fouquier-Tinville had his office. Below the Palais, and an integral part of it, was the Conciergerie, for the most part a collection of small rooms, but including a great vaulted chamber, at that time divided with wooden partitions. That was the Souricière, the Mousetrap, where so many spent their last night on earth. Beyond, in the courtyard, was a bell—still there today—which was rung to inform all concerned that the tumbrils had arrived to transport the latest batch of victims to their deaths in the Place de la Révolution.

Some hours previously Madame Richard, the wife of the gaoler at the Conciergerie, had taken her young maid aside and warned her, "Rosalie, we shall not go to bed tonight. You are to sleep in a chair. The Queen is going to be moved to this prison from the Temple."

Marie Antoinette was to be placed in the cell occupied by General Custine. The General had succeeded the traitorous Dumouriez as commander of the armies in the north, but after his withdrawal from Mainz he too fell from favour and on July 22nd had been arrested. Now he was hastily turned out of his cell, half below ground and permeated with damp. An arched window looked out on to the Cour des Femmes, used by the women prisoners for exercise.

Quickly it was refurnished, and a folding bed, two mattresses, a bolster, an eiderdown, two chairs, a table and a wash-basin were put in for the Queen's use. Three o'clock in the morning found both Rosalie Lamorlière and the turnkey Lariviere fast asleep in their chairs. Knocking woke Larivière, and on opening the iron grating in the main door he saw "a tall beautiful woman being brought in by several officers and officials of the prison. She was dressed in a long black garment, which enhanced the extraordinary whiteness of her skin."

At the same moment Madame Richard was shaking the young girl by the arm.

"Come, Rosalie, come, wake up! Take this candlestick—they are coming!"

The two women went to the cell and found Marie Antoinette had already reached it ahead of them, and details of her admission were being entered in the prison register. "Widow Capet, aged 38." Soon the Queen was alone with Madame Richard and Rosalie Lamorlière. It was stiflingly hot, and Rosalie noticed the perspiration running down Marie Antoinette's face. From time to time she wiped it away with her handkerchief. "She looked around with astonished eyes at the awful bareness of the room, and with a certain amount of interest at the gaoler's wife and myself." Then she stood on a stool which Rosalie had brought from her own room, and hung her watch on a rusty nail quite high up on the wall. It was the watch she had retained ever since she left Vienna so many years ago, in what must now have seemed another existence. But Marie Antoinette had at least one familiar face with her. Evidently she entered the Conciergerie with a pug dog, though curiously enough no one seems to have mentioned its existence in the Temple. It lived on in the prison as the pet of the gaoler after the Queen's execution and was still there in 1796.

All the clothes the Queen had on arrival were those she stood up in: a mourning dress and a large mourning bonnet. For the first few days Madame Richard dared not compromise herself by even lending the Queen a few of her own clothes. Who could blame her? Later, when another gaoler called Bault tried to obtain a decent eiderdown for Marie Antoinette, Fouquier-Tinville went into a rage. "How dare you ask for such a thing? You deserve to be sent to the guillotine." Coming from such a man, he undoubtedly meant what he said. Finally it was Michonis, the inspector of prisons, who went to the Temple and arranged for clothes to be sent to the Conciergerie. Ten days after her arrival Marie Antoinette received a parcel. "It contained some lovely cambric chemises, some handkerchiefs, some fichus, stockings of black silk or filoselle, a white wrapper to wear in the morning, some nightcaps and coloured pieces of ribbon of various widths. Turning to Madame Richard and me she said: 'From the careful way in which all these things are arranged, I can recognise the thoughtfulness and the hand of my poor sister Élizabeth.' "

Thanks to Madame Richard, the Queen's very large mourning bonnet was unpicked and made up again into two smaller and more practical caps. As souvenirs she gave Rosalie the wire frame and cambric left over and returned by the seamstress. In her cell Marie Antoinette had neither a cupboard nor a drawer in which to put her clothes, and so she asked for a box to keep them from getting dusty. "Madame Richard did not dare pass on this request to the prison authorities, but she allowed me to lend the Queen a cardboard box, who welcomed it as though she had been give the most beautiful piece of furniture in the world." Nor was she allowed to have a mirror, so the goodhearted Rosalie lent her her own. "It made me blush to offer it, for I had bought the mirror on the quays and it only cost twenty-five sous in assignats. I can see it still. It was edged with red, and had Chinese faces painted on each side of it."

In addition to Rosalie, the turnkey's old mother helped look after the Queen. Madame Larivière was horrified at the state of her dress—torn under both arms and with the hem frayed from the stone flags on the floor of the Temple, and sent out her son to buy half a yard of cloth, needles and threads. For the first time in many months Marie Antoinette was among humble people who had no desire to hurt or insult her feelings. On the debit side were the two gendarmes, one a sergeant, who were permanently on duty in her cell. Decent enough in themselves—the gendarme Gilbert used to bring her flowers—it was an affront to her dignity and feelings as a woman that the only privacy she had was behind a screen four feet high. That was all that stood between her and the gendarmes when she dressed, undressed and relieved nature. Sometimes the men played picquet, but for most of the day they just sat, smoking, drinking and staring in her direction.

One by one the few remaining links with her former life were broken: the first to go was her gold watch, confiscated only four days after her arrival in the Conciergerie. Later Madame Richard told Rosalie that the Queen had wept bitterly at its loss. At least she still had a locket on a cord round her neck of which the authorities were unaware. It was of the Dauphin, and also contained a lock of his hair. Also, for a few weeks she still had her rings. "Although she was unaware of the fact, the two diamond rings made a kind of plaything for her. As she sat dreaming, she would take them off and put them on again, passing them from one hand to the other several times in a minute."

By now Marie Antoinette looked more like a woman of sixty than one of nearly forty, though, according to Rosalie, her hair was not entirely white. "I noticed patches of white hair on her temples. There was none on the top of her head nor in the rest of her hair. Her Majesty told us that this was due to her distress on the 6th of October."

The narrative dictated by Rosalie Lamorlière, for she was illiterate, is full of such details which though perhaps unimportant in themselves are both touching and pathetic. On one occasion Madame Richard thought it would provide a diversion if she took her youngest son for Marie Antoinette to see. Fanfan, as he was nicknamed, was an attractive, fair-haired child; but at the sight of him the Queen took him in her arms, smothered him with kisses and burst into tears. Then she started to talk about the Dauphin, admitting that she thought about him night and day. Afterwards Madame Richard regretted bitterly that, unwittingly, she had caused such unhappiness to Marie Antoinette.

Another eyewitness was a glazier sent to replace two panes of glass in her cell. "I saw the Queen seated in front of her bed with her eyes fixed on her work (knitting or needlework). Two gendarmes, armed with swords and muskets, were in the opposite corner, with their faces towards the Queen, and a woman of the people, sitting between the Queen's chair and the door, watching me closely. While I was putting in my first pane of glass the sound of a harp came from the upper windows of the prison. Her Majesty put down her work and listened to the music, which I thought seemed to please her. Then this great princess said to me: '*Monsieur le Vitrier*, do you think that the harp we hear is being played by some woman in the prison?"

"Madame," I answered at once, "the person playing does not belong to the prison. She is the daughter of one of the registrars . . ." The woman Harel looked at me in an irritated way, and reduced me to silence. The Queen noticed by my expression that there had been an order of this nature, and lowered her eyes."

Harel, the "woman of the people", was the woman brought in to take over from old Madame Larivière. Marie Antoinette disliked this hard bitten wife of a police official, as well she might, for she was an informer.

Harsh though her living conditions were, the food served to Marie

Antoinette was unexpectedly good. "Her Majesty had quite a good appetite. She cut her chicken in two, that is, to make it last two days. She stripped the bones with incredible ease and care. She never left any of the vegetables that composed her second dish." When the market women knew for whom M. Richard was shopping, they always selected the best poultry and fruit, saying, "For our Queen."

Although it was still summer, the damp in the cell rotted Marie Antoinette's clothes and covered her shoes with mildew. Usually the Queen wore a pair of low slippers, but she also had a pair *à la Saint-Huberty*, with two-inch heels. "One day, to my astonishment," Rosalie dictated years later, "the officer (on duty) took up one of the Queen's shoes himself and using the point of his sword scratched off the mildew from the damp bricks, as I was doing myself with my knife. The imprisoned priests and nobles watched our proceedings from the yard, through the grating that divided us from them. Seeing that this officer of the constabulary was a good fellow they begged me to come nearer so that they could see the Queen's shoe close to. They took it from me, and passing it from hand to hand, covered it with kisses."

Another time when Rosalie was carrying the remains of Marie Antoinette's meal across the courtyard, an American who had business at the registrar's office came up and asked:

"Did the Queen drink the water that has gone from this glass?" Rosalie said "yes". The American bared his head, and drank the remainder.

In spite of the bolts, bars, guards and spies the Conciergerie was by no means sealed off from the outside world. At this time, the summer of 1793, it was not occupied exclusively by political prisoners; in fact, offenders of all kinds mixed freely. Letters continually passed to and fro, and occasionally visitors were smuggled in. Considering the strictness of the surveillance under which Marie Antoinette had to live, it is remarkable how many people gained entry to her cell. Michonis made frequent calls, apparently to satisfy himself that the security measures were being maintained, but also to whisper what news he could about her children and Madame Élizabeth in the Temple.

Some of those who came were merely curious to see the Queen in her misfortune, but one was a painter, believed to be Prieur, who painted what was to be her last portrait. In it she is simply dressed in a black gown, her neck and shoulders covered by a white wrap and wearing one of the two caps made from her large mourning bonnet. Considering her privations the face is remarkably unaltered, and fuller than might have been expected. It is the eyes that are changed. In Kucharski's unfinished pastel they had a look of weariness, but now there was a gentleness never seen before, almost humility. No longer the hint of arrogance, but the air of one who has come to accept whatever the future may hold. "Nothing can hurt me now," said Marie Antoinette after hitting her head as she left the Temple, and her eyes show the truth of that simple statement.

Before long Monsieur Richard followed the example set by the inspector of prisons and started allowing people into the Queen's cell when it was safe to do so. One who saw the Queen was a Mademoiselle Fouché, after bribing Richard with gold.

"There are four gendarmes who guard the prisoner," warned the gaoler, "two are devils, but the other are two good lads. They relieve each other at midnight, so come at half past."

Mademoiselle Fouché not only visited Marie Antoinette, but if her story is true it was she who arranged for the Queen to receive the Abbé Magnin, a non-juring priest who on several occasions had entered the Conciergerie, with the Host in a box round his neck, to minister to those under sentence of death. According to his own testimony, given years later, he twice entered the Queen's cell, heard her confession and gave holy communion.

Suddenly, on August 28th everything was altered for the worse. Michonis had brought yet another visitor with him on his rounds. This time it was the self-styled Chevalier de Rougeville, who had led Marie Antoinette, Madame de Lamballe and others to safety during the demonstration in the Tuileries on June 20th the previous year. Almost at once Marie Antoinette recognised him and flushed with excitement. Taking two carnations from his buttonhole he threw them on the floor, and looked intently at her. She showed no comprehension, so as he left with Michonis he whispered to her to pick up his note.

Michonis was standing outside the window, and Marie Antoinette asked Gilbert, the gendarme on duty, to complain about her food. While the man's back was turned she picked up the carnations and discovered a note in each. One assured her of de Rougeville's loyalty, and asked if she wanted three or four hundred louis for bribes; the other apparently contained a plan of escape.

A quarter of an hour later de Rougeville returned with Michonis, and asked if she was prepared to attempt to escape. She was. He promised to return in two days' time with the money. Immediately he had gone Marie Antoinette decided to try and enlist Gilbert's help. The man was sympathetic, and had not reported Mademoiselle Fouché or the Abbé Magnin for visiting the Queen. What happened next is confused and contradictory. According to Gilbert, Marie Antoinette at once pricked out an answer with a pin on a piece of paper, which was handed to Madame Richard with the instruction that it was to be given to the stranger—de Rougeville—when he returned. Madame Richard lost her nerve and told Michonis. Since he was undoubtedly in the plot, the information was not likely to go any further as far as he was concerned. However, after a week had elapsed, Gilbert decided it was his duty to report the matter to the authorities. This he did on September 3rd, but the night before there had already been an abortive attempt to rescue the Queen from the Conciergerie. According to de Rougeville, he and Michonis went to the prison late that night saying they had come to take Marie Antoinette back to the Temple, but in reality to take her to General Jarjays' house outside Paris, before escaping to Germany. But because of the threatening attitude of one gendarme the whole scheme foundered. Rosalie gives quite another version, saying that the informer Harel saw de Rougeville trying to slip the Queen a note and told Fouquier-Tinville, who ordered an inquiry. Anyway, officials appointed by the Convention cross-examined Marie Antoinette, who at first denied everything. Michonis was also interrogated when he returned to the Conciergerie. He still had the note (which survives), but had made it quite illegible with additional pinpricks. He tried to dismiss the whole affair as a storm in a tea cup, though admitting he had been talked into conducting some man, whose name he didn't even know, along to the Queen's cell, Madame Richard admitted handing him the note, but insisted she knew nothing more about the affair.

When Marie Antoinette realised that Gilbert, Michonis and Madame Richard had at least in part admitted there was something curious going on, she too admitted that de Rougeville had given her a note in a carnation. But she refused to implicate Michonis. However he was arrested, as were Richard and his wife, though the latter couple was not imprisoned until a week later. On September 4th a minute search was carried out in the Queen's cell, the furniture even being overturned in search for clues.

Life for Marie Antoinette would now become harsher than it had ever been at any time before. Another cell was prepared, further away from the entrance to the Conciergerie, from which escape would be impossible. Of the three windows it contained, only one was left and that was boarded up to about half its height. Iron bars were fitted and a massive new door, two inches thick, set in place. On September 14th Marie Antoinette was moved into her new quarters. Now, instead of having gendarmes in the room with her, one was posted outside the door, while the other stood in the courtyard watching her every move through the window. At least she still had Rosalie to look after her as best she could.

"She thought deeply, and sighed, as she walked to and fro in the cell. One day she noticed in a room with iron bars opposite her own that there was a woman prisoner praying with hands clasped and eyes turned up to heaven. 'Rosalie', this noble and good princess said to me, 'Look up there at that poor nun. How earnestly she is praying to God!' No doubt the nun was praying for the Queen. This was the way the ladies in the prison spent all their time."

Years before Marie Antoinette had lacked the patience to read all but the lightest novels to the end, yet since her incarceration she had become an avid reader of travel books—*Captain Cook's Adventures*; *The History of Famous Shipwrecks*; and one which gave particular pleasure, *A Voyage to Venice*. In it she found many places mentioned she had known in her childhood in Vienna.

In place of the kindly Richard and his wife the new gaoler was Monsieur Bault from La Force Prison. The Commune had made it clear that he was responsible for the Queen's safety with his own life, and consequently he appeared unnecessarily severe, not to say on edge. The first time he came into the cell, wearing a carmagnole jacket, bareheaded and holding his keys, he found Rosalie about to dress Marie Antoinette's hair for the day.

"Rosalie, I want you to put up my chignon for me today," she said. But Bault pushed forward, took the comb and said loudly: "Leave it alone, leave it alone; that's my job." Marie Antoinette looked at him with surprise, and said, "No, thank you." Then she dressed it herself. Taking up a white ribbon she handed it to Rosalie, saying, "Take this ribbon, and always keep it in memory of me." When Bault and the girl had left the cell he turned to her and said, "I am very sorry to have annoyed that poor woman, but my position is so difficult that the least thing is enough to frighten me. I can't forget that my comrade Richard and his wife are in prison. For Heaven's sake, Rosalie, don't do anything silly, or I'm lost."

Hardly anything was left to the Queen; even her underclothes were confiscated, and she was only allowed one chemise at a time at infrequent intervals, as instructed by the Revolutionary Tribunal. Again Rosalie tried to help, by slipping her own chemises under the Queen's bolster when she made her bed. A worse privation was not being allowed candles. The evenings were drawing in, but Marie Antoinette could not even pass the time reading. The only light to enter her cell was from a lamp in the Cour des Femmes outside her half boarded-up window.

"I spun out as long as possible the various little preparations for the night," recalled the young girl many years later, "so that my revered mistress might not be left alone in the dark until the last possible minute." All too soon Marie Antoinette would be quite alone, sitting in the near-dark, remembering the past, and thinking of those she had known and loved—so many of them were dead now.

In August it was the heat that had troubled her, but now at the beginning of October it was the cold and damp.

"She complained of it in her gentle way; and as for me I was so upset because I could do nothing to make things easier for her. In the evenings I took her nightgown from under the bolster and ran up to my room to get it really hot at the fire. Then I put it back under the bolster along with the large fichu the Queen wore at night."

If Marie Antoinette had only one real friend in the Conciergerie, perhaps it is true to say she had only one other in all Europe—Fersen. Even Mercy was indifferent to the Swede's pleas begging him to exert all his influence with Vienna. The old Austrian had never liked the Queen's lover, and chose this time to show it. Fersen turned to the *émigré* Comte de la Marck and begged him to try his powers of persuasion. Mercy finally agreed, and a letter was written to the Commander in Chief of the Austrian forces, pointing out that Marie Antoinette's death might be only a matter of days. "Do you think posterity will find it credible that such a crime could be carried out within a few days' march of the victorious armies of Austria and England without some effort being made to stop it?" The only reply Mercy received was to the effect that if anything did happen to Marie Antoinette the four members of the convention held prisoner by the Austrians would be put to death.

Mercy then wrote direct to the Austrian Emperor, pointing out that future generations would hold him to blame if he did nothing to try to save his aunt. Francis, if he even saw the letter, never replied. Like the other crowned heads of Europe, he was prepared to bear with fortitude the misfortunes of the helpless woman—whose sight was now starting to fail—locked away in the innermost part of the Conciergerie.

CHAPTER TWENTY-TWO

Le Palais de Justice

"A woman, the shame of mankind and of her sex, the Widow Capet, must at long last pay for her crimes on the scaffold. Many think that she has been transferred to the Temple, that she has been tried secretly, and that she has been whitewashed by the Revolutionary Tribunal. The thought that a woman responsible for the deaths of thousands of Frenchmen could ever be acquitted by a French Court is preposterous. I demand that this week the Revolutionary Tribunal shall pass judgement on her case."

Not only did Billaud-Varenne demand the death of Marie Antoinette as an act of revolutionary justice, but as a terrible example which should stiffen morale; a warning not only to the enemies of France beyond its frontiers, but also to the city of Lyon, which like the Vendée, was in a state of revolt.

Hébert, writing in *Père Duchesne*, was equally outspoken in his demands: ". . . we must satisfy the *sans-culottes*. They will kill all our enemies, but their ardour must be fed with Marie Antoinette's death. Remember that the way to make them risk all is by persuading them that in such a crisis as this, whatever the outcome, their anonymity is their safeguard and only we are answerable for everything. In this way they will give us every help, since they take the profits while we run the risks."

Even if the outcome of the trial was a foregone conclusion, the gesture must still be made. Now judges and jurors were appointed to the Revolutionary Tribunal, and on October 5th Fouquier-Tinville informed the Convention that he required documents on which to ground his case for the prosecution. But surprisingly little documentary evidence was available, and none of it sufficiently overwhelming to send Marie Antoinette to the guillotine on a wave of public disapproval.

Hébert decided that he must be able to bring a charge so devastating that there could be no chance of an acquittal. In history there was the precedent he required, though whether he used it consciously is another matter. When Henry VIII tired of Anne Boleyn and wished to be rid of her without the delays of a protracted divorce, she was charged with having an incestuous relationship with her brother. Marie Antoinette would be charged with a similar relationship with her eight-year-old son. The Revolution had reached its lowest ebb, so for that matter had human nature.

In the two months since his separation from Marie Antoinette the young Louis had been alternately coaxed and bullied, made to feel like a grown-up, and treated like a criminal. He may well have reached the point when he would say whatever his interrogators wanted to hear, in the hope of being left alone. Also, even his mother had been aware when he was still only four years old that he was something of a liar. When Madame de Tourzel took up her duties as governess, Marie Antoinette wrote: "Quite often he will elaborate what he has heard, without meaning to tell lies. This is indeed his chief fault, and the one above all others which must be corrected."

Now Hébert was with him in the Temple, firing questions he could not understand, and putting answers into his mouth. Both Daujon and Goret were present at the cross-examination: in fact Daujon had to take down the notes.

"The young prince," recorded Daujon, "was sitting in an armchair, swinging his little legs, for his feet did not reach the ground. He was examined about the statements in question, and was asked if they were true: he answered affirmatively. At once Madame Élizabeth, who was present, cried out, 'Oh, the monster!' " "As for me," added Daujon, "I could not consider this answer came from the child himself, because of his air of uneasiness and his whole manner made me feel it was a suggestion put to him by another person—and that he may have been threatened with punishment or ill-treatment if he did not comply."

The venom contained in the obscene and scurrilous pamphlets published over the last fifteen years was really working now, fed in particular by the vitriolic pen of Madame de la Motte—until her timely death in London in 1791. That, then, would be the explosive charge to be hurled at Marie Antoinette by the unspeakable Hébert.

Since her transfer to another cell she had been alone, though continually watched through the window, but after October 5th Lieutenant de Busne of the gendarmerie was on duty, separated from her by a screen. Some two hours after going to bed on October 12th, Marie Antoinette was made to dress again, and taken to the Grand' Chambre in the Palais de Justice. There, seven years before, Madame de la Motte and her accomplices had stood their trial. Now, by the light of only two candles Marie Antoinette found herself facing Fouquier-Tinville, the deputy public prosecutor, and Hermann, the President of the Revolutionary Tribunal. At this point he was only presiding as an examining magistrate at the preliminary hearing which would precede the trial itself.

Calmly and clearly Marie Antoinette answered the first question:

"I was Marie Antoinette of Lorraine-Austria, widow of Louis Capet, sometime King of the French, thirty-eight years old." First she was questioned about her political activities before the Revolution on behalf of the Emperor of Austria, though Hermann pointedly referred to him by his lesser title of "King of Bohemia and Hungary". The charge of acting against the interests of France was all too true, though naturally Marie Antoinette denied the accusation. Hermann moved on to the equally well-founded charge of squandering the country's finances on her pleasures and intrigues. Again she denied that such statements were justified, so Hermann declared that she had led her husband astray, and taught him to dissemble and deceive the French people, "who could not believe that wickedness and perfidy could be carried to such lengths."

Marie Antoinette agreed that the people had been deceived, but not by her or the King: "By those who had an interest in deceiving them, but it was not in our interests to deceive them." Her answer was collected, and with an edge.

"Never for a moment since the Revolution," declared Hermann, "have you stopped intriguing with foreign powers and against liberty at home."

Again her denial, but this time Hermann could refer to concrete evidence: the papers in the secret cupboard in the Tuileries, though he did not tell Marie Antoinette of the discovery itself. Next there was the escape to Varennes. Outright, Hermann blamed her:

"Beyond doubt it was you who ruled Louis Capet and talked him into escaping." When charged with engineering the war between France and Austria, the Queen reminded Hermann that it was France which made the declaration, and that Louis had only done so on instructions from his councillors. Then Hermann doubled back four years to the banquet given in the opera house at Versailles for the officers of the Flemish Regiment. The rumours that she had trampled on the tricolour were revived as concrete facts. Marie Antoinette pointed out that her only part in the proceedings that evening was to walk from one end of the tables to the other, not once but twice. The preliminary investigation drew to a close with more questions about the affair of the carnation—but no mention of the charge Hébert was preparing concerning herself and the ex-Dauphin.

Hardly had Marie Antoinette returned to her cell before Fouquier-Tinville set to work to write out the indictment. The inaccuracies began with the first sentence, for among others he likened Marie Antoinette to Messalina, whom he described as a French Queen. Had the outcome not been tragic, the document would merely have been ludicrous—and indecent. She was supposed to have helped the Swiss Guards to manufacture cartridges the night before the storming of the Tuileries on August 10th, and to have bitten the bullets, presumably as an offensive gesture to the "patriots" they would kill. A few hours later she was supposed to have called Louis a coward, and herself given the order to fire on the revolutionaries. After the storming of the Tuileries was all over it was claimed that empty bottles were found under her bed, and that during the night she had cemented the loyalty of the Swiss officers by making them drunk. In fact the whole indictment is a terrifying example of how in an atmosphere bordering on hysteria people will believe the most blatant nonsense. Blatant nonsense is the only description for the charge alleging that at Versailles, in the days before the Revolution, Marie Antoinette went around with two pistols concealed about her person, with which to assassinate the Duc d'Orléans, and that when Louis found out she was confined to her rooms for a fortnight.

Meanwhile, two counsel had been appointed to defend the Queen, and one of them, Chaveau-Lagarde, was already on his way to the Conciergerie. The cell, he noted, was divided into two halves by a screen; in one half sat an armed gendarme, while in the other was Marie Antoinette herself, wearing a simple white dress. Almost in tears he introduced himself, and she received Chaveau-Lagarde in a manner that was both "majestic and kind". Together they read the indictment, and Marie Antoinette showed no emotion, even at Hébert's appalling charge. Then Chaveau-Lagarde went upstairs to see the documents to be used at the trial. By then the prosecutor had gathered together a large pile of papers, some of doubtful relevancy, but all requiring careful reading. Back once again with the Queen, her counsel explained that they must apply to the Convention for a delay of three days, so he could go through them meticulously. Marie Antoinette wanted to ask no favours from that body, but her young counsel, only twenty-eight, insisted, and finally she wrote a letter requesting the delay for the sake of her children and Madame Élizabeth. It concluded: "I owe it to my children to do everything in my power to justify the conduct of their mother. My defence counsel asks for a delay of three days, and I hope the Convention will grant it." The letter was given to Fouquier-Tinville to deliver, but it was never handed on. Already the trial had been fixed for eight o'clock the following morning, October 14th, and nothing would stop it now.

Consciously and with great dignity Marie Antoinette was gathering strength to face the last days of her life. The trial was a foregone conclusion, and the outcome inevitable; all she had left was dignity and courage. The following morning she entered the Grand' Chambre of the Palais de Justice wearing the white dress and one of her small white caps, to which she had attached black crêpe. Her judges could see that she was in mourning for her husband, the late King of France. Spectators filled the public gallery, all watching the prematurely aged woman sitting on a hard wooden chair, and running her fingers over the arms as though playing the harpischord while listening to the Clerk of the Court reading the indictment. Two hours were spent detailing ruinously expensive banquets and festivities held at Versailles in the decade before the Revolution, culminating in the banquet for the Flemish Regiment.

"It is widely known in France that at that time you visited the three armed corps at Versailles in person, urging them to defend your rights to the throne." Marie Antoinette said there was no charge to answer. Then she was questioned about the presence of troops around the National Assembly at Versailles when it was addressed for the last time by Louis XVI on June 23rd, 1789. The Queen insisted she knew nothing of any plan to kill a number of the deputies, nor was she aware what lay behind troop movements in the capital forty-eight hours before the fall of the Bastille.

The questioning jumped about from one subject to another: one was about money acquired out of the treasury by the de Polignac family, and was followed by more probings into her part in influencing the Swiss Guards shortly before the attack on the Tuileries. That in its turn was followed by the old rumour that she had sent gold to her brother the Emperor to help him finance a war against the Turks. Then it came—the charge of incest. Marie Antoinette heard herself described as being so perverted and so used to all crimes, "that forgetting she was a mother and disregarding the limitations set by the laws of nature, she had not been afraid to practise with Louis Capet, her son, indecencies whose very idea and whose mere name arouse a shudder."

Even Madame Élizabeth's name was dragged into the catalogue of indecencies, and then Hébert got up to testify as a witness. The warped ingenuity of the man's reasoning is unparalleled, even in this century. According to him these activities, which resulted in physical injury to the Dauphin, were indulged in by Marie Antoinette as part of a scheme to undermine his physique, so that when restored to the throne, she could "dominate his morale", so enabling her to remain the real ruler.

Whatever Marie Antoinette must have felt, she never betrayed her feelings, but refuted the charges with dignity.

"I have no knowledge of the incidents of which Hébert speaks," was all she said in a quiet voice.

The charge was not proving the bombshell the Court had hoped it would. Hermann sensed the spectators in the public gallery were not reacting with shocked indignation. Fearing the prosecution had badly overshot the mark, he passed on to cross-question Marie Antoinette about the way she and Madame Élizabeth had given the boy precedence as though he were King after the execution of his father. One of the jurors cut in:

"Citizen President, I must ask you to draw the attention of the

The Affair of the Diamond Necklace brought enormous unpopularity and vilification upon Marie Antoinette. Although she was only indirectly involved, the affair epitomised her extravagance and frivolity. 39 and 40 (*Above*) The two principal characters in the affair: Louis-René Edouard, Prince of Rohan, Cardinal and Grand Almoner of France, and Jeanne de Saint-Rèmy, Comtesse de la Motte. 41 (*Below left*) The diamond necklace made by Bohmer and Bassenge from 540 diamonds. This engraving shows the multi-tiered necklace when it was made. 42 (*Below right*) The diamond necklace as it survives today. The stones were taken to London and sold by Monsieur de la Motte.

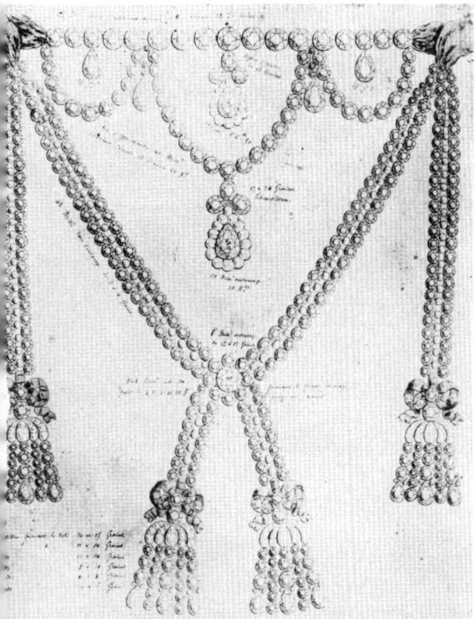

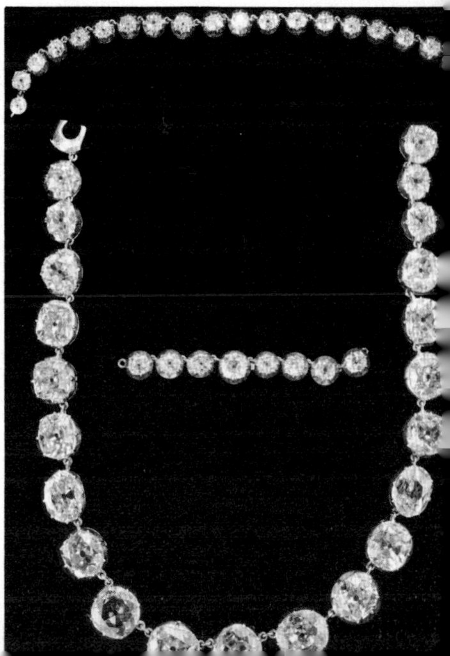

43 (*Above*) Royal troops firing upon rioters in the Paris suburb of St Antoine, on the evening of 27 April 1789.
44 (*Below*) Political cartoon showing the three estates of the *ancien-régime* in France.
45 (*Right*) The first attack on the fortress of the Bastille, 14 July 1789.

46 (*Above*) The departure of the *tricoteuses* to Versailles on 5 October 1789. The cannon shown in this popular engraving was looted from the Châtelet of Versailles.
47 (*Below*) The woman of Paris in the Cour d'Honneur of Versailles, demanding that the King and Queen should return to Paris with them. In the foreground are Lafayette's National Guard.
48 (*Right*) On the first anniversary of the storming of the Bastille, a *Fête de la Federation* was held in the Champ de Mars. In this engraving, the King is shown helping to raise an earthwork for the altar.

49 and 50 (*Above*) On 20 July 1791, the royal family fled to Varennes. These engravings show the interception of the royal coach and the arrest of the King and Queen in the house of Monsieur Sauce.

51 (*Above right*) Anonymous cartoon of Louis XVI in a cage, published on 2 June 1791, fourteen days before the King's flight. It is entitled 'Mais que faîtes-vous là ?' 'Je suis en penitence'.

52 (*Above, far right*) Barnave, one of the Deputies of the National Assembly who escorted Louis along the last stages of his return journey from Varennes to Paris. He showed much sympathy towards the royal family and was thus attacked by Robespierre and Pétion for selling out to the Austrian Committee. This cartoon shows how many regarded Barnave as a two-faced politician.

53 (*Right*) Cartoon of the flight of the royal family.

La
L'HOMME
DE LA COUR.
1791.
L'HOMME
DU PEUPL
1789.
LISTE CIVILE
PATRIOTISME
LIBERTÉ
VERTU
JANUS.
SERMENT DU
JEU DE
PAUME.

54 (*Above left*) Jean-Paul Marat, editor of the Jacobin paper, *Ami du Peuple*; portrait by Garnesay.

55 (*Above*) Bailly, President of the National Assembly and Mayor of Paris, who welcomed the royal family back to the Tuileries from Varennes with the words 'The town is delighted to see you in the palace of our kings'; portrait after David.

56 (*Left*) Mirabeau, who in 1791 tried to act as intermediary between the National Assembly and Marie Antoinette. He declared of the Queen, 'She is great, she is noble and unfortunate, but I shall save her'; portrait by Boge.

57 (*Above*) On 20 June 1792, a revolutionary mob stormed the Tuileries Palace and forced the royal family into the Council Room. This engraving shows Louis XVI wearing a red cap of liberty and drinking the health of the *sans-culottes*.
58 (*Below*) The attack upon the Tuileries on the night of 9–10 August 1792, when the Swiss guards were massacred by the revolutionary troops.

59 (*Above*) While the Tuileries was being stormed, workmen demolished the statue of Louis XVI which stood in the centre of the Place Vendôme.

60 (*Below*) On 13 August 1792, the royal family was taken to the Temple, the last stage in their journey to the guillotine. This cartoon shows a *sans-culotte* driving 'le Ménagerie Royale' to the Temple.

61 (*Right*) Portrait of Louis XVI painted by Ducreuse, during the last weeks of the King's life while he was imprisoned in the Temple.

62 (*Below*) Maximilien Robespierre, the incorruptible patriot who led the committee of Public Safety.

63 (*Above*) The Dauphin Louis; portrait painted in the Temple.
64 (*Below*) The last portrait of Marie Antoinette, probably painted by Prieur at the Temple.

65 (*Above*) The first meal taken by the royal family in the Temple prison.
66 (*Below*) English cartoon of Louis XVI taking leave of Marie Antoinette and his family before his execution. This was published in March 1793.

67 (*Above*) The execution of Louis XVI, which took place in the Place de la Révolution on 21 January 1793.
68 (*Left*) Jacobin 'tricoteuses' who sat beneath the guillotine to witness the executions.
69 (*Above right*) Simon, Louis XVII's 'tutor' in the Temple, who brought about the horrifying change in the child's character; portrait by Gros.
70 (*Above, far right*) Hébert, the Deputy Public Prosecutor and author of the journal *Père Duchesne*, who also had charge of Louis XVII. He wrote of the royal children, 'the best thing would be to maroon the young snake and his sister on a desert island'.
71 (*Right*) Water-colour showing Louis XVII with his 'tutor' Simon. Louis is reputed to have died on 8 June 1795 in his cell in the Temple.

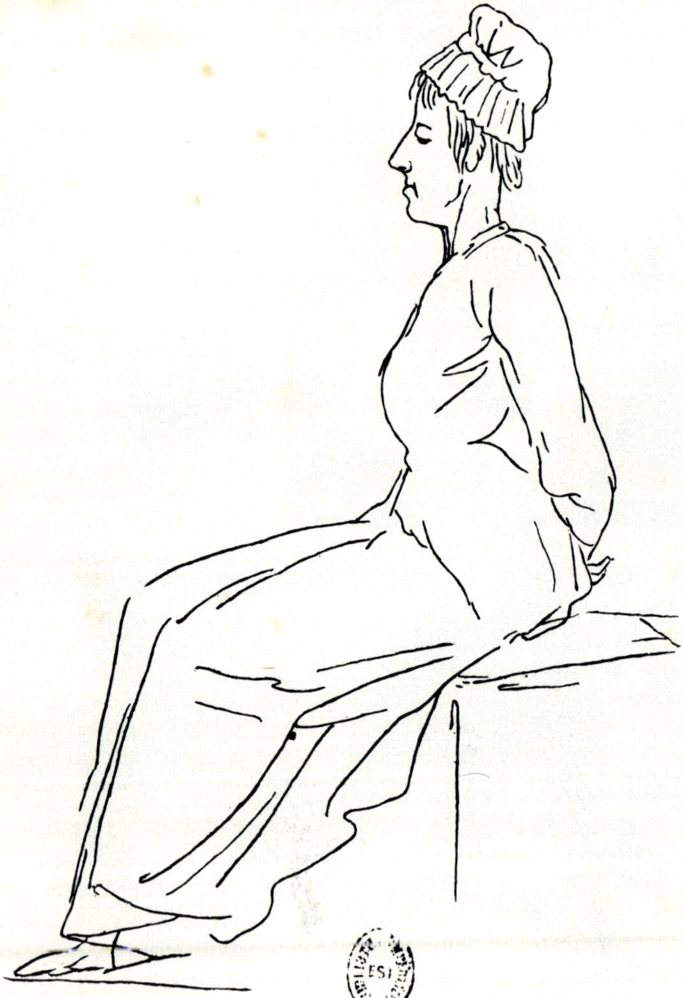

72 The artist J. L. David watched the procession carrying Marie Antoinette to the guillotine from the window of 'citoyenne Julliene'. He drew this pen portrait of the Queen during the last hours of her life.

accused to the fact she has not answered Citizen Hébert's question about what went on between herself and her son."

Marie Antoinette rose to her feet.

"If I did not answer, it was because nature cannot answer such a charge brought against a mother." She paused, and then turned towards the spectators: "I appeal to all mothers who are here!" For a moment there was silence, then such a buzzing that there were calls for order. Hébert almost slunk back into his place.

"Was there too much dignity in my answer?" the Queen asked her counsel. Chaveau-Lagarde assured her that she would be all right so long as she was true to herself. Soon after that incident there was a break in the trial, which was resumed in the late afternoon. Now the Court was listening to hearsay evidence from a one-time servant at Versailles who claimed to have been told that Marie Antoinette had sent vast sums in gold to her brother for his campaign against the Turks. It was not until eleven o'clock that Marie Antoinette returned to her cell, having been in court since 8.00 a.m., with only a two-hour break in the early afternoon.

The following morning the Queen was back in her wooden armchair at 9.00 a.m. Among the witnesses that morning was Simon, but all he spoke about was the way his mother treated the boy as though he were King; nothing else was mentioned.

An attempt to prove that Marie Antoinette had signed vouchers for large sums of money drawn from the Civil List misfired when a witness claimed that one of them was dated August 10th, 1792. As Marie Antoinette pointed out, that day she and the rest of the royal family went to the National Assembly early in the morning.

The questioning went on—irrelevant and time wasting. Even the personal possessions taken from her when she left the Temple on August 2nd were exhibited in Court, including miniatures of two friends from her childhood in Vienna and one of Madame de Lamballe. Now Hermann was back to the question of the Queen's expenses, and in particular the Petit Trianon. Where did the money for that come from, he asked, and for the parties "at which you were always the goddess"?

Marie Antoinette replied that there was a special fund. "It is possible that the Petit Trianon cost huge sums, perhaps more than I would have desired. By degrees it came to cost more and more." Next she was questioned about Madame de la Motte, whom she asserted she had never met in her life. That was followed by interrogation about the way she used to nominate ministers and obtain posts for her friends and their relations. The second afternoon had nearly gone now, and at four o'clock the proceedings were adjourned for three-quarters of an hour.

"Marie Antoinette will get off," Rosalie overheard someone saying. "She answered like an angel. She will only be banished." Bault, the gaoler, told the girl to take a bowl of soup up to the Queen, who was to remain in Court. Just as she was about to enter the Grand' Chambre a police officer whisked the bowl out of Rosalie's hands, "and gave it to his mistress, a very overdressed young woman. 'This young woman,' he said, 'is very anxious to see the Widow Capet, and this is a grand chance for her to do so.' At which the woman went off with the soup, spilling half of it."

At midnight the case for the prosecution was over, ending in a mass of trivial detail. Some two hours later Chaveau-Lagarde sat down after making his defence, and Marie Antoinette remarked gently that he must be very tired. Then and there Fouquier-Tinville ordered his arrest, followed shortly after by that of his colleague.

Hermann summed up; cleverly he never mentioned Hébert's disgusting charges, but concentrated on the Queen's political activities to the detriment of France both before and after the outbreak of the Revolution. Although he could not prove it, since the evidence for the most part was in letters to Mercy, the charges were undeniably and regrettably true. All through the trial not one letter or document in the Queen's own hand could be produced to be used against her. Now the jury had to decide whether she was guilty on the four questions put to them.

1. Is it true that there were plots and communications with foreign powers and with other outside enemies of the Republic, the which said plots and communications intended to give them financial assistance, to make it possible to invade French territory and facilitate the advance of their armies?

2. Is it true that Marie Antoinette of Austria, widow of Louis Capet, took part in these plots and helped in their furtherance?

3. Is it true that there was a plot and a conspiracy to cause civil war inside the Republic?

4. Is it true that Marie Antoinette of Austria, widow of Louis Capet, took part in this plot and conspiracy?

The jury retired, and Marie Antoinette was taken into an adjoining room to await the verdict. Lieutenant de Busne, who had been on duty in her cell for the last week, was still with her. Thoughtfully he brought a glass of water, something that no one else did during the whole trial. An hour dragged by; then at four o'clock in the morning she was brought back into the Grand' Chambre and returned to the wooden chair she had occupied for so many hours.

"Guilty"—that was the verdict of the jury. Fouquier-Tinville demanded the death penalty. Hermann condemned "the said Marie Antoinette, called Lorraine-Austria, widow of Louis Capet, to the pain of death . . . the present judgement to be executed in the Place de la Révolution and printed and displayed throughout the Republic."

What had begun on October 6th, 1789, when the market-women marched on Versailles, was now nearly over. After some fifteen hours in the courtroom, Lieutenant de Busne led Marie Antoinette out, guiding the woman who was now almost unaware of herself or her surroundings. Perhaps it was an unconscious gesture, but as he walked beside Marie Antoinette he held his hat in his hand. Suddenly, on some stairs, her sight failed: "I can hardly see to walk," she told him. A moment later she nearly fell, but he managed to save her. Soon it would be dawn, and at midday all would be over.

CHAPTER TWENTY-THREE

'How many there are'

"October 16th, at half past four in the morning.

It is to you, my sister, that I am writing for the last time. I have just been sentenced to death, but not one that is shameful, for it is only shameful for criminals, and I am going to rejoin your brother. Innocent like him, I hope I shall exhibit the same firmness that he did in his last moments. I am calm, as well I may be with a clear conscience, though it upsets me deeply to have to leave my children. You know I lived only for them and for you, my good and loving sister. In the kindness of your heart you sacrificed everything to be with us, and now I leave you in a terrible situation. It was only during the trial that I learned my daughter had been separated from you. Alas! Poor child. I dare not write to her, since she would not receive the letter. I do not know whether this will reach you. Even so, I send them both my blessing through you, and hope that one day when they are older, they will be reunited with you in your tender care."

With only a few hours left to her, every minute was precious to Marie Antoinette. By the light of two candles she was writing her last letter, to Madame Élizabeth in the Temple. Was she really the same woman who years before had exclaimed: "I am terrified of being bored?" Adversity had transmuted arrogance into courage, and superficiality into an understanding of the world in which she found herself. Tears were falling on the pages, blurring the writing. She continued:

"If only they will go on thinking in the way I tried to teach them, which is that right principles and devotion to duty are the basis of life, and that mutual love and confidence will bring its own happiness. I hope my daughter is now old enough to realise it is her duty to help her brother to grow up, and give him advice as an elder sister;

and that he in his turn will try to help her and show affection; that whatever situation they find themselves in, they will look to us as an example, and only find happiness in being together. How much consolation we have gained from our mutual affection in our troubles. Again, in happier times, to share one's enjoyment with a friend is to double it, and where can one find a more loving or intimate friend than in one's own family? I hope that my son will never forget his father's last words which I now repeat: He must never try to avenge our death!

"I have to mention something that is extremely painful to me, because I know how much the boy must have hurt you. Forgive him, my dear sister: remember how young he is, and how easy it is to put words into his mouth and make him say what is wanted. I hope that one day he will realise the value of your kindness towards them both.

"All that is left is for me to tell you my last thoughts. I should have liked to have written them before the start of the trial, but quite apart from the fact I was not allowed to write, things have happened so quickly I should not have had time.

"I die in the Catholic, Apostolic and Roman religion, that of my father in which I was brought up, and which I have always professed. Having no hope of spiritual consolation, and I do not even know if there are still priests of this religion here, and feeling that even if there were they would run great risks in coming to me, I sincerely ask God's pardon for all transgressions that I may have committed since my birth. I hope that He will at last hear my prayers, as well as my wish for a long time now that in His mercy and goodness He will receive my soul.

"I ask all those known to me, especially you, my sister, to forgive me any unhappiness which I may have caused them. I forgive my enemies the wrong they have done me. I say farewell now to my aunts, brothers and sisters. I used to have friends. Among my greatest regrets in dying is the thought of being separated for ever from them, and of their unhappiness. Let them know, at least, that I thought of them till the end.

"Goodbye, my good and loving sister. I hope this letter will reach you. Think of me always. I send you my deepest love, and also to my poor, dear children. It is unbearable to leave them for ever. Goodbye.

Goodbye. I must now attend to my spiritual duties. Since I am not free perhaps they will bring me a non-juring priest. If that is so, I shall have nothing to do with him and treat him like a complete stranger."

Worn out physically and emotionally Marie Antoinette stretched out on her bed, and lay there sleepless and in tears. Watching from a corner was a gendarme, but not Lieutenant de Busne. He was under arrest, denounced by a fellow officer simply for having saved her when she nearly fell on the stairs, and also for having fetched a glass of water while awaiting the verdict.

At seven o'clock Rosalie came in. Marie Antoinette still lay on her bed, staring up at the window, her head resting on her hand.

"Madame," said the girl, "you didn't eat anything yesterday evening, and hardly anything during the day. What would you like to have this morning?"

"I shall never want anything more, my child," Marie Antoinette answered through her tears. "It is all over for me."

"Madame, I have been keeping some soup and vermicelli hot on the kitchen stove, let me bring you some."

Marie Antoinette agreed, though hardly able to speak. When it came, she could not eat, and gave up after a few spoonfuls. At eight o'clock Rosalie returned yet again, to help the Queen dress. Once it had required at least two ladies of noble birth and several waiting-women to dress the Queen: now she slipped between the bed and the wall while she tried to put on a clean chemise. At a sign Rosalie stood between her and the prying eyes of the gendarme, but he came to the head of the bed.

"In the name of decency, Monsieur," said Marie Antoinette gently, "let me change my linen without being watched."

"That's impossible," the man replied. "I've got my orders to keep an eye on you, whatever you do."

Without another word she continued to dress, putting on a black petticoat under a white skirt, a white jacket usually worn in the mornings, and a white bonnet. Hating the thought that all of her few possessions would be examined and itemised by men such as Fouquier-Tinville and Hébert, she screwed up the chemise she had taken off and furtively slipped it into a hole in the matting fixed to the wall beside her bed.

There was nothing more for Rosalie to do.

"I left without daring to say a word of farewell, or make even one curtsy, for I was afraid of compromising or upsetting her. I went to my room to cry, and pray for her."

As Marie Antoinette had feared, the priest who came to her at about eight o'clock was one who had taken the oath to the Constitution, and in her eyes was a traitor to his Church. She treated him "as a stranger", and within minutes the news was all over the Conciergerie.

Like her husband at the end of his life, Marie Antoinette could remember to thank those who had tried to ease her imprisonment. Larivière, the turnkey, had just come into her cell. She said:

"Larivière, you know that they are going to put me to death? Tell your good mother that I thank her for her care of me, and that I beg her to pray for me."

It was ten o'clock.

Hermann, two of Marie Antoinette's judges and the Clerk of the Court entered. The Queen, who had been praying beside her bed, rose to her feet.

"Pay attention," said Hermann. "Your sentence is about to be read to you."

"It is unnecessary to read it. I know it only too well," answered Marie Antoinette.

"No matter," said one of the judges. "It must be read to you again."

Someone else had come into the cell. Young and extremely tall, it was Henri Sanson, whose father had guillotined Louis.

"Hold out your hands," was all he said.

"Must my hands be bound?" asked Marie Antoinette "Louis XVI's were not bound."

But they were being tightly tied behind her back. For a moment it looked as thought she would weep, but her courage returned. Next her hair, now almost white, was cut short by Sanson, who afterwards replaced her bonnet. It was time to leave.

Outside the heart of Paris was at a standstill: guns were mounted on the bridges and in the squares, and since ten o'clock streets along which Marie Antoinette would pass had been closed to traffic.

Followed by Sanson, the one-time Queen of France and daughter of the Empress Maria Theresa of Austria walked out of the Conciergerie. There was one thing for which she had not prepared herself. Louis had been driven to the Place de la Révolution in one of his own closed carriages. There standing in the Cour de Mai she caught sight of an open tumbril, pulled by two carthorses. In death, as in life, the Republic had decreed that there should be equality even on the journey to the scaffold. Also, it was inflicting the last ounce of mental cruelty on the Widow Capet. Even now, it could not resist just one more opportunity to be vindictive.

With help from Sanson she climbed up into the tumbril, but instead of being allowed to face the front of the cart. Marie Antoinette was made to sit on a plank with her back to the direction in which she was going. A constitutional priest, in ordinary clothes, seated himself beside her, but was ignored. Behind her stood Sanson, still holding the end of the rope which bound her wrists, while his assistant stood at the back. Both men, perhaps without realising what they were doing, held their hats under their arms during the terrible forty-five-minute drive.

The autumn morning had a nip in the air, which brought a touch of colour to Marie Antoinette's face. Rouy, a republican, noted: "Though she looked rather downcast as she got into the cart, she never lost the proud, haughty expression and bearing that were so characteristic of her."

Over the Pont au Change, and towards the Rue Saint-Honoré the tumbril went at a walking pace, surrounded by gendarmes, mounted and on foot. There were cries of "*Vive la République!*" and "*A bas les tyrans!*" At the entrance to the Rue itself there was something approaching a demonstration, in spite of the thousands of troops and police. For a moment the tumbril came to a stop, and it may have been then that the painter David sketched in a few mordant lines the likeness of Marie Antoinette: old and drawn, but with her spirit unbroken.

A one-time actor, Grammont, now in the uniform of the National Guard and flourishing a sabre, pushed through the gendarmes and shouted at her:

"There she is, the infamous Antoinette. She's done for at last, my friends."

Past the church of Saint-Roche, with the *tricoteuses*, those women who were forever knitting, shouting abuse from the steps. Past the house occupied by Robespierre, and on towards the Rue Royale, mercillessly jolted as the wheels ground over the cobbles. Then left down the lower half of the Rue Royale into the crowded but silent Place de la Révolution, and the end of the journey that had begun twenty-three years earlier in Vienna when she was still little more than a child.

For the first time since leaving the Conciergerie Marie Antoinette's face betrayed real emotion—when she caught sight of the Tuileries through the bare branches of the trees in the Gardens. "At that moment she changed colour and grew much paler than before." Perhaps she remembered her remark as she had gazed at the crowd from the balcony of the Palace at the culmination of her first visit to Paris twenty years before: "My God, how many of them there are!"

"The cart drew up before the scaffold," wrote Rouy, "and she got down easily and quickly without needing any help, though her hands were still tied. In the same way she ascended the scaffold with an air of bravado; she seemed calmer and more undisturbed even than when she left the prison."

Marie Antoinette was wearing her better pair of satin shoes with the high heels *à la Saint-Huberty*. Accidentally she trod on Sanson's foot, and he cried out.

"Monsieur, I beg your pardon. I did not do it on purpose." They were the last words she uttered.

Rouy continued his account of the scene:

". . . she submitted to the final preparations, shaking her cap from her head herself. Her execution and the horrible prelude took about four minutes. At a quarter past twelve exactly her head fell under the iron avenger of the law, and the executioner showed it to the public amid repeated shouts of '*Vive la République! Vive la Liberté!*' "

CHAPTER TWENTY-FOUR

The Aftermath

Twenty-three years earlier a huge but happy and excited crowd had filled the Place Louise Quinze, watching the fireworks display to celebrate Marie Antoinette's marriage to the Dauphin. But suddenly the carnival atmosphere had turned to tragedy as scores fell underfoot in the rush to leave the Place for a fair held close by. One hundred and thirty-two were trampled to death and interred in the Cemetery of the Madeleine, not far away. For fourteen days, in October 1793, the body of Marie Antoinette lay unburied in the same grass-covered plot, apparently forgotten by the very authorities who had been so anxious to encompass her death. Finally a gravedigger named Joly, acting on his own initiative, went to work and gave the Queen burial that, if not Christian, was at least decent. Not more than a few yards away was the similarly unmarked grave of her husband, close to the wall by the Rue d'Artois.

Apart from the King and Queen, the Cemetery of the Madeleine was the burial place of the five hundred or so Swiss Guards killed during the storming of the Tuileries, of Charlotte Corday, and in the following month of November, of Philippe-Égalité—the one-time Duc d'Orléans. In fact, it was the last resting place of nearly all those executed in the Place de la Révolution until December, 1793.

As soon as the Terror had run its self-consuming course the cemetery was acquired by a Monsieur Desclozeaux, whose property adjoined. There was a tradition concerning the spot where Louis and Marie Antoinette lay, and M. Desclozeaux planted weeping willows on the site. Napoleon rose to power, became Emperor, was defeated finally at Waterloo and sent into exile on St. Helena. One of the first acts after the restoration of the Bourbons to the throne was to exhume the royal couple so that they could find a proper resting place in the vaults of St. Denis. On January 18th, 1815, the bones of

Marie Antoinette were found, and positively identified by some scraps of black filoselle stockings and the garters she was known to have worn. The next day the King's grave was also located. The search had been successful, and tradition was vindicated.

The date chosen for the final ceremonies in the histories of Louis XVI and Marie Antoinette was fateful: January 21st, which was the twenty-second anniversary of the King's execution. From Monsieur Desclozeaux's house adjoining the cemetery of the Madeleine the leaden coffins were taken in a long procession of blacked-plumed horses, court carriages and minute guns to the ancient Abbey Church of St Denis on what was then the northern outskirts of Paris. Part of the route from the centre of the city was that traversed in the opposite direction by Louis on his last journey that misty morning in 1793.

There they still lie, in the crypt below the choir of St Denis, which since its erection in the twelfth century had been the burial place of the Kings and Queens of France, though only the coffin of Louis VII remained undisturbed from pre-revolutionary times.

What of the others whose paths had crossed that of Marie Antoinette, either as friends or enemies or simply by chance encounter? Every day, as the Terror ran its nightmare course, more and more names that were either famous or infamous disappeared from the scene. Among the revolutionaries, nearly all those responsible for sending Marie Antoinette to the guillotine followed the same route within the next twelve months. Hermann, the President of the Revolutionary Tribunal, Fouquier-Tinville, the Deputy Prosecutor, Hébert, the editor of *Père Duchesne*, most of the judges, and five of the jurymen would all know what it was like to ride in a tumbril. Simon, the Dauphin's so-called tutor, and Michonis, the Inspector of prisons, were only two of those who had their names called out in the "Mousetrap" in the Conciergerie. Madame Roland, Danton, Desmoulins, Bailly, the one-time Mayor of Paris, and eventually on July 28th, 1794, Robespierre himself, all were to be destroyed by the monster they had raised up.

Of those who had known Marie Antoinette during her imprisonment in the Temple and the Conciergerie, the officials Goret and Daujon outlived the Revolution, as did Lieutenant de Busne, who had been arrested for fetching a glass of water and assisting the Queen on a flight of stairs. Another who saw the return of better days was her counsel, Chaveau-Lagarde; but his colleague, Tronson-Ducoudray, was deported to Guiana, where he disappeared. Some time after the death of Marie Antoinette, Richard and his wife were reinstated at the Conciergerie, where they retained the services of Rosalie Lamorlière. The girl remained with them until the death of Madame Richard, after she had been stabbed by a prisoner. Then she left, but thanks to Madame Royale a place was found for her in her old age in a Home for Incurables, together with a small pension. History even recorded what happened to the gendarme Gilbert: he may have brought Marie Antoinette flowers, but according to the turnkey Larivière, whose sister he married, "he was the most depraved gendarme that ever lived", and ended by blowing out his brains after gambling away all the money belonging to the firm which then employed him.

On May 10th, 1794, Madame Élizabeth suffered the same fate as her sister-in-law. Condemned for having a treasonable correspondence with her brothers in exile, it was only as she was leaving the Conciergerie that she learnt that Marie Antoinette was no longer alive. Would Richard please remember her to her sister, asked Madame Élizabeth. "Madame," said one of her fellow-victims, "your sister has suffered the fate that we are about to suffer ourselves."

The last letter written by Marie Antoinette had never been delivered. Bault, the gaoler, had given it to Fouquier-Tinville, who had handed it over to Robespierre. Then, after the Incorruptible fell, his room was searched by Courtois, the Deputy for Aube. The letter and a number of other papers came to light from under Robespierre's mattress, and were pocketed by Courtois, who foresaw the day might come when they could be used to his advantage. That day came in 1816: the Bourbons ruled once again, and Courtois felt sure Marie Antoinette's letter would be worth a pardon. However, admission that it even existed and was in his possession brought not a pardon but a magistrate and several gendarmes to his house. The letter was appropriated and given to Madame Royale. At the sight of the two pages of closely-written tear-stained manuscript Marie Antoinette's daughter fainted away. For the last surviving member of the ill-fated royal family the sight of it was too much. Imprisonment for Madame Royale had ended in 1795, when she was exchanged for members of the National Convention captured by the Allies during their advance into eastern France. Among the latter was Drouet, the posting-master at Ste Menehould who had recognised the royal family during the flight to Varennes. While in exile, this frozen-up and withdrawn young woman married her cousin the Duc d'Angoulême, son of Louis XVI's youngest brother the Comte d'Artois. She died in 1851.

Adelaide and Victoire, the Mesdames who had plagued Marie Antoinette's young years at Versailles, died in exile, and their bodies were brought back to lie in St Denis in 1817. The rule of the de Polignac family lived on, for Yolande de Polignac's second son Jules was to exercise the same kind of meddlesome and reactionary influence over Charles X as his mother had exercised over Marie Antoinette. Indeed it was his interference with the Constitution in 1830 that resulted in the July Revolution, which toppled Charles X from the throne. Two others from the halcyon days at Court were Madame Campan and Madame de Tourzel; both survived the Revolution and lived on well into the nineteenth century. But the one who had meant most of all to Marie Antoinette was now far away from France. What Fersen suffered when he heard the news from Paris—however expected—can be imagined. He returned to Sweden, where he became a Marshal and a man of power. The fire, even the life, had gone out of him; now he was cold and reserved, an embodiment of the *ancien régime* who did not try to hide his dislike of the ordinary people. They were, to him, the kith and kin of those who had sent Marie Antoinette to her death. In 1810 the Crown Prince, the King's popular brother, died suddenly. A rumour circulated that he had been poisoned by Fersen, who wished to become king in order to make war on France, the murderer of his beloved Marie Antoinette. Friends advised him not to go to the Crown Prince's funeral, but Fersen brushed aside the story as a malicious invention. His carriage was brought to a stop by the mob, he was dragged out and battered to death, and left for hours lying in the street. The date was June 20th, the nineteenth anniversary of the Flight to Varennes.

Both Louis XVI's brothers, Provence and Artois, mounted the throne; Provence in 1814 as Louis XVIII, and Artois in 1824 as Charles X. For Provence the route had certainly been long and devious. It really began when he assumed the title of Louis XVIII after the Dauphin's death in the Temple in 1795. But there followed nineteen years of wandering around Europe before he really became king in his own capital. During the Hundred Days he fled to Ghent, and Napoleon contemptuously remarked that Madame Royale was the only man among them. Back on his throne once more after Waterloo, Louis XVIII grew fat and gouty—a puppet to be manipulated by the Ultras, the reactionary faction headed by his brother Artois. "Cold, unsympathetic and calculating," was Leopold of the Belgians' description of him when he heard of his death. But if anything, Artois, once the most irresponsible of Marie Antoinette's companions in the days of the Petit Trianon, had even less to recommend him. He too wandered round Europe, spending most of his time in England or Scotland during the First Empire. His coronation at Rheims in 1825 was the magnificent swan song of the old order, and his attitude to changed times was summed up in the remark, "I would rather hew wood than be a king under the conditions of the King of England." In 1830, due to the influence of Jules de Polignac, he practically suspended the Constitution but the calendar could not be turned back to 1789, and after the July Revolution he abdicated in favour of his son, Henri. But he was reckoning without Louis Philippe, son of the Duc d'Orléans—Philippe Égalité—who did so much to undermine Louis and Marie Antoinette in the days before and after the outbreak of the Revolution. For the father at least, his scheming had come to nothing: within a month of Marie Antoinette's death he too was guillotined in the Place de la Révolution, accused of being involved in a conspiracy with the traitorous General Dumouriez.

In exile Charles X repented of his misspent youth by indulging in religious austerities, and died half-forgotten in Prague in 1836. Until 1848 Louis-Philippe's bulk occupied the throne without either honour or glory. Then he too was forced to make a hasty and ignominious exit, telling his wife on board the ship taking them to Newhaven not to pray so loudly, as people might become suspicious. And so the Bourbons ceased to rule in France, though in a sense the dynasty really ended with the tragedy at the end of the eighteenth century; what came after was in the nature of an epilogue and of no consequence.

A coffin in the crypt of St. Denis bears the simple inscription: "Marie Antoinette of Lorraine-Austria, wife of Louis XVI, King of France." Perhaps her best epitaph is the last sentence she ever spoke.

"I beg your pardon, Monsieur. I did not do it on purpose."

Historical Appendix

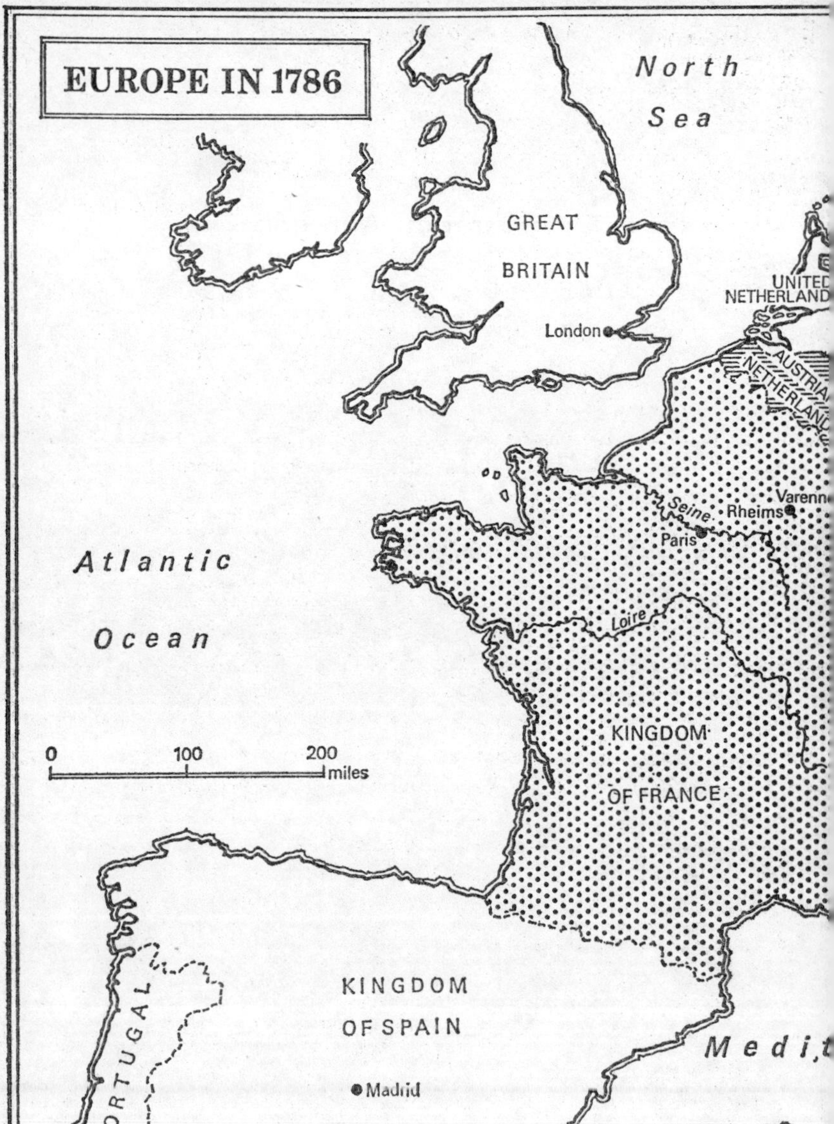

EUROPE IN 1786
North Sea
GREAT BRITAIN
London
UNITED NETHERLAND
AUSTRIAN NETHERLAND
Atlantic Ocean
Seine
Rheims
Varenn
Paris
Loire
KINGDOM OF FRANCE
0
100
200
miles
PORTUGAL
KINGDOM OF SPAIN
Madrid
Medi,t

KINGDOM OF DENMARK
Baltic Sea
MECKLENBURG
HANOVER
DOMINIONS OF THE HOHENZOLLERNS
Berlin
Vistula
KINGDOM OF POLAND
Warsaw
Elbe
SAXONY
Oder
Rhine
DOMINIONS OF THE HABSBURGS
Danube
Vienna
ancy
Strasbourg
BAVARIA
Augsburg
Budapest
SWITZERLAND
SAVOY
Po
Venice
VENETIAN REPUBLIC
OTTOMAN EMPIRE
Adriatic Sea
TUSCANY
PAPAL STATES
Rome
KINGDOM OF THE TWO SICILIES
rranean Sea

THE HOUSE OF BOURBON 1589–1830

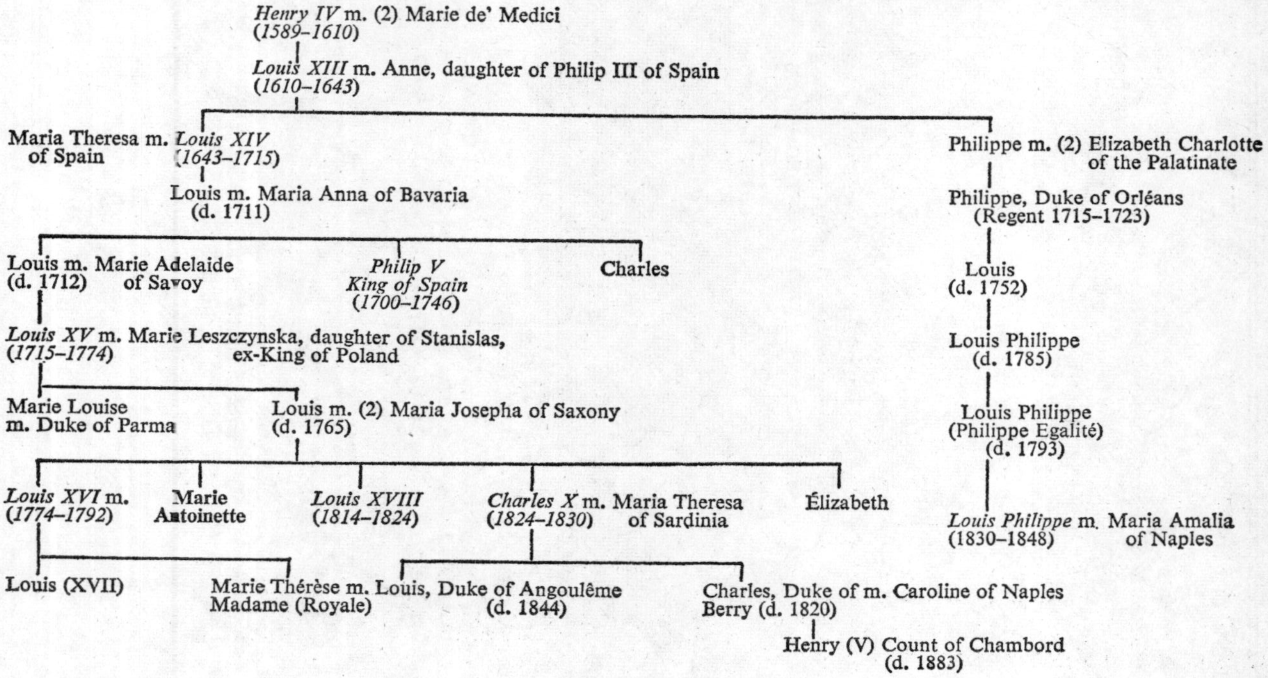

THE GERMAN HABSBURGS 1519–1848

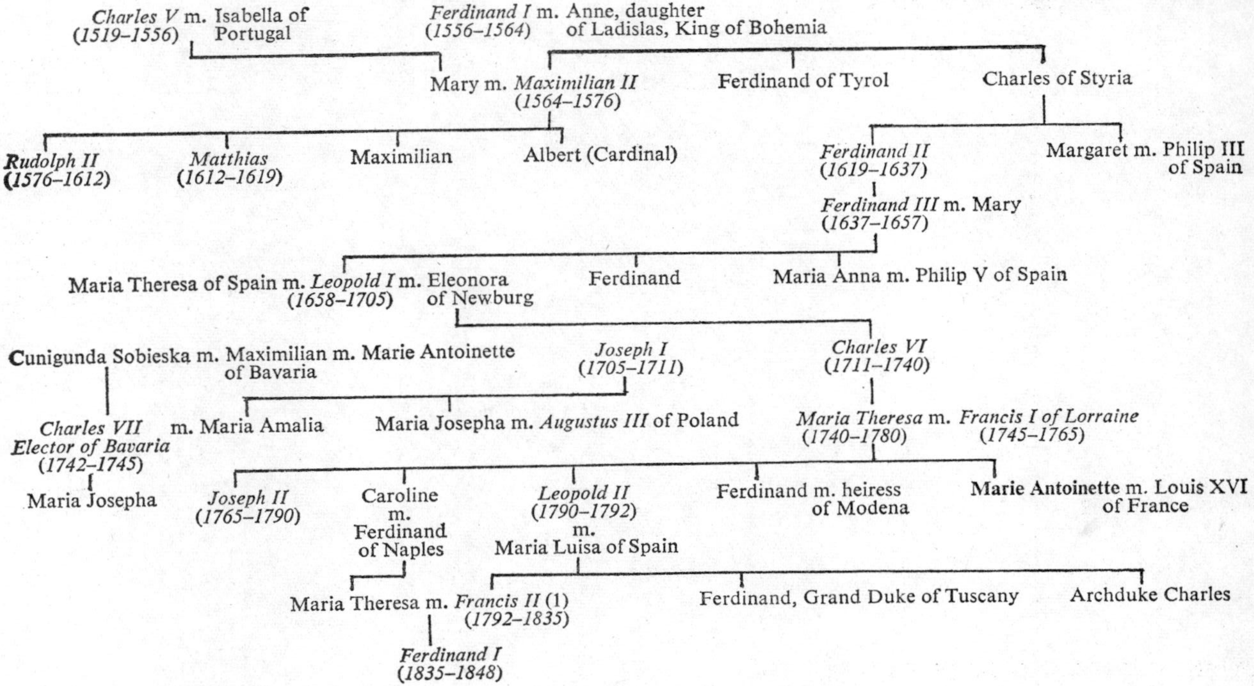

Towards Revolution

On September 22nd, 1792, began Day One of Year One of the First French Republic; thenceforward all Frenchmen, the National Convention decreed, must use the familiar *tu* and *toi* forms of address, all titles were abolished, all persons were to be known as *citoyen* and *citoyenne*, and all *émigrés* were placed under sentence of perpetual banishment. A year later the names of the old months went the way of the old titles: they were replaced beginning with September, by Vendémiaire, Brumaire, Frimaire, Nivôse, Pluviôse, Ventôse, Germinal, Floréal, Prairial, Messidor, Thermidor, and Fructidor; in each month there were thirty days, which left five intercalary days in each year, familiarly dubbed the *sans culottides*. Sundays shared the fate of God: His worship was abolished on November 10th, 1793, and starting from that date, every tenth day, *décadi*, was to be a holiday. Today, such revolutionary thoroughness seems uncalled for, naïve, certainly not aimed at Liberty—rather at Equality. But then the Revolution was not so much impelled by an ideal of Liberty as by a fierce desire to destroy Privilege, to substitute in place of administrative *laisser aller* laws that were applicable to ALL, with no exceptions. From the *ancien régime* the pendulum had swung to the other extreme.

What was the nature of the hated *ancien régime* which the revolutionaries attempted so violently to extirpate? The roots of the Revolution could be traced back into the Middle Ages, but for practical purposes the special flavour of the *ancien régime* under the reigns of Louis XV and Louis XVI—that is from 1715 until the outbreak of the Revolution—may be explained by the uneasy co-existence of feudalism with centralisation, the former a rotten shell retaining its framework and none of its virtues, the latter centred on Paris and gradually absorbing like a vast spider all administrative authority. Louis XIV, *Le Roi Soleil*, has been blamed for much of this, not least for having effectively deprived his nobility of its power and influence in return for sinecures and privileges. Thereafter administration became increasingly bureaucratic, until no town or village in all France was exempt from government interference—even in such a triviality as deciding upon the source of funds for repairing a village steeple; in this case two and a half years went by before the workmen took up their tools.

It becomes overwhelmingly obvious, when studying the channels of power under the *ancien régime*, that nothing short of a revolution could have purged France. No legislation was passed but that thousands of exceptions were made, no taxes levied that remained constant or were equally applied from one village to the next. Town guilds and corporations, traders, merchants, shopkeepers financiers, hordes of public servants and governmental officials and, of course, nobles and clergy, claimed and got exemptions of one kind or another; indeed, each regarded himself as having a positive right to be treated as an exceptional case. For instance, no government employee, from the Intendant himself to the merest underling, could be brought into the civil courts, whose judges were for the most part conscientious and competent; he would instead claim his right to be tried by governmental tribunal and could thus be assured of a mitigated sentence, even if he were found guilty. Not only did the government shield its members from the law, but even interfered on occasion with private court proceedings. Provincial records reveal that the Intendant of each province at one time or another had either arrogated judical powers to himself, made arbitrary judgements, or issued warrants for arrest and imprisonment without trial—and the central government had turned a blind eye. For a long time *Jacques Bonhomme* had been squeezed and flouted not only by the two traditional masters but also by a third—the all-powerful government official, usually in the person of the Tax Collector, against whom he had no means of constitutional redress.

The state machinery, which operated with relative efficiency towards the last decade of the old regime, was controlled in theory by the King, in practice by the Royal Council and Controller General. The authority of thirty Intendants radiated from the Controller General, unequivocally key minister of the Royal Council because all financial matters in whatever connection had ultimately to be brought before him. Each Intendant appointed subdelegates in all areas of his province, and numerous lesser minions orbited around individual subdelegates—the subdivisions of public authority were endless.

Town corporations, usually bodies of bourgeois notables working in conjunction with a subdelegate or with the Intendant himself, wielded their local influence in such a way as to prevent the peasant from gaining an official hearing. These men, usually of considerable substance, made only token tax-returns—scandalously disproportionate to their means—on the grounds that they were unsalaried servants of the committee, then ensured the perpetuation of their privileges by electing only men of their own sympathies to sit in the provincial assemblies. Rarely were the nobility members of any town corporation. In fact they regarded public office, even that of Intendant, as more befitting a commoner. Straitened circumstances, though, often forced them to ask favours of their low-born masters, and many such requests are a strange blend of conciliation and hauteur.

Since most governmental measures throughout the eighteenth century were dictated by constant financial crises rather than by political necessity, the State was obliged to impose taxes only upon those who were unable to throw up a barricade of rights and privileges against taxation, either direct or disguised as forced labour. In a similar way the Church's prerogatives were financial and feudal ones, not spiritual, and the same mixture of indulgence and stringency prevailed here as in the secular field: in some districts the tithe or *dîme* amounted to as much as one fifth and in other parishes diminished to one thirteenth. As to the government, it was not blind to the fact that France's annual revenue would double if taxes were levied in proportion to individual means. Increasingly during the last decade before the crash, provincial assemblies, lawyers and many members of the clergy voiced sympathy for the peasant's lot and pleaded his cause most eloquently. They little realised that their largely unimplemented condolences repeatedly nudged *Jacques Bonhomme* nearer the brink of revolution by making him more conscious of and more convinced of his grievances.

Agriculture was the basis of France's economy; the price of bread, rising or falling according to the harvests, largely determined the annual revenue, because when bread was in short supply and high in price the common people, living as they did at the edge of starvation, could not afford to pay for bread and taxes too. Hence the tax yield was totally insufficient to finance army, navy, armaments, public works, industrial state enterprises, let alone poor relief. Faced with such a situation the government created new saleable public offices overnight, and imposed emergency taxes which, needless to say, became temporary *in permanentio*. France's agriculture could not long stand the strain of the country's growing population: 19 million in 1715 and 26 million in 1789.

In addition, agricultural methods were backward, crop rotation was never practised, and land lay fallow for months on end. Colonial import schemes, designed to alleviate the situation, generally failed, and the land itself had not only been subdivided and chopped about by land-hungry bourgeois and peasants but had been abandoned by considerable numbers of both, who had left to work in industry. Most damning of all, taxes were so burdensome that all incentive melted at the approach of the Collector. Indeed, the peasant's position in eighteenth-century France was appreciably worse than it had been in the thirteenth, although unlike most other peasants in Europe he was a free man and generally better off than they were; sufficiently well off in fact to wish himself better still. Yet still he could not pay his dues in full, which meant an ever-decreasing income for his seigneur, most of whose minimal feudal dues were swallowed up by the expenses of enforcing their collection. The aristocracy, too was poorer just before the Revolution than it had ever been, and indeed looked upon the impoverished peasant as far more tolerable than the comfortable middle-class snob.

The peasant's obligations in eighteenth-century France would fill several volumes—suffice it to say that they varied from one village to the next, from the *pays d'état* to the *pays d'élection*. It is not possible to gauge to what extent the French peasant was injured to the fact that he was *né pour la peine* (born to suffer) yet the opposite must have gradually become apparent to him during the last decade of the old order. Briefly, he was subject to minimal feudal dues (which were nevertheless sufficient to cause annoyance), to the *taille*, to a purchase tax on certain articles, to the *gabelle* or salt-tax, and to indirect taxes in the form of seigneurial or state *corvées* (which meant unpaid labour, including harvesting, work on roads, waterways and public buildings, revictualling and transport operations on behalf of the army or the marine, and the escorting of convicts) for all of which he received next to nothing.

The peasant's subjection did not end there. The *seigneurie* system represented a multitude of rights which sorely tried the peasant: hunting, fishing and pasturing rights, ferry and toll rights, traditional rights on marketable produce. On top of this, despite the state of France's agriculture and the peasant's growing inability to pay his taxes in times of stress, the declining feudal revenues were in turn subject to a capitation tax and to the *vingtième*, another tax devised to levy one twentieth of a landholder's landed income; and this had tripled since its introduction in 1749. This outrageous system crippled not only the aristocrat but also the bourgeois scheming to become a landed seigneur and the occasional peasant who had himself laboriously accumulated some land.

Industry on the other hand was stimulated by tax exemptions, an arrangement of mutual advantage both to government and to the industrialist, for merchants could plump their own pockets unhindered and invest their money at interest in government projects, while the government conveniently provided itself with a reliable source of capital—on which it rarely paid the appropriate interest. Many such loans dragged on without being repaid; as a result numerous creditors of the government were ruined and joined forces with its most bitter opponents.

With money and education a man could rise; without either he must grovel. France was split into thousands of little groups, each one grimly hanging on to its own rights and privileges—a rat-race which rendered impossible the country's peaceable political development. More reforms were passed in the last decade of the *ancien régime* than ever before in France's history, but these, rather than eradicating, merely brought to light, aggravated and enflamed the glaring social injustices, making every institution seem an anachronism. The result was a vast destructive surge of indignation, intent upon smashing all the established institutions in order to replace them with something better. Napoleon rose to the crest of this revolutionary wave and eventually harnessed its power.

Ever since the publication of Montesquieu's *L'Esprit des Lois* in 1748, France's most brilliant writers, the most influential of whom were the group known as the *Philosophes*, had been putting forward their own, often eccentric, solutions to the problem of good government. It had become almost an obsession to bypass appearances and to probe deeper into the origins of human society, into the legitimacy of authority, custom, and law. Although few writers made political theory their exclusive study (whereas many toyed with the idea of the perfect state), the point of departure for all their writings was a strong desire to erect a system of government guided by clear and simple precepts derived from the exercise of natural law and human reason; to sweep away social patterns hide-bound by centuries of tradition. The means by which this miraculous change was to be accomplished they left vague. And so the nobility and the bourgeoisie, finding these new-coined doctrines of equality so entertaining, so witty, light-heartedly helped to propagate the seeds of their own destruction. They did not foresee, and neither did France's over-abstract political theorists, that once these same ideas were grasped by the masses the result would be catastrophe. To the privileged, the new principles were a delightful novelty, but to the oppressed they became passionate ideals.

From the *cahiers*, or lists of grievances, drawn up by the three orders of the States General in readiness for its opening at Versailles on May 5th, 1789, it can clearly be seen that what in fact was proposed by *all three* orders, not only by the Third, was precisely the systematic and simultaneous abolition of all existing laws and customs. However, when it came to the test, the States General was still befogged by the old rivalry of nobleman versus commoner. So the Third Estate broke away to form the National Assembly which, until the very last minute, imagined that a radical transformation of their ancient, complex social system could be effected through constitutional means, quite painlessly. Under the dynamic lead of Mirabeau and the Abbé de Sieyès, the Assembly pledged itself "not to disperse until it had given a new constitution to France". This first concerted movement, in open defiance of King, clergy and nobles, marked the bloodless dawn of the new day; a stand had been made, and to that rallying point flocked the men who were to shape the course of the Revolution.

The Ancien Régime

A Glossary of Terms and Personalities

ANCIEN RÉGIME
(lit: "Old Order")
It is generally understood that the *ancien régime* in France ended with the Revolution, but when it began is not so clear. To revolutionaries, the old regime began with feudalism; to others, it began with the reign of Louis XIV, the Sun King and chief exponent of absolutism and divine right. Still others date the *ancien régime* from the death of Louis XIV in 1715.

BOURGEOIS
(adj. "pertaining to the town")
In its old legal sense the word was applied only to persons who had lived in a town for a specified period, owned property and paid municipal taxes. The minute criteria that distinguished the bourgeois from the rest of the Third Estate were often so arbitrary as to appear absurd. Even in the eighteenth century, however, the term was commonly used in the modern sense when referring to certain professions and attitudes of mind—depending of course on the speaker's social standpoint.

CAHIERS de doléances
(lit: "lists of grievances")
Lists drawn up by each of the three orders or estates for presentation at the meeting of the States General.

CONDORCET, 1743–1794
Marie Jean Antoine Nicolas Caritat, Marquis de
Born into the aristocracy, Condorcet was a brilliant mathematician and one of the more radical of the *Philosophes*. During the revolution he was a member of the Legislative Assembly, and became its president in 1792. He acted as deputy in the National Convention and in 1793 sided with the Girondins. When the Girondins were overthrown in June, 1793 he was arrested and died in prison on March 28th, 1794. Whilst in prison he wrote his *Esquisse d'un tableau historique des progrès de l'esprit humain*

(Historical Outline of the Progress of the Human Mind), a work which traces nine epochs of human development, predicting the perfectability of man in the tenth.

CONTROLEUR GÉNÉRAL des finances
(Controller General of Finance)
The most important post in the government; its holder was in charge of the country's entire financial administration as well as its agriculture, commerce, industry and communications. Both Turgot and Necker held this post prior to the outbreak of the Revolution.

CORVÉE
A term applied to compulsory labour enforced upon "roturiers" (members of the Third Estate other than the privileged bourgeoisie) and justified by the government on the assumption that this type of work was only imposed upon them at times when agricultural work was slack. Not only the peasants themselves but also their animals and implements were frequently commandeered at short notice. This alternative to direct taxation was difficult to enforce and became the most notorious of the peasants' complaints.

D'ALEMBERT, 1717–1783
Jean Le Rond
D'Alembert's scepticism and his brilliance as a mathematician were put to practical use in the great *Encyclopédie*, begun in 1751, which he produced in collaboration with Denis Diderot. As a leading proponent of the Enlightenment, he helped to cultivate in intellectual circles a passion for facts, a craving for exact and detailed knowledge in all fields. He was a member both of the Academy of Science (1741) and of the Académie Française (1754).

DIDEROT, 1713–1784
Denis
Denis Diderot's *Encyclopédie, ou Dictionnaire Raisonné des Sciences, des Arts et des Métiers* (Encyclopedia, or Universal Dictionary of the Arts and Sciences), started in 1751 and completed twenty years later, was a unique achievement in the eighteenth century and a powerful force in disseminating the ideals of the Enlightenment. Diderot's materialist philosophy, his often profoundly original and intuitive thought, his critical attacks on existing society, encouraged a spirit of inquiry and nourished in his readers the will to improve their intellectual and social conditions.

DÎME

Derived from Vulgar Latin, meaning a tenth or tithe; the old form of "dixième" and in current use before the French language was remodelled on Classical Latin. The term was retained to indicate the special nature of the tenth paid to the Church.

DROIT DE SEIGNEUR

Sometimes known as the *droit de cuissage*, denotes the right of a feudal overlord to deflower the bride of any of his tenants on her marriage night, a right rarely, if ever, taken advantage of in eighteenth-century France.

ÉTATS GÉNÉRAUX (STATES GENERAL)

The French National Assembly, with representatives from each state or province of France, each province being classed as either a *pays d'état* or as a *pays d'élection*. The calling of regular sessions of the States General had lapsed after 1614. Vastly disproportionate in representation, the privileged majority were able to ensure that the voice of the plain peasant would not be heard. In the 1789 meeting the States General, after two months spent in arguments, crumbled, and the Third Estate proclaimed itself the National Assembly.

FRANCIS II 1768–1835

Francis II, nephew of Marie Antoinette, succeeded his father Leopold II in 1792 as Holy Roman Emperor, but was the last to use that title; two years before the formal dissolution of the Holy Roman Empire in 1806 he had already assumed the title of Francis I, Emperor of Austria. Austria's successive trouncings by the French from 1797 to 1809 were smoothed over by Napoleon's marriage in 1810 to Francis's daughter, Marie Louise, who provided him with an imperial heir, the King of Rome. Francis permitted Metternich to deal with foreign affairs, but himself manipulated Austria's internal administration, never deviating from his policy of conservatism, enforced by police, censors, and informants. He was succeeded by his son, Ferdinand I, who lacked his father's mettle and left Austria almost entirely in Metternich's hands.

JOSEPH II

In his impetuous but relatively short reign Joseph strove to bring his empire out of the Middle Ages into the Age of Reason; he abolished serfdom and feudal dues and personally saw to the overhauling of the educational system, the abolition of judicial torture and the humanising of the penal code. Joseph became Emperor in 1765 on the death of his father,

Francis I, and ruled jointly with his mother Maria Theresa until her death in 1780. His idealistic bursts of energy during his ten-year reign as sole monarch were largely unsuccessful; his plans to centralise administration were only half fulfilled and gradually fed the radical discontent which finally flared into revolution in 1848, overthrowing Metternich and the reactionaries.

LEOPOLD II 1747–1792

Leopold, eight years older than his sister Marie Antoinette, succeeded his brother Joseph II in 1790. To pacify his subjects Leopold was obliged to revoke most of his brother's reforms; in face of the degree of autonomy enjoyed by Hungary, Bohemia and the Austrian Netherlands he found it impossible to realise his brother's dreams of a centralised imperial administration. He died before war between Austria and France broke out in April, 1792; but the previous year he had negotiated an alliance with Prussia, obliging him to intervene in French affairs only with the unanimous consent of all the powers, including England. He even found himself reluctant to intervene on behalf of his brother-in-law, Louis XVI, King of France.

LETTRE DE CACHET

An order signed by the King and countersigned by a Secretary of State for the arrest and imprisonment, for an indefinite period of time, of any undesirable individual, without trial held or reason given; a notorious practice in direct opposition to the contemporary English law of *habeas corpus*.

MARIANNE

Just as Jeanne d'Arc became the symbol of pre-revolutionary France, so Marianne, symbolising Liberty, became the emblem of France during the Revolution.

MONTESQUIEU, 1689–1755

Charles Secondat, Baron de La Brède et de

Montesquieu's greatest contributions to the spirit of the Revolution were his *Lettres Persanes*, 1721, a set of critical, satirical letters on French society as seen through the eyes of two Persian travellers, and *L'Esprit des Lois* (The Spirit of Laws), published in 1748. As a practising lawyer he was well qualified to analyse the relationship between human and natural law. *L'Esprit des Lois*, the first authoritative study of social institutions, acted as a powerful stimulus to all eighteenth century political thought. Even today it is still one of the most lucid political treatises in existence; it profoundly influenced the Founding Fathers in their framing of the American Constitution, and this in turn served as model for subsequent European constitutions.

NECKER 1732–1804

Jacques

Swiss-born Jacques Necker, father of the celebrated Madame de Staël, succeeded Turgot as Controller General in 1776 and held the office for five years until the injudicious publication of his *compte rendu* (balance sheet) in 1781. Necker's stringent measures as Controller to systemise administration and to apply taxes more equitably made him unpopular with the *privilégiés*. When, in response to popular feeling, he was recalled in 1788 to avert France's complete bankruptcy, he recommended the convening of the States General. But the meeting of the States General in May, 1789 gave rise, not to urgently needed legislation, but to the consolidation of Third Estate power in the National Assembly. Necker's dismissal brought on the storming of the Bastille, and again he was recalled. He definitively tendered his resignation in September, 1790, however, and retired to his estate in Geneva.

PAYS D'ÉTAT AND PAYS D'ÉLECTION

Navarre, Burgundy, Brittany, Béarn and Languedoc came into the *pays d'état* category, and enjoyed more administrative and political freedom than the *pays d'élection,* particularly where taxation was concerned. In the former the provincial assembly, composed of members of the three estates, superintended the collection of taxes, an operation which was carried out by royal officials in the *pays d'élection*. While this procedure was followed the *pays d'états* avoided too great a tax burden, but in return raised considerable loans for the Crown. The distinction between *pays d'état* and *pays d'élection*, despite all attempts by the Crown to curtail the powers of the former, was preserved until 1789.

PHILOSOPHES

In the eighteenth century, philosophy meant the study of the world and mankind including the natural sciences. The *philosophes*—the name given to the leaders of the French Enlightenment, Diderot, d'Alembert, Condorcet, Rousseau, Voltaire and others—therefore treated all knowledge as their domain. They believed their main function to be the education of public opinion, not the pursuit of knowledge for its own sake. The *Philosophes* helped, through their writings and personal influence, to foster a spirit of inquiry which proved conducive to revolutionary thought. The

Encyclopédie, the "Bible" of the *Philosophes*, attacked established principles and paved the way for more dynamic thought and action.

ROUSSEAU, 1712–1778
Jean Jacques
Rousseau's second philosophical essay, *Discours sur l'origine et les fondements de l'inégalité parmi les hommes* (Discourse on the Origin and Bases of Inequality among Men), written in 1754, provided literary authority for the Revolution's bloody indictment of private ownership and the political system as the causes of oppression and inequality. But of all his works *Le Contrat Social* (The Social Contract) drove the longest nail into the coffin of the *ancien régime*: the work assumes *a priori* that all men are born equal, and hence that no man has any natural authority over his fellows. Rousseau concludes that only moral and practical considerations should determine a country's government. His collectivist theories have frequently been adduced to explain the "democratic despotism" of the Revolution itself and of succeeding regimes.

SEIGNEURIE
Under the *ancien régime*, the *seigneurie* usually consisted of two kinds of property—the *domaine proche* and the *domaine utile*. The *domaine proche* was an area of land part of which the seigneur, or lord, cultivated for his direct use, letting out the remaining portion to tenant farmers. The *domaine utile* was wholly cultivated and inhabited by peasant farmers who were required by law to render "feudal dues" (payment and services) to the seigneur in return for the use of the land. This system vested control of the land in the hands of the privileged classes; it was almost impossible for a peasant who worked a piece of land to own it outright.

TAILLE
This tax, although designed to be levied on all commoners, fell almost entirely on the shoulders of the peasants because of the exemptions granted to towns and members of the First and Second estates. The *taille* was levied on all peasants' possessions and on the land which he cultivated—but did not own because of the practice of *seigneurie*. The tax brought the government its major revenue through direct taxation and was one more reason for the frustration of the peasant.

TURGOT, 1727–1781
Anne Robert Jacques (Baron de L'Aulne)
Turgot, one of the founders of political science, was Controller General

from 1774 to 1776; his policies were based on these principles: "No bankruptcy, no increase in taxation, no borrowing." In the face of strong opposition from Court, clergy, nobles and bourgeoisie, he tried to put France upon a sound financial basis by attempting to introduce certain constants in the economy, abolishing certain feudal privileges, and restoring internal free trade. Opposition to his policies hastened his dismissal from office in 1776. He devoted the rest of his life to scientific and literary studies.

VIGÉE-LEBRUN, 1755–1842
Madame Louise Élizabeth
Madame Vigée-Lebrun was one of the most successful of all women painters. She was trained by her father and was elected to the French Academy in 1783. Because of her connection with Marie Antoinette, she was obliged to escape from France at the outbreak of the Revolution and thereafter earned herself a reputation abroad as a gifted portraitist. Today her best-loved portraits are those of Marie Antoinette, Lady Hamilton, and Lord Byron.

VOLTAIRE 1694–1778
(François Marie Arouet)
François Marie Arouet, who wrote under the name of Voltaire, was one of the leading *Philosophes* and was famous throughout Europe in his own day for his biting wit and his total lack of respect for entrenched institutions and authority of any kind. During his long life he poured out a torrent of plays, dialogues, light verse, pamphlets, historical and philosophical works and a total of over 12,000 letters. Of his works the best known is the short novel, *Candide*, which embodies the essence of his satiric attack upon established institutions, in particular the Church and the Monarchy of his native France. Naturally Voltaire paid for his unorthodox opinions with persecution and imprisonment. But the meaning of his works was not lost upon a generation which was preparing itself for the Revolution, for it was not hard to discern behind the savagery of Voltaire's attack a profound concern for just those ideals we prize today—tolerance, justice, equality and liberty. Voltaire's later years were spent in retirement in Ferney, on the borders of France and Switzerland. His pen remained sharp, but he was also noted for his generous help for the victims of persecution. In 1778, in his old age, he returned in triumph to Paris, now recognised as the arch apostle of that creed which was to lead so soon to the Revolution: turn out the old and bring in the new.

The Revolution

A Glossary of Terms and Personalities

BONNET ROUGE

(lit: "red cap")

Made of red wool and worn by all truly militant revolutionaries, the *bonnet rouge* was adopted in 1789 at the same time as the *carmagnole* jacket, and was regarded as a symbol of liberty. It was often decorated with the tricolour *cocarde* or cockade. The *bonnet rouge* enjoyed its greatest vogue during 1792 and 1793 and was the subject of much tendentious argument as to whether it should be used by women, and whether or not the cockade should be worn with it. This symbol *par excellence* of *sans-culottisme* gradually disappeared after the end of the Reign of Terror.

BRISSOT, 1754–1793

Jacques Pierre (surname de Warville)

Brissot's pre-revolutionary journalistic activities had already acquainted him with the inside of the Bastille; on July 14th, 1789, he was one of the mob that stormed it. After this—together with Vergniaud and Gaudet, both like himself brilliant orators and natives of Bordeaux in the Gironde—he formed the Girondin party in the Legislative Assembly. The struggle between the Girondins and the Montagnards climaxed in 1793 when the National Convention, coerced by the Jacobins and by an uprising carefully engineered by the Paris Commune, arrested and condemned Brissot and thirty other Girondin deputies. Brissot was guillotined on October 31st, 1793.

ÇA IRA

This was the name of a popular patriotic song of the French Revolution, whose refrain ... "*ça ira*" ... is supposed to have originated with Benjamin Franklin. When referring to the American Revolution he used to say, "*Ah, ça ira!*" meaning "we'll succeed!"

CARMAGNOLE

The costume of the French revolutionaries, consisting of a wide-collared jacket, wide black pantaloons, red cap, and a scarlet or tricoloured waistcoat or sash. The jacket, regarded as a symbol of liberty, was adapted in 1789 from that worn by French galley slaves after they had been freed. The *Carmagnole* was also the name of a dance and of a song popular during the revolution whose chorus ran:

"*Dansons la Carmagnole—vive le son, vive le son*
(trans: Let's dance the Carmagnole—long live the sound, long live the sound)
Dansons la Carmagnole—vive le son du canon . . ."
(Let's dance the Carmagnole—long live the sound of the cannon . . .)

CITOYEN, CITOYENNE (fem.)

Meaning "citizen", signifying loyalty to the Republican cause. Many heads rolled in consequences of their owners' refusing or forgetting to address their fellows as "citizen".

COMMITTEE OF GENERAL SECURITY

Working beside the Committee of Public Safety, this Committee was the chief instrument of the secret police. During 1793 and 1794 all power was concentrated in these two Committees, the Committee of General Security becoming increasingly subordinate to the Committee of Public Safety.

COMMITTEE OF PUBLIC SAFETY

Originally the Committe of General Defence, which had acted as the executive body of the Revolutionary Tribunal, it was reorganised and renamed by Danton in April, 1793. It was composed at first of nine members, of which Danton at once became the most influential. He gradually consolidated his position until the Girondins were ousted from the Committee and replaced by his own associates. For the first time all real power had been gathered into the hands of a few resolute and competent men, so that when Robespierre replaced Danton as leader of the Committee it controlled, under the National Convention, all foreign policy and the entire administration of France. The Committee's repressive measures, which swept away all legal protection for persons accused of political offences, soon culminated in the Reign of Terror. The fall of Robespierre, due mostly to jealousy within the committee, was followed by more moderate leadership.

THE COMMUNE

The Commune represented the smallest of the Paris administrative districts. After the storming of the Tuileries in August, 1792, it established, jointly with the Jacobins, a provisional ministry under the Legislative Assembly. Following the execution of Louis XVI, the Commune reorganised itself on the basis of manhood suffrage and its voice in the succeeding National Convention was entrusted to its elected committee of twenty, under the leadership of Hébert and Chaumette. The influence of the Commune precipitated the fall of the moderate Girondins and by June, 1793 the Commune dominated even Robespierre and the Montagne party. But by March, 1794 the all-powerful Montagne Committees (Public Safety and General Security) had turned on both the Hébertists and the Dantonists. Hébert, Chaumette and Cloots were guillotined on March 24th) thereafter the influence of the Paris Commune dwindled and in July was extinguished by the Thermidoreans.

CORDELIERS

An extremist club founded in 1790 by Danton and named after the monastery of the Cordelier friars, a Franciscan order, where the club held its meetings. Danton, Marat and Robespierre were the main speakers. Together with the Jacobins, the Cordeliers formed the Montagne party under the Legislative Assembly and the National Convention. Having played their part in the overthrow of the Girondins in 1793, the club was closed in 1794 when its leading members were guillotined at the instigation of Robespierre and his lieutenants, Couthon and St Just.

DANTON, 1759–1794

George Jacques

Danton, a powerful orator, was the principal leader of the revolutionary left. As a founder of the Cordeliers, he advocated extreme action and his name was associated with both the Tuileries riots of 1792 and the September Massacres of the same year. Elected President of the Jacobin Club in March of 1793, his place as one of the most influential revolutionaries in the National Convention was steadily usurped by Robespierre and his extremist associates. Danton, along with Desmoulins and Herault de Seychelles, was seized and imprisoned during the Reign of Terror and died beneath the guillotine on April 15th, 1794.

DÉCADI

(lit: "tenth day"; an artificial word compounded of the Latin *decimum diem.*) The *décadi* denoted a holiday. The revolutionary ten-day week was therefore called, quite logically, *décade*.

DUMOURIEZ, 1739–1823
Charles François
Dumouriez was fifty when the Revolution broke out. He had seen service under Louis XVI as Commandant of Cherbourg from 1778 to 1788, and in 1789, then a major general, he joined the Jacobin Club. In 1792 he became minister of foreign affairs, his policy leading to war with Austria and Prussia. In the same year, he was made lieutenant general of the Army of the North and conducted the campaign that checked the Duke of Brunswick at Valmy in September, 1792, the first of a series of French successes. In 1793, however, he was defeated by the Austrians at Neerwinden. His subsequent desertion to the Austrian side was inevitably denounced by the watchful National Convention. Thereafter he wandered through Europe an exile, until his departure for England in 1804. He died in 1823.

ÉMIGRÉS
(lit: "emigrants")
Term used to denote members of the nobility of France who took refuge abroad during the Revolution. The first wave of *émigrés* was headed by the Comte d'Artois, and the Princes of Condé and Polignac, their flight taking place shortly after the storming of the Bastille in July, 1789. When the Terror ended many *émigrés* returned to France to join the royalist cause, and were variously known as Les Chouans, Les Vendéens or as the Paris Royalists.

ENRAGÉS
(lit: "rabid" revolutionaries)
Revolutionary followers of Jacques Roux and Varlet, who violently condemned all monopolists and speculators and agitated for the forced subdivision of large agricultural estates for the benefit of small independent producers. This doctrine was known as the *loi agraire* or agrarian law.

FEUILLANTS
A political club founded in 1791 by breakaway moderates of the Jacobin Club (including Lafayette), and named after the convent of the Feuillants, a branch of the Cistercian Order, where their meetings took place. They strongly supported a monarchy under the revised Constitution of 1791, and distrusted the political force of the *sans-culottes*, the Parisian mob. The Feuillants, or constitutionalists, formed a ministry in 1792 during the Legislative Assembly only to be replaced by the Girondins over the question of war with Austria. Their power declined rapidly and they were finally suppressed by the Jacobins after the abolition of the monarchy in September, 1792.

GIRONDINS

The middle-class republican party founded in 1791 and so named because many of its members came from the *département* of the Gironde in Guienne, southwest France. Led by Jacques Brissot, Vergniaud, Gaudet and Pétion, it strongly advocated the abolition of the monarchy and in March, 1792 formed a ministry under the Legislative Assembly which pursued aggressive foreign and anti-clerical policies. For a time the Girondins shared the views of the majority group of moderate republicans and timid monarchists, but were forced to assume a position more to the right of centre to oppose the rising fanaticism of the Montagne faction. By October, 1793 almost all Girondins and the followers of Brissot, the "Brissotins", had either been guillotined or imprisoned; the survivors lived to form the Council of the Five Hundred under the Directoire, 1795–1799.

GUILLOTINE

The instrument of execution perfected by and named after the French physician Joseph Ignace Guillotin who, in defending capital punishment, proposed the use of this device. Most towns in Revolutionary France possessed their own guillotine. On occasion the accelerating force of the falling blade, blunt in most cases, was not enough to decapitate the victim straight away. Heads fell into baskets provided for the purpose.

JACOBINS

A political club founded in 1789 and named after its original venue in the hall of an ex-monastery of Dominican friars in the Rue St Jacques. Only moderately democratic at first, its propagandists, led by such men as Robespierre, Danton and Marat, became increasingly radical—in fact the Jacobins were the driving force of the Revolution. The Jacobins, the dominant faction of the Montagne and the two committees (The Committee of Public Safety and The Committee of General Security) governed dictatorially during the Reign of Terror until the coup of 9 Thermidor which destroyed Robespierre, Couthon and St Just. Jacobin clubs spread throughout France and although the Paris club closed immediately after the death of Robespierre and the end of the Terror, the Jacobins, still representing extremism, remained a constant force to be reckoned with, even under the Directoire.

JACQUES BONHOMME

Nickname for the French peasant, used at the time of the "jacquerie" or peasants' revolt of 1358 and revived by revolutionary propagandists in 1789 to mean the long-suffering but good-hearted peasant, "born to stagger beneath clergy and nobles."

LAFAYETTE, 1757–1834

Marie Joseph Paul Yves Roch Gilbert du Motier, Marquis de

As famed for his personal vanity as for his military and political ambitions, Lafayette had already served the cause of American Independence before becoming a member of the Legislative Assembly. His Jacobin sympathies were nevertheless moderate, and, supported by Bailly, he broke with the Club to form a group known as the Feuillants. The adoption of the tricolour and the organisation of a National Guard in 1789 were largely due to his efforts. When France declared war on Austria on April 20th, 1792, Lafayette was given command of a third of France's military strength. In spite of his tactics, the Austrians were successful in the field and the revolutionary authorities impeached and proscribed him; he fled to Flanders, was captured by the Austrians and kept prisoner at Olmütz until 1796. He returned to France in 1799 but took no part in politics until after the fall of Napoleon.

LEGISLATIVE ASSEMBLY (1791–1792)

The Legislative Assembly, formed on October 1st, 1791, like the preceding National Assembly was still primarily representative of the middle class, although the tide was now turning in favour of republicanism. The Assembly's right wing was composed of an ever-diminishing Royalist or Constitutional party; the Plain, a middle-class majority group, assumed a position slightly right of centre, while the Girondins formed a moderate left; the Montagne, or the combined Cordelier and Jacobin elements, represented the extreme left. The ominous assertion of mob influence during the Storming of the Tuileries and the September Massacres of 1792 rendered the authority of the Assembly ineffectual and it abdicated its short-lived power to the National Convention.

MARAT, 1743–1793

Jean Paul

Marat was one of the most vicious and inflammatory of the revolutionary leaders. His paper, *L'Ami du Peuple*, published in 1789, openly called for mob violence and even after its suppression circulated secretly; its ferocious articles were no doubt in part responsible for the abolition and fall of the monarchy in 1792. As leader of the extremist Cordeliers, Marat was elected to the National Convention in the same year and managed to survive Girondin opposition which culminated in his arrest and trial and final acquittal on April 24th, 1793. In consequence he joined Robespierre and Danton, whose energies were then directed at crushing the Girondins. Charlotte Corday, horrified at the revolutionary excesses sanctioned by Marat and his fellow terrorists, stabbed him in his bath on July 13th, 1793.

(Apparently a skin disease obliged Marat to spend hours at a time in a warm bath.) Charlotte was guillotined four days after Marat's assassination.

MIRABEAU, 1749–1791
Honoré Gabriel Victor Riqueti, Comte de
Although notorious for his wild excesses in early life, Mirabeau, from 1789 until his death in 1791, exerted a definite moderating influence on revolutionary fervour. He was a Third Estate deputy for Aix and Marseilles at the States General of 1789 and from June, 1789, until his death became the National Assembly's leading figure. With his powerful oratory and strong personality, he was an eloquent advocate of a constitutional monarchy for France. No matter how often rejected, his constitutional measures restrained the Assembly. He was nevertheless playing a double game; although President of the Jacobin Club in 1790 and President of the National Assembly in 1791, he sold his advice and support to Louis XVI and Marie Antoinette. This, fortunately for himself, was not known until just after his death.

MONTAGNE
(lit: "the mountain")
A political party under the Legislative Assembly and National Convention, most of whose members were extremists. Because the seats they occupied in the Legislative Assembly had been the highest on the left side of the Hall, they were commonly known as Montagnard (of the Mountain). Montagnard history is largely that of its two constituent groups, the Cordeliers and Jacobins.

NATIONAL OR CONSTITUENT ASSEMBLY (1789–1791)
The National or Constituent Assembly, the first Revolutionary government, lasted from June 17th, 1789, until September 30th, 1791. Most of its members, for whom Mirabeau and Sieyès acted as spokesmen, were upper middle class and envisaged a constitutional monarchy with restricted powers as the best compromise between despotism and democracy. A minority group among the Assembly's members were the future leaders of the Girondins, Jacobins and Cordeliers, namely Brissot, Robespierre and Danton. True to its oath on assuming office, the Assembly dissolved itself when Louis XVI accepted the revised version of its Constitution of 1790.

THE NATIONAL CONVENTION (1792–1795)
The National Convention, which first met on September 21st, 1792, was

the longest-lived of the three revolutionary assemblies. Its 749 members were elected by manhood suffrage and were entirely republicans. Under the National Convention the Girondins now formed the right while the left was formed by the Montagne under Robespierre and his associates. During the run of the Convention, Louis XVI and Marie Antoinette were guillotined and the Reign of Terror was unleashed. In order to quiet opposition, the Convention placed General Bonaparte in charge of its troops but only a few months later, on October 25th, 1795, dissolved itself and was replaced by the Directory.

THE PLAIN

The name given to an unorganised majority group in the Legislative Assembly, comprised of moderate republicans and timid monarchists. They were alternately swayed by Girondins and Montagnards and much scorned for their diffidence by both parties. The Plain played the same role in the National Convention where it had numerical superiority but no real influence.

REIGN OF TERROR

The Reign of Terror, lasting from 1793 to 1794, began with the fall of Brissot and the Girondin deputies, leaving Robespierre and the Revolutionary Tribunals supreme. While the Terror lasted, thousands lost their heads for offences, real or imagined, against "the people". The almost omnipotent Committee of Public Safety, headed by Robespierre, directed the Terror; one after another of his political opponents were arrested and guillotined while more and more repressive measures were introduced. Purge followed purge until 9 Thermidor (July 28th), when Robespierre himself fell victim to hostile groups within the Committee. His execution ended the Reign of Terror; public opinion then forced the remaining leaders to adopt more moderate policies.

ROBESPIERRE, 1758–1794

Maximilien François Marie Isidore de

For many the name Robespierre conjures an image of the more violent aspects of the French Revolution. He gained notoriety as a lawyer and radical in the Legislative Assembly and became leader of the Jacobin Club in 1791. Crowned "Incorruptible Patriot" by the people of Paris, his strong influence upon the more irresponsibile sections of the populace seems difficult to disentangle from actual mob violence. He gained dictatorial power within the Committee of Public Safety in 1793 and took advantage of his position to dispose of his chief rivals, notably Hébert, Danton and

Desmoulins. The Committee, which directed the Reign of Terror, was the most dreaded enforcer of his exterminatory policy. His excesses at last roused the Convention; the Terror was turned upon its leader and he was arrested and guillotined.

SANS-CULOTTES, SANS-CULOTTERIE, SANS-CULOTTISME
(lit: "without breeches")
Breeches were the mark of both the aristocracy and the upper echelon of the Third Estate, who were graphically described as *culottes dorées* (Francy breeches) or as *bas de soie* (silk stockings). All revolutionaries, of course, wore trousers although some, known as the *Muscadins,* displayed more sartorial elegance, even foppishness in their attire. To a great extent appearance indicated political sympathies. The influence of the *sans-culotterie* reached its peak under the two Committees created in 1793, which were designed to better the social conditions of all citizens by promoting *l'égalité des jouissances,* i.e. an equal opportunity for every man to enjoy the benefits conferred by society. The daily life of a militant *sans-culotte* was a busy one, spent between the Convention and his local *societé sectionnaire.*

SOCIÉTÉS SECTIONNAIRES
These societies, forty-nine of which are recorded, were formed as a means of evading the law of September, 1793, which forbade general assemblies in the *sections* of Paris. For the *sans-culottes* these societies provided popular political education. Gradually, through their contact with the work and ideas of the main political clubs, these popular and patriotic societies came to have a measure of influence, especially in the Commune.

THERMIDOREANS
Name given to the moderates who eventually broke the power, not only of the Commune but of the Jacobins, on 9 Thermidor (July 28th, 1794) when Robespierre was openly accused of despotism and soon afterwards arrested and guillotined. Thus ended the Reign of Terror. Although called "moderates", the Thermidoreans were in fact rival extremist leaders out to break the dictatorship of Robespierre. But Robespierre's execution relaxed the political atmosphere; the results of 9 Thermidor were therefore a move from extremism to moderation.

TRICOTEUSES
(lit: "knitters")
Parisian women who, during the Revolution, attended all executions, meet-

ings of the Convention and other popular assemblies. They represented the *sans-culotterie*, the Parisian mob, and ensured that the revolutionary leaders bowed to the will of the mob; they looked on while some of the bloodiest excesses of the Revolution were committed.

TU AND TOI
(lit: "you")
In French, there are two ways of saying "you". *Vous*, the plural form, is used formally, to denote respect. *Tu* (emphatic, *toi*) is the familiar form. During the Revolution, *tu* was used in favour of *vous* because the latter smacked too much of the formality of the old order; *tu* also stimulated more fellow feeling and republican solidarity. To use the general *vous* would have rendered one suspect to the vigilant *sociétés sectionnaires* and to the Committee of General Security. Towards the end of the Terror, however, *tu* was felt in some circles to detract from the dignity and moral decency of Revolutionary achievements and the time-honoured *vous* regained its prestige.

VENDÉMIAIRE, BRUMAIRE etc.
Names invented for the French Republican Calendar by the poet Fabre d'Eglantine and arranged chronologically by Gilbert Romme. Year I began with the Autumnal Equinox of 1793. The whole system, in many ways unsatisfactory, became obsolete on January 1st, 1806. The names of the months pay tribute to France's agricultural economy:

Vendémiaire	month of the grape harvest
Brumaire	,, ,, mist
Frimaire	,, ,, frosts
Nivôse	,, ,, snows
Pluviôse	,, ,, rains
Ventôse	,, ,, winds
Germinal	,, ,, sowing
Floréal	,, ,, blossoms
Prairial	,, ,, haymaking
Messidor	,, ,, harvesting
Thermidor	,, ,, heat
Fructidor	,, ,, fruitpicking

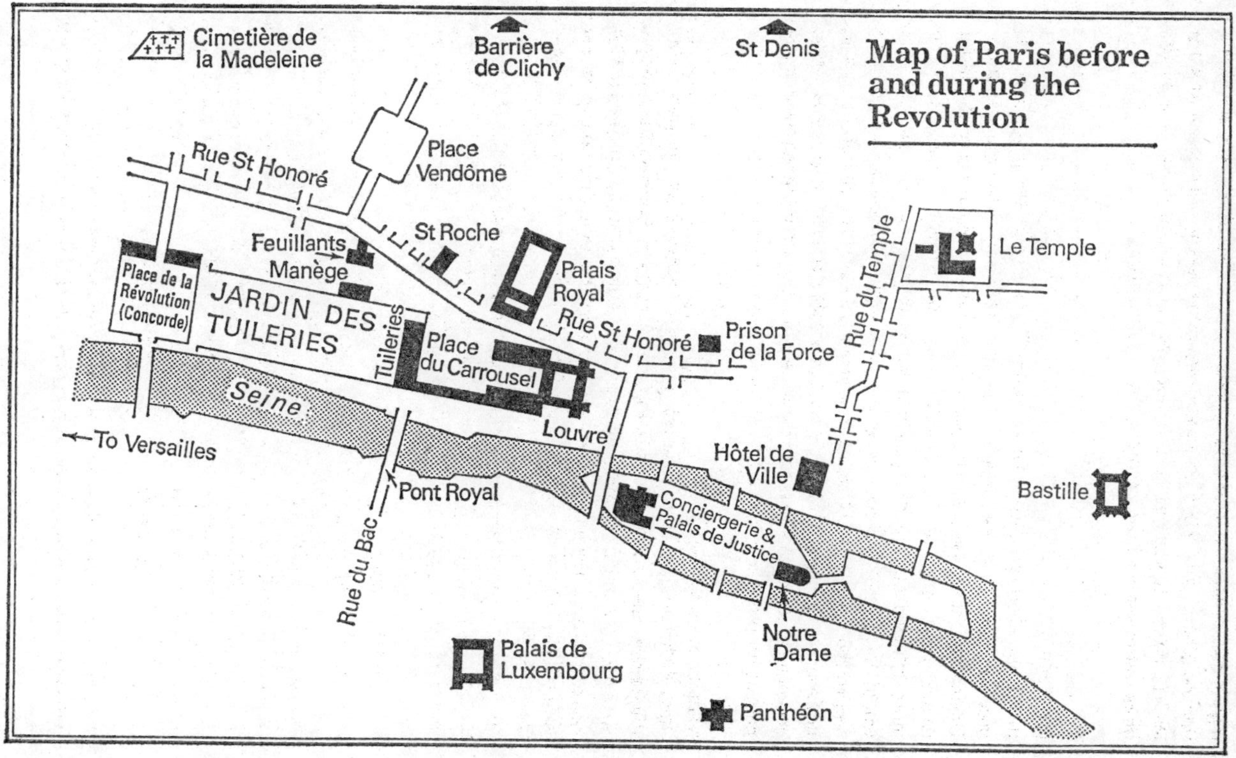
Map of Paris before and during the Revolution
Cimetière de la Madeleine
Barrière de Clichy
St Denis
Place Vendôme
Rue St Honoré
St Roche
Feuillants
Manège
Palais Royal
Rue St Honoré
Prison de la Force
Rue du Temple
Le Temple
Place de la Révolution (Concorde)
JARDIN DES TUILERIES
Tuileries
Place du Carrousel
Seine
Louvre
To Versailles
Hôtel de Ville
Pont Royal
Conciergerie & Palais de Justice
Bastille
Rue du Bac
Notre Dame
Palais de Luxembourg
Panthéon

Index

THE WORLD OF ROME

MICHAEL GRANT

The historical background and astounding cultural and political achievements of the Roman Empire, resulting in a fascinating contribution to our understanding of the important role Rome played in the evolution of the modern world.

£1·00 *Illustrated*

THE BYZANTINE COMMONWEALTH

DIMITRI OBOLENSKY

'Outstanding ... Obolensky has provided what must, for many years, remain the most authoritative and comprehensive textbook on the history of Eastern Europe'
Times Literary Supplement

£1·25 *Illustrated*

THE MEDIEVAL WORLD

FRIEDRICH HEER

A brilliant and comprehensive picture of two and a half centuries of European civilisation, discussing all the facets of Medieval life, which laid the foundations for modern society.

£1·50 *Illustrated*

THE CENTURY OF REVOLUTION 1603–1714

CHRISTOPHER HILL

In England between the years of 1603 and 1714 a transformation took place which embraced the whole of life, thought and taste. This book attempts to reassess what happened, penetrating below the surface of seventeenth-century events to show how our modern society began to take shape, and how England's position in the world was considerably altered. It outlines the changes which set England on the path of Parliamentary government, economic advance and imperialist foreign policy, of religious toleration and scientific progress, and shows the century as the greatest age in English literature.

While not setting out to provide an exhaustive compendium of facts, it considerably broadens and enriches our concept of a brilliant and bewildering century of change, heralding the modern world—'the world of banks and cheques, budgets, the stock exchange, the periodical press, coffee-houses, clubs, coffins, microscopes, shorthand actresses and umbrellas'.

60p

LADY CAROLINE LAMB

Elizabeth Jenkins

A sensitive and colourful portrait of the wife of William Lamb, Viscount Melbourne and later Prime Minister, whose wayward disregard for convention made her the topic of conversation in fashionable salons throughout England.

45p

THE FALL OF THE HOUSE OF HABSBURG

Edward Crankshaw

A vivid portrayal of the history of the Habsburg monarchy from 1848 to 1918.

'Authoritative, lucid and utterly absorbing'
Evening Standard

90p

A GUIDE TO PREHISTORIC AND ROMAN MONUMENTS IN ENGLAND AND WALES

Jacquetta Hawkes

A detailed account, region by region, of the prehistoric as well as the Roman monuments to be found throughout England and Wales, enabling the visitor to find the most interesting sites and to understand the importance of what he sees.

£1·25 *Illustrated*

THE LIFE AND DEATH OF MOZART

Michael Levey

'An original and scholarly biography which succeeds in bringing Mozart alive'
Contemporary Review

90p *Illustrated*

THE WASHING OF THE SPEARS

Donald E. Morris

'An excellent study of Zulu-European relations from Shaka's time to the Zulu wars of 1879'
New Statesman

£1·00

PRINCES OF JADE

Edmund Capon

A fascinating account of Han China, examining every aspect from the political background to the foundation of the Han State to the court life, art and culture.

£1·50 *Illustrated*

HUMBOLDT AND THE COSMOS

Douglas Botting

A vivid biography of Humboldt, scientist, explorer and diplomat, the last truly Universal Man.

£1·75 *Illustrated*